THE LOST LANGUAGE OF SYMBOLISM

THE
LOST LANGUAGE
OF SYMBOLISM

AN INQUIRY INTO THE ORIGIN OF
CERTAIN LETTERS, WORDS, NAMES,
FAIRY-TALES, FOLKLORE, AND
MYTHOLOGIES

BY

HAROLD BAYLEY

"The English mind, not readily swayed by rhetoric, moves freely under the pressure of facts."

E. B. TYLOR.

"One may, for a moment, arouse interest by a new hypothesis, but it is only by the accumulation of facts that public opinion is perceptibly influenced in the end."

WALTER JOHNSON.

VOL. II

A CITADEL PRESS BOOK
Published by Carol Publishing Group

First Carol Publishing Group Edition 1990

A Citadel Press Book
Published by Carol Publishing Group

Editorial Offices
600 Madison Avenue
New York, NY 10022

Sales & Distribution Offices
120 Enterprise Avenue
Secaucus, NJ 07094

In Canada: Musson Book Company
A division of General Publishing Co. Limited
Don Mills, Ontario

Manufactured in the United States of America
ISBN 0-8065-1163-x

10 9 8 7 6 5 4 3 2 1

CONTENTS

CHAPTER XIV

THE HEAVENLY TWINS

CHAPTER XV

THE WHITE HORSE

CHAPTER XIX

THE GARDEN OF ALLAH

CHAPTER XX

THE TREE OF LIFE

CHAPTER XXI

VIA DOLOROSA

CHAPTER XXII

CONCLUSION

THE LOST LANGUAGE OF SYMBOLISM

CHAPTER XIV

THE HEAVENLY TWINS

"The ONE remains, the many change and pass."
SHELLEY.

"One is all alone
And ever doth remain so."
Old English Folk-Song.

IT was customary among the ancients to regard the Great Spirit under the dual aspect of GEMINI the Twins, or, as they were called in Sanscrit, the AHANS or ASVINS. In EGYPT, as elsewhere, the palpable dualism of Nature—Male and Female, Day and Night, Morning and Evening, Summer and Winter, Sun and Moon, Light and Darkness, Heaven and Earth—was typified as a double Being. "In most of the [Egyptian] hymns," says De Rougé, "we come across this idea of the double Being who engendereth Himself, the Soul in two Twins—to signify two Persons never to be separated."[1]

The innumerable forms under which the duality of the ONE was typified may be judged from the following Vedic invocation :—

[1] *Hibbert Lectures,* 1879, p. 90.

"Like the two stones you sound for the same object. You are like two hawks rushing toward a tree with a nest ; like two priests reciting their prayers at a sacrifice ; like the two messengers of a clan called for in many places.

"Coming early, like two heroes on their chariots, like twin-goats, you come to him who has chosen you ; like two women, beautiful in body ; like husband and wife, wise among their people.

"Like two horns, come first towards us ; like two hoofs, rushing on quickly ; like two birds, ye bright ones, every day, come hither, like two charioteers, O ye strong ones !

"Like two ships, carry us across ; like two yokes, like two naves of a wheel, like two spokes, like two felloes ; like two dogs that do not hurt our limbs ; like two armours, protect us from destruction.

"Like two winds, like two streams, your motion is eternal ; like two eyes, come with your sight towards us ! Like two hands, most useful to the body ; like two feet, lead us towards wealth.

"Like two lips, speaking sweetly to the mouth ; like two breasts, feed us that we may live. Like two nostrils, as guardians of the body ; like two ears, be inclined to listen to us.

"Like two hands, holding our strength together ; like heaven and earth, drive together the clouds. O Asvins, sharpen these songs that long for you, as a sword is sharpened with a whetstone."[1]

The two eyes of the Spectacles (illustrated *ante*, p. 22) were probably understood to denote respectively Love and Knowledge, but prior to the invention of spectacles twin wheels or circles were regarded as a symbol of the Deity. The examples of this emblem, reproduced herewith, are classed by Mons. Briquet as "cars, chariots, or ploughs."

---

[1] Quoted in *Science of Language*, Max Müller, p. 540.

From some of them descend the customary three rays, and they all doubtless represent the Solar Chariot, the "Great Vehicle" of esoteric Buddhism.

Dr INMAN, referring to an uncomprehended two-circle ornament found frequently on the sculptured stones of SCOTLAND, writes: "It is spoken of as 'the spectacle

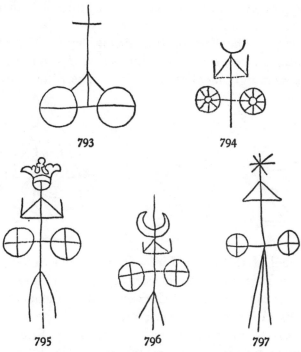

793   794

795   796   797

ornament,' and is commonly associated with another figure closely resembling the letter Z. It is very natural for the inquirer to associate the twin circles with the Sun and Earth or the Sun and Moon. On one Scottish monument the circles represent wheels, and they probably indicate the solar chariot. As yet I have only been able to meet with the Z and the 'spectacle ornament' once out of Scotland; it is figured on apparently a Gnostic gem. In that we see in a serpent cartouche two Z figures, each having the down-stroke crossed by a horizontal line, both ends terminating in a circle ; beside them is a six-rayed star, each ray terminating in a circle. I can offer no satisfactory explanation of the emblem."[1]

In the paper-marks herewith the letter Z is associated, as on the Scottish monuments, with two circles. In fig. 800 these appear beneath the figure of ZEUS, the All-Father, who is represented sitting upon a five-rayed zigzag, crest, or cockscomb. The hair of this sitting figure is portrayed like *four*fold Fire ; the Danish for *four* is *fire*, and the word *four*[2] is seemingly identical with *fire*. The Roman numeral

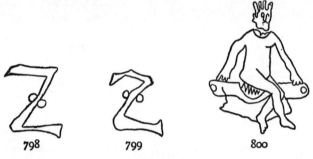

798   799   800

4—symbol of the divine Fire—is the Indian letter *ch*, the initial of *chatur*, the Sanscrit word for *four*.   *Chatur* resolves itself into *cha t ur*, the "Ever-existent resplendent Fire." The Persian for *four* is *chehar* ; the Breton is *puar*, " Father Fire," or *peder*, " Father of Resplendent Fire."   The Lithuanian for *four* is *peturi*, which may be equated with *pater*, and the Greek is *tetras*[3] or *tettares*.   The sacred *four* or *tetraktis* stood among the Pythagoreans for the Supreme Deity, and this symbolism is presumably responsible for the names of the Number.   The Mexican for *four* was *can*, and *caan* meant *heaven*.   KAN, *i.e. ak an*, the " great ONE," was the Mexican title for the Being to whom the Creator had

[1] *Ancient Pagan and Modern Christian Symbolism*, p. 59.
[2] In *far*thing it becomes *far*.   [3] *Tat Horus* or Father HORUS?

entrusted from the beginning the keeping of the pillar that supported the Sky — hence *kan* meant also *yellow*, the colour of fire, and *kin* meant "the vivifying, the life sustainer, the God."¹ *Khen* was Egyptian for *good*; *kin* was Celtic for *good*—whence, no doubt, our adjective *kind* and the word *kine*, a generic term for cattle. In Irish KEAN means *vast*.

The poets feigned that ZEUS, in the form of a swan, loved a maiden named LEDA, who gave birth to an egg— whence sprang the twins CASTOR and POLLUX. These beneficent, star-browed brethren, known to the Greeks as the DIOSCURI, are generally represented as riding upon white horses, and their reputation is expressed by Macaulay's well-known lines :

> " Back comes the chief in triumph,
>   Who, in the hour of fight,
> Hath seen the great Twin Brethren
>   In harness on his right.
> Safe comes the ship to haven
>   Through billows and through gales,
> If once the great Twin Brethren
>   Sit shining on the sails."

The name LEDA may be equated with LADA, the heroine of a Slav version of CINDERELLA entitled "The Princess with the Gold Star on her brow."² According to one version of CINDERELLA, she becomes the mother of a twin boy and girl, the girl having, like the DIOSCURI, a star on her brow.³ From the "fair unspotted side of PSYCHE two blissful twins" were born.⁴ Of the Bride of King SOLOMON the poet says : "Thy two breasts are like two young roes that are *twins*, which feed among the lilies,"⁵ and the teeth of the Bride are twice likened to "a flock of sheep which go up

¹ Le Plongeon, *Queen Moo*, 93.
² *Cinderella*, p. 418.   ³ *Ibid.*, p. 281.
⁴ Bulfinch, *Age of Fable*, p. 96.   ⁵ iv. 5.

from the washing, whereof every one beareth *twins*, and there is not one barren among them." [1]   *White* (washed ?) *lambs*

801

802

were the particular offering of the Dioscuri, who were symbolised not only by twin circles, but also by the twin cherubs [2] that are so familiar a feature of Renaissance ornament.

---

[1] vi. 6 ; iv. 2.
[2] The word *cherub*=CHOREB, an alternative name of Mount Sinai.

In fig. 801 these two children are flourishing on either side of their Parent, the Bird of Light, and in fig. 802, associated with their white horses, they are supporting LEDA's Swan. The fable of the Swan's enchanting death-song probably had some such similar symbolic basis as that of the Panther's alluring breath.

The Old Irish for *swan* was *geis*, which is cognate with *geese*, and as a symbol the swan and the goose were no doubt equivalent.

803

In fig. 803 the Twins are represented piping upon fifes on either side of the Vase of Abundance, and in fig. 804 they appear "like twin goats" with PAN, the Great Trunk, or *Torso*. The word *Torso* reappears in the place-name THURSO. To the north of THURSO is the ORKNEY Island named POMONA, "sole Father," and the principal town on POMONA is named OP. North of POMONA, a word meaning *apple*[1] in Latin, is a small island named PAPA WESTRAY—an extended form of PAPÆUS, one of the names of JUPITER.

---

[1] The root *apple* in such English place-names as APPLEBY, APPLE-CROSS, APPLEDRAM, APPLETON, etc., may often be equated with APOLLO. In the parish of GODSHILL, Isle of Wight, is an APPLEDURWELL, alternatively known as APPULDURCOMB. Compare surname APPOLD.

In the SHETLANDS is PAPA STOUR, *i.e.* Father STEER, the " STEER of Day."

THURSO, a name cognate with the Greek word *thyrsus*, meaning a stem, stalk, or *ashera*, is allied philologically to THIRSK in Yorkshire, which is overlooked by a hill named Great HAW, and by another named SIMON SEAT, an eminence evidently comparable to SIMONS YAT on the River WYE.

804

THIRSK is situated on the River CODBECK, an affluent of the SWALE ; and the Gaelic for *whale* is *ork*.   In days of *yore* the River OUSE flowing through YORK was known as the EURE or YORE, and YORK was originally YUREWICK or YORICK. There are several rivers named the YAR in England ; YORA is a river in GEORGIA ; and the town of AXMINSTER is on the River YARTY.   The great Asiatic River OXUS was alternatively called ARAXES ; in Hebrew *iar* is a generic term for river, and the syllables fundamentally meant the " Ever-existent Fire or Light." Most rivers, great or small, were once held sacred as symbols of the life-giving Sun, and it was by frequent usage that *iar, ock, exe, usk, isis, ysel,* etc., became generic terms for *river.*

The holy estimation in which rivers were once held may be judged from extant Hymns to the NILE, in which the Egyptians express their adoration in practically the same terms as they used in worshipping the Sun. Among other invocations the NILE is hailed as "a healing balm for all mankind." "He *shines* when he issues forth from the darkness to cause his flocks to prosper. It is his force that gives existence to all things ; nothing remains hidden from him. . . . He causes all his servants to exist. . . . Hail to thee, O Nile, who manifesteth thyself over this land and comest to give life to Egypt."

According to EDMUNDS the River TEIGN derives its name from TAN, "the sacred fire of the Druids,"[1] and religious nomenclature is elsewhere very generally traceable in river names.

In Egypt the TWINS were spoken of as two Lions whose solar phases constituted Day and Night. OSIRIS was entitled "Lord of the Double Lions," and the solitary solar disc was surnamed the "Lion of the Double Lions." ATEN, the Sun, may be equated with WOTAN or ODIN of WEDNESDAY and the Great World ASH.[2]

Within the city of EDINBURGH or ODIN'S BURGH (?) is a famous *Lion* Rock known alternatively as "Arthur's Seat"; and five miles south of BRECON in North Wales rise two mountain-peaks designated "Arthur's Chair." The semi-fabulous ARTHUR or ARTURIUS, whose mystic land was LYONESSE and whose seat was CAERLEON, was

---

[1] *Traces of History in the Names of Places,* p. 294.
[2] The Christian festival of ASH-Wednesday cannot but be a survival of some ceremony in connection with WODAN'S ASH.

identified with ARCTUS,[1] the Great Bear, and the legends of ARTHUR of BRITAIN preserve many relics of prehistoric theology.

The mother of King ARTHUR is said to have been IGRAINE, and as *graine* is Celtic for *love*, the name IGGRAINE(?) presumably meant "the Mighty Love." The Father of King ARTHUR, according to most versions, was UTHER PENDRAGON. The word UTHER, like AITHER, the Father of PAN, may be equated with Ether, the superfine, all-permeating atmosphere.

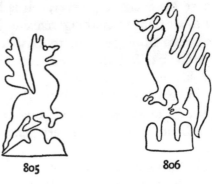

805   806

Figs. 805 and 806, consisting of a Dragon surmounting a "pen," may be understood as a rebus reading "PENDRAGON." This title was given to an elective sovereign paramount over the many kings of Britain, and was equivalent to "King of Kings." A dragon was the standard of the West Saxons, of the Welsh, of the Phœnicians, and of the Chinese MANCHU dynasty.

The Three Queens associated with King ARTHUR may be equated with the three maidens seated at the root of the World's Ash, and with the Triple Light-ray. Tennyson refers thus to them as a triple flame:

[1] *Chronicle of Gildas.*

"Down from the casement over Arthur, smote
Flame-colour, vert and azure, *in three rays,*
One falling upon each of three fair queens,
Who stood in silence near his throne, the friends
Of Arthur, gazing on him, tall, with bright
Sweet faces, who will help him at his need."

These three Queens, Good Thought, Good Word, and Good Deed, the builders of mystic Camelot, are said to have come "from out a sacred mountain, cleft toward the Sunrise." Twin mountain-peaks figure in nearly all ancient

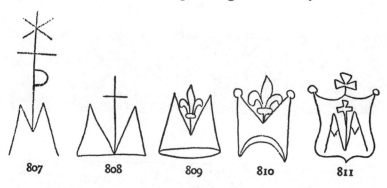

807   808   809   810   811

mythologies. In INDIA are MERU and KAILASA, the Sunrise mountains; in CHALDEA a sacred mountain in the East was contrasted with a second in the West, and, according to the Egyptians, the Western mouth of Hades consisted of a double mount between whose peaks the Sun rose and set. The emblems herewith imply that the twin mountains were simply another symbol of the Asvins.

The twin-peaked M was a letter called *san* in the Dorian alphabet, and its value was equivalent to *s*. The word *San*—primarily meaning the Light of the One, and secondarily *Holy*—is the radical of *san, santa, sainte, saint, sanctus, santé, sanitas, sane, sanguine,* etc.

The twin peaks of fig. 811 are marked with the A A of

the AHANS or ASVINS invoked *ante*, "like two breasts, feed us that we may live." The HEBRIDES contain two mountains named "the Paps of JURA."

In Egyptian the word *aa* meant *great*, and in the emblems

812

813

814

herewith the divine Asvins are portrayed lolling blissfully upon two A's. In nearly every case one of these A's is represented as dark and the other as white, presumably an allusion to the idea expressed in the Vedas : "One of them shines brightly, the other is black ; twin sisters are they, the one black, the other white." [1]

[1] *Mythology of the Aryan Nations*, Cox, p. 207.

The Chaldean "God of *Life*" was sometimes entitled AA and sometimes Aos.[1] The name Aos is probably connected with *ayus*, the Sanscrit for *life*, and also with Eos, the

[1] Pinches, *Rel. of Bab. and Ass.*, pp. 32, 50.

Greek name for the Dawn. CHAOS, the Infinite Space (not confusion)—whence Gods, men, and all things else arose, and which existed, according to ancient cosmogonies, previous to the creation of the universe—may be resolved into AK Aos, the Light, Spirit, or Essence of the Great A.

The Chaldean Aos was known alternatively as HOA, and it would seem that in his dual aspect the Holy ONE came to be known somewhat indiscriminatingly as OA,[1] Ao,[2] or AA.[3]

One of the Gnostic's terms for the Supreme Spirit was IAO, *i.e.* the ever-existent Ao and TAO, a Chinese name for the Supreme Spirit—may be resolved into T-AO, the "resplendent Ao."

The legends of TAO declare that he existed in the Great Absolute prior to the birth of the elements, that he is the "pure essence of the *teen*," the "original ancestor of the prime breath of life," and the giver of form to the heavens and the earth.[4] Chinese mythology represents TAO as a divine emanation incarnate in a human form. He is termed "the most high and venerable prince of the portals of gold of the palace of the genii," and is said to have condescended to a contact with humanity by becoming incorporated with the "miraculous and excellent Virgin of Jasper."

Among the Greeks the Twins were denominated *anakes*, *i.e.* the One Great Light, and sometimes, instead of as Two, the *anakes* was invoked as Four, under the names AXIEROS (The Great Fire EROS ?), AXIOKERSA (The Great Fire, The Great URSA or Bear ?), AXIOKERSOS, and KADMIEL. The Celestial children of the Creator were regarded as the conquerors of darkness, the lords of light, ever youthful,

---

[1] The Polynesian word *aloha* means *love, friendship, gratitude,* and *benevolence.*

[2] HEIGHO is an English surname ; *Ao* is Polynesian for the *Sunrise.*

[3] PHARAOH'S alternative title was PERAA.

[4] Sir T. Thornton, *History of China,* i. 134.

swift as thought, and possessed of a profound wisdom. In INDIA they were termed the VRITRAHANA because they ushered in the Sunlight and destroyed VRITRA, the darkness. The VRITRAHANA were symbolised by two V's as in the designs herewith.

In fig. 821 they are supported upon the Diamond of their Father, DYAUS, *i.e.* the resplendent AYUS or *Life*, and

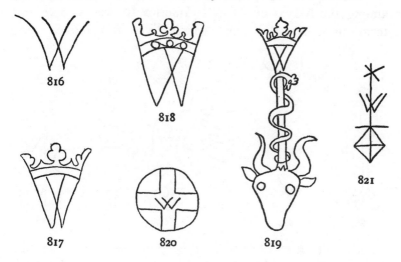

this emblem may be equated with the Twin Circles attached to the Z.

The designer of figs. 823 and 824 evidently identified the two strokes of the X with the Twin Circles, and the P surmounting the two V's on fig. 825 is simply another form of the Labarum, *i.e.* P surmounting X. *Ekse* is the Latin numeral for *Ten* or *Aten*, and the figure X is composed by the combination, point to point, of two *fives* or V's.

The Druids used to invoke the Omnipotent and All-preserving Power under the symbol I.O.W., and among the Cabalistic names for the Deity occurs the word IHOH, said to mean "The Eternal, absolute principle of creation and destruction, the male and female principle, the author and *regulator of* time and *motion*."[1] The circles of Supreme Love and Knowledge represented in fig. 826 exhibit a singular resemblance to the regulating balls of a steam-engine.

Among the Egyptians Io was identified with Isis, and among the Mayas of Central America Io was a sacrosanct term implying "all that which lives and moves," the

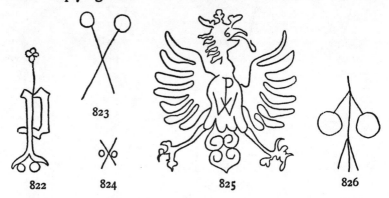

822   823   824   825   826

"Spirit of the Universe, the Boundless, the Infinite One."[2] Of the Maoris of NEW ZEALAND, who to this day worship a First Cause under the name Io, Mr Cowan writes, "Beneath all the personifications of natural things, of the Sun and Moon and Stars, the Winds and the Ocean, there are faint traces of some still more ancient faith, the belief in a Great First Cause. This supreme Being or Power is Io, a name occasionally to be heard in ancient chants and genealogies. The resemblance of the name to Devus, Deo, Zeus, Iouis, and other forms of the Old World names for the Supreme God, has frequently been remarked upon, but probably the likeness is merely

[1] *Lexicon of Freemasonry*, Mackey, p. 229.
[2] *Queen Moo*, pp. 151, 216, 221.

verbal ; Io is no doubt a form of *iho*, the core or animating force of all things, the primal energising principle." [1]

The letters Io are exhibited in the emblems below, and in fig. 829 they appear upon the Vase of Light in conjunction with the Twin Circles.

To the MAORI mind Light was the primal Father and Po was the passive " Mother Darkness." The North American Indian for *water* is *po ; po* is the Chinese for *lake*, and the European river-name Po is probably assignable to the same root. [2] *Eau*, the French for *water*, is phonetically O, *i.e.* the feminine moiety of Io. In Old English *yeo*, as in YEOVIL near AXMINSTER, meant *water*, but

827   828   829

in *yeoman* and the surname YEO it is probable that the word had an older signification.

OHIO is an Indian place-name, and in Indian language *ohio* means *beautiful*. IOWA is also an American place-name, and in Hebrew the word IHOAH means " Who is and who will be (?)." The Druidic invocation I.O.W. seemingly implied the Male and Female Spirit of Creation and their Offspring, the Twin Spirits of Love and Knowledge.

In fig. 830 the Celestial Twins are supported by the

[1] *The Maoris of New Zealand*, J. Cowan, p. 103.

[2] The River PO was alternatively known as the PADUS, the " Parent of Resplendent Light " ; the British *ay* or *ey*, meaning *water*, may be compared with the Norse *a*, meaning *river*, and all three terms may be equated with the primal A. The Babylonian Goddess EA or the Great Deity may perhaps be responsible for *ea*, another British form of *ay* or *ey*. TAW, a Celtic term for *river*, is apparently resplendent *Aw*.

Flower of Light ; in figs. 831 and 832 they are springing from between its lobes. Sometimes the Fleur-de-lys is represented with twin stars upon it,[1] and sometimes, as in

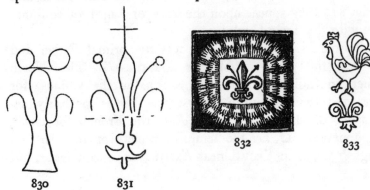

the arms of the city of FLORENCE, bursting with golden seeds. On fig. 833 is standing the Cock, "Chanticler"—a name apparently compounded of *chant* and *éclair*—"the singer of the lightning." Note the minute symbolism of

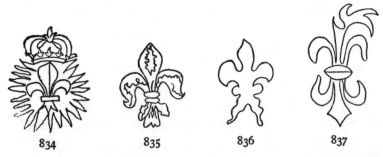

this cock ; his tail feathers are the *five* of light ; his wing is inscribed S ; and his comb is a combination of three and two.

That the IRIS symbolised the Primal Fire is abundantly evident from the examples herewith. Figs. 832 and 834 are encircled by a blaze of Flame ; fig. 835 is decorated with

[1] This emblem has been adopted as the crest of the Boy Scouts.

the flickering lines of Fire; and figs. 836 and 837 are designed in a form that suggests Fire.

Associated with figs. 838 to 840 are the Circles of Perfection,[1] and the S or SS of the Supreme Spirit is artfully introduced into the forms of figs. 840, 841, 843, and elsewhere. Our letter S is the Greek *sigma*, and the earliest form of *sigma* was practically the same as our modern Z. This letter subsequently assumed what Dr Isaac Taylor calls "the ordinary lunar form C."[2]

Fig. 843 is surmounted by a new moon or C. The

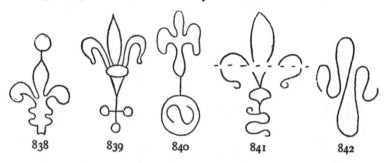

| 838 | 839 | 840 | 841 | 842 |

name *see* is phonetically identical with *sea*, the ocean, Dutch *zee*; and *sinus*, the Latin for a curving *sea*, is evidently cognate with Sin, the God of Light, whose emblem was the crescent moon or letter C. According to Plutarch, the Egyptian

---

[1] A *Fleur-de-lys* associated with two circles is the arms of the town of Liskeard in Cornwall. The main street in Liskeard is Luxe Street; one of the boundaries of the borough is "a certain cross which is called Luxycross." In the same district are Luxstowe and Luxulyan. In Liskeard—*i.e.* the Caer or Seat of Elis, the Lord of Light—St Luke's Day used to be a prime festival.—See Allen (J.), *Hist. of Bor. of Liskeard.*

Elis was essentially the Holy Land of ancient Greece. Watered by the River Alpheus, it was the centre of peace and religion, and the site of the Olympic games. Armies were compelled to lay down their arms before being permitted to pass through the favoured and sacred land.—See Buckley (T. A.), *Great Cities of Anc. World*, pp. 327–30. Compare also Lisbon or Lisboa, the capital of ancient Lusitania. Lisbon or Olisipo is still known in its most ancient part by the Moorish name Alfama, *i.e.* Alif, the Sun A?

[2] *The Alphabet*, ii. 105.

priests considered the sea " to proceed from fire," [1] and it is seemingly this idea which is preserved in the words *sinus*, *sea*, and *zee*.

The spear or rod-like core of figs. 844 and 845 represents *iho*, the primal, energising, and animating force of Light or Rod of JESSE. In fig. 844 it transfixes the wavy M of *mare*, the Sea ; in other words, it is a combination of I, the Holy One, and O or *eau*—a variant of the symbolism known to underlie the Maypole and its Ring. Under fig. 846, designed with the suggestion of a fiery Backbone, is the

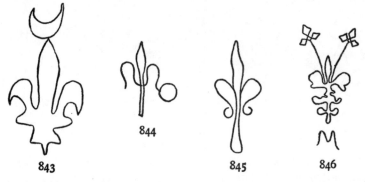

843   844   845   846

M of the Great Mother, and the divine Twins are denoted by the outspringing diamonds of DYAUS.

The word *sigma* resolves into *is ig ma*, the "light of the Mighty Mother." In the Arabian alphabet the equivalent of *sigma* is named *za*, which must be cognate with the European *zee* or *sea*.

The idea that Z, the original sign of *sigma*, once represented the zigzag lightning-flash or mighty Light, is to some extent supported by the Greek and Hebrew names for Z. In Greek Z is *zeta*, which resolves into *zee t a*, the Fire of the resplendent A.

The earliest forms or signs of *zayin*, the Hebrew for Z,

[1] *Isis and Osiris.*

are admittedly either a flame of fire or a duck.[1] The duck
was, as has been illustrated, identified with the Primal
Spirit floating on the primeval Ocean. The duck was
associated with Isis, who is said to have brought forth the
Sun ; and *nessa*, the Greek for *duck*, may be equated with
Nissa, the name of the Nymph who, according to Greek
legend, was the Mother of the Sun. According to Russian
fairy-tales, it was a duck and not a goose that laid the golden
eggs ; and in fig. 844 the attached circle may, no doubt, be
regarded either as the Sun or as the Golden Egg laid by the
primeval Goose. *Zasis*, the Lithuanian word for *goose*,
must be allied to Zas, the Chinese Sun-god whose trumpeter
was the Golden Cock, and Zas must be allied to Zeus and to
za, the Arabian *sigma*.

We meet with the *zig* of *zig*zag and *sig*ma in the names
of the Northern Solar hero Siegfried and of his parents
Sieglinde and Siegmund. The prevalence of twin heroes in
mythology is a fact that has often aroused comment, and
not infrequently the hero—as in the case of Siegfried—is
the fruit of what the critics deprecate as "an incestuous
union " of brother and sister.

At Dodona, perhaps the oldest of all Greek Sanctuaries,
Zeus was worshipped as immanent in the sacred oak, and the
rustling of its leaves in the wind was his voice. The worship
of the oak prevailed almost universally in Europe, and the
peculiar sanctity of this tree in all probability arose from the
form of its parts. The Acorn in its cup—which in fig. 848
surmounts the Bull of the Creator, and in fig. 847 is identified
with the P or Pa—was no doubt regarded as a lingam or combination of I, the Holy One, and O, the generative cup or
crater. It would also appear that the leaves of the oak were
regarded as flaming and *eight*-lobed, a suggestion borne out

[1] "For Zayin (Z) we have to choose between the Flame and the Duck."
—*The Alphabet*, Taylor, i. 111.

by the Celtic word *tan*, which means not only *oak*, but also
fire. In fig. 849 a Trinity of Acorns are associated with two
leaves ; in fig. 850 the eight-lobed parent Flame is balanced
by Twin Acorns ; and fig. 851, the Holy Family of I.O.W.,
consists of Four Acorns.

Among the Celts, Germans, and Slavs, it was strictly
prescribed that the sacred fire should be annually ignited by
the friction of two pieces of *Oak*wood, and in some countries
the new fire for the village was made on Midsummer Day
by causing *a wheel* to revolve rapidly round an axle of oak

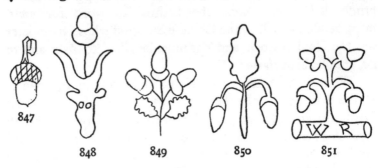

till the axle took fire.[1] This curious custom may have had
its origin from the idea that the Oak-tree symbolised the
Core, Pole, or Axis of Immaculate Fire. In fig. 852 the
three Acorns and two Leaves surmount a Solar Wheel, and
in fig. 853 this WHEEL, identified with Jesus Christ, is supported by the Twin Leaves of the Creative Unit. It was
the custom of the Druids to seek studiously for an oak-
tree having *two* principal boughs in the form of a cross ; if

---

[1] Frazer, *Golden Bough*, p. 293. Sometimes instead of a wheel the
machinery was " of a *square* form, in the centre of which was an axle-tree.
In some places three times three persons, in others three times nine, were
required for turning round by turns the axle-tree or wimble. If any of
them had been guilty of murder, adultery, theft, or other atrocious crime,
it was imagined either that the fire would not kindle or that it would be
devoid of its usual virtue."—*Golden Bough*, ii. 255.

the two horizontal arms were not sufficiently adapted to the figure, they fastened a cross beam to them, and the tree was then consecrated by cutting upon its right branch the letters HESUS, upon the middle stem TARANIS, upon the left branch BELENUS, and over them the word THAU[1]—*i.e.* seemingly *t au*, the resplendent Aw or A.[2]

In fig. 854 an Oak-tree is represented with three leaves, arms, or boughs, and the Flower of Light thence springing may be regarded as a diagram of the prophecy, "And there shall come forth a rod out of the stem of Jesse, and a

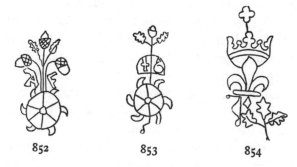

852   853   854

Branch shall grow out of his roots."[3]   The designer of fig. 854 would thus appear to have identified Christ, the Healer of the World, with the "Golden Bough," the Branch or offshoot of the Oak.   Mistletoe used to be called ALL HEAL, as it was supposed to be a universal healer, and a remedy against every kind of poison.   According to PLINY, "the Druids esteem nothing more sacred than the mistletoe

---

[1] *Veil of Isis*, W. Winwoode Reade, pp. 60, 151.
[2] Compare *Slav Fairy-Tale*:
    "O Oak Tree so green and with acorns of gold,
      In my helplessness I to thee cry ;
    In Heaven's great name now to beg I make bold,
      My pressing needs pray satisfy."
                Slav Tales, p. 339.
[3] Isaiah xi. 1.

and the tree on which it grows, provided that the tree is an Oak. They believe that whatever grows on these trees is sent from Heaven, and is a sign that the tree has been chosen by the God himself. The mistletoe is very rarely to be met with; but when it is found they gather it with solemn ceremony. . . . They hail it as the universal healer." [1]

It was until lately the custom at YORK Minster to carry Mistletoe to the High Altar at Christmas Eve, and to proclaim at the gates of the City towards the four quarters of Heaven, a public and universal pardon. [2]

The *twin* leaves and translucent, pearl-like berries (usually twins) of the Mistletoe, or Missel*dew* [3] as it is alternatively called, probably symbolised the celestial semen, dew, or sap of the Supreme Spirit. The mistletoe plant was regarded as the vital seat of the Oak-tree's life, and it was believed by country people that a potion prepared from mistletoe would make barren animals fertile.

In the oldest Vedic hymns the Celestial Twins are worshipped with a peculiar reverence as able not merely to heal sickness, but also to restore the aged to youthfulness.

ALL HEAL, the European mistletoe, corresponds to SOMA, [4] the God of the Eastern Soma plant, who is said to clothe the naked and *heal the sick*. His attributes are summed up in the lines :

---

[1] Cf. *Golden Bough*, ii. 286.

[2] Winwoode Reade, *Veil of Isis*, p. 238.

[3] Among the scintillating many-meanings of the word INDRA, the "Enduring A," are "dew" and "sap." The mediæval English word for dew was DYAU, and it would thus appear that our "dew" is cognate, if not identical, with the Sanscrit DYU (brilliant) and DYAUS (the Sky), so named a being the glistering offspring of the brilliant sky. The Cornish for *God* was *Dew*, and the French DIEU has evidently the same ancestry as the English *dew*.

[4] SOMA, the personification of the plant, is extolled as the *Creator* and *Father* of the Gods, *Hindoo Mythology*, W. J. Wilkins, p. 59.

" This Soma is a god ; he cures
The sharpest ills that man endures.
He heals the sick, the sad he cheers,
He nerves the weak, dispels their fears ;
The faint with martial ardour fires,
With lofty thoughts the bard inspires ;
The soul from earth to heaven he lifts ;
So great and wondrous are his gifts,
Men feel the god within their veins,
And cry in loud exulting strains :

    ' We've quaffed the Soma bright,
      And are immortal grown ;
    We've entered into light,
      And all the gods have known.
    What mortal now can harm,
      Or foeman vex us more ?
    Through thee, beyond alarm,
      Immortal god, we soar.' " [1]

Although SOMA is here hailed as masculine, the name Soma was and still is given to the Moon. " How and why this change took place," says Wilkins, " is unknown, but in the later of the Vedic hymns there is some evidence of the transition." [2]

It was said that " SOMA is the Moon, the food of the Gods," and that " the Sun has the nature of AGNI, the Moon of SOMA." [3] The Israelitish Manna, described by the Rabbis as like pearls, and in the Old Testament as a honey-sweet, small, round seed resembling hoar-frost, fell *during the night* and had to be gathered before the rays of the Sun became so hot as to melt it.

At the solemn ceremonials of the Druids the Chief Priest wore a golden crescent on his breast, and the Mistletoe,

---

[1] *Hindoo Mythology*, Wilkins, p. 60.
[2] *Ibid.*, p. 62.   [3] *Ibid.*

at full moon, was reverently cut from the Oak by means of a golden sickle—evidently the emblem of the crescent Moon, or *So ma*, the "Fire Mother."

Part of the Imperial insignia of Japan is three crescent-shaped agates, one red, one white, and one blue. The meaning of red is Love, of white, Purity, and of blue, Truth. In fig. 845 the three C's of "SOMA" or "SIGMA" are linked into a rose-surmounted Trinity.

During the Festival of the Mistletoe-cutting, *two white* bulls were brought to the foot of the oak-tree, and these

855

twin Bulls are curiously referred to in a Druidic folk-song current in France and England. The English version runs :

> "I will sing you my one O !
> (*Chorus*) *What is your one O ?*
> One is all alone,
> And ever doth remain so.
> (*Chorus*) *What is your two O ?*"

To this query the answer returned is "two white boys clothed in green," but in the French version it is *deux bœufs attelés à une coque, ils vont expirer—voyez la merveille ?*[1] The custom of kissing under the mistletoe was once associated with the *two* circles looped into each other, as shown in fig. 682, p. 289, vol. i. A writer in *Notes and Queries* describing old English Christmas customs says, with regard

[1] See Reade, *Veil of Isis*, p. 234.

to the mistletoe " Kissing-bunch," that it was " always an elaborate affair. . . . The size depends upon the couple of hoops—*one thrust through the other*—which form its skeleton. Each of the ribs is garlanded with holly, ivy, and sprigs of other greens, with bits of coloured ribbons [1] and paper roses, rosy-cheeked apples, and oranges. Three small dolls are also prepared, and these represent our Saviour, the Mother of Jesus, and Joseph. These dolls generally hang within the kissing-bunch by strings from the top, and are surrounded by apples and oranges tied to strings, and various brightly-coloured ornaments. Occasionally the dolls are arranged to represent a manger scene. Generally a bit of mistletoe is obtainable, and this is carefully tied to the bottom of the kissing-bunch, which is then hung up in the middle of the house place." [2]

It is still a custom to pluck a mistletoe berry for every kiss taken, and it is fairly evident that the Christmas mistletoe kiss was originally a quasi-sacramental pledge of atonement, reconciliation, and goodwill. The Christmas Tree, garlanded with bright balls, decked with candles and gifts, and surmounted by a Father Christmas or a Fairy Queen, is obviously a symbol of the Great Giver.

In Nursery-tale the Celestial Twins figure as the Babes in the Wood, and in many versions these two innocents are banished by their ignorant parents, because—like the Goose of the golden egg—every morning a piece of gold falls from the children's mouths. According to some accounts, the boy Babe when grown up plays the rôle of a SIEGFRIED or a PERSEUS.

But a still larger cycle of mythology deals with brothers, one of whom quarrels with and slays the other. The

---

[1] These may be compared with the many-coloured streamers of the Maypole and the Tambourine.

[2] 1877, 5th series, viii. p. 481.

Hebrew sign for Cain and ABEL[1] is " the Twins,"[2] and the murder of ABEL, the "keeper of sheep," by CAIN, the "tiller of the ground," apparently typifies the death of Love at the hands of his brother Learning.[3]   Similarly BALDUR was done to death by the machinations of LOKI—a form of LOGOS or Reason.

In Egyptian mythology SET, the Darkness, is figured fighting against HORUS, the Light, and at a later period the myth was transferred to TYPHON and OSIRIS.   AHRIMAN and ORMUZ were said to be twin brothers, and probably LUCIFER, the fallen angel, was originally the twin brother of his opponent MICHAEL.   In all these and many other instances the idea underlying is that the brothers were primarily Twin Rulers ; that subsequently one revolted against the other, and that ultimately this rebel came to be regarded as the Devil—Prince LUCIFER, the fallen star.[4] The Asvins were said to be one white and the other black, and it will be remembered that the riddle of the " Princess with the Golden Hair " was correctly guessed in the words, " You must be Time, including *night* and *day*."[5]   Tennyson catches this idea in the lines :

---

[1] ABEL and CANE or KANE are English surnames.

[2] *Bible Folk-Lore*, p. 10.

[3] The Polynesians in their traditions of the genesis of humanity record that there was "darkness from the first division unto the tenth, to the hundredth, to the thousandth—that is for a vast space of time ; and *these divisions of time were considered as beings and were each named*."—(*Polynesian Mythology*, Sir George Grey, p. 1.)   In all probability the Semitic Patriarchs will prove to be personifications of various past eras and epochs.

[4] The names of the most noted Brethren yield very curious results, *e.g.*, in ancient Mexico King CAN is said to have had three sons, two of whom quarrelled, and Prince AAC (*i.e.* A the great?) slew Prince COH (*i.e.* the great O?).   ABEL or OBEL, the Ball O, was murdered by Cain, the great one A. JACOB, the great ORB, supplanted ESAU, the light A.   BALDUR, the enduring BALL, was done to death by LOKI, Lord Great I.   LUCIFER or DIABOLUS, the resplendent OBULUS, struggles with MICHAEL—OM-IK-A-EL.

[5] Symbolised in fig. 856.

". . . The Bright one in the highest
Is brother of the Dark one in the lowest,
And Bright and Dark have sworn that I, the child
Of thee, the great Earth-Mother, thee, the Power
That lifts her buried life from gloom to bloom,
Should be for ever and for evermore
The Bride of Darkness." [1]

Among nearly all primitive peoples it is believed that
the Earth and Sky were once wedded, but that long ages ago
something—in some instances a snake—cut them asunder.
The Hindoos speak of the marriage between Dyaus, the
glistening sky or ether, and Nishtigri, the Earth ; and a
legend of the Polynesian " savages" records that : " Up to

856

this time the vast Heaven has still ever remained separated
from his spouse the Earth.   Yet their mutual love still
continues—the soft warm sighs of her loving bosom still
ever rise up to him, ascending from the woody mountains
and valleys, and men call these mists ; and the vast Heaven,
as he mourns through the long nights his separation from
his beloved, drops frequent tears upon her bosom, and men
seeing these, term them dewdrops." [2]

The poetic marriage of Earth and Heaven is identical in
idea with the theologic marriage of Christ and His mystic
Bride, the Church on Earth.   It is alternatively expressed
in the passage, " Mercy and Truth are met together ;
Righteousness and Peace have kissed each other.   Truth
shall spring out of the earth ; and Righteousness shall look
down from Heaven." [3]   This marriage, reconciliation, or

---

[1] *Demeter and Persephone.*
[2] Sir George Grey, *Polynesian Mythology*, p. 10.   [3] Psalms.

atonement—*i.e.* a making one—*not* an "expiation," was
denoted by the two linked circles of the All-healing
Mistletoe-Bunch, and it is again denoted in fig. 857 by the
kiss of the Twin Cherubs ;[1] the scattering flowers, like the
many-coloured ribbons of the Maypole and the Mistletoe-
Bunch doubtless symbolise the resulting joys and pleasures.
In figs. 859 to 861 the Twin Children of Light are represented by C's, which in figs. 862 to 864 are clasped in an
embrace. The centres of fig. 862 are twin-balls or circles,
and from the extremities spring seeds, berries, or dewdrops.

857

858

The double cross on which the C's or crescents of fig. 864
are interclasped is the ancient form of the Greek Z, *i.e.*
Zeta, the parent Flame. That this word meant *zi tau*, the
light of the Tau or resplendent Au, is confirmed by the
form T introduced into fig. 863.

The Celestial Twins of Love and Knowledge or Religion
and Science were not only expressed by two circles, two
children, and two eyes, but also by the twin pillars ; and
these twin pillars thus, Π, are the Zodiacal sign of Gemini.

In Egypt the two pillars known as the North Pole of
Day or Light and the South Pole of Night or Darkness,[2]

[1] The Two Golden Cherubim guarding the Ark were no doubt the same
symbol.

[2] *Signs and Symbols of Primordial Man*, Churchward, p. 201.

symbolised the Portals of Eternity, the Gateway of Life, the Door of Heaven.

In fig. 865 the two pillars are bridged by a rosary of perfections, and in figs. 866 and 867 the pillars are intertwined.

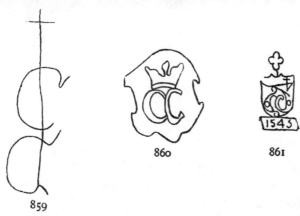

859
860
861

In fig. 868 the Holy Four are expressed by a Flower of Light, the sides of which are C's or Sigmas.

The symbol of the Twin Pillars bears a general re-

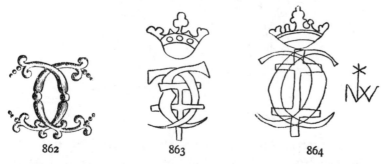

862
863
864

semblance to the sign H, the letter of stability (*a-t-ch*), A, the resplendent Self-Existent; and from the fact that the twin circles are at times found associated with a capital H, it is reasonable to infer that H, the *eighth* character of our alphabet, was looked upon as peculiarly the letter of Regeneration or Atonement. The regenerating 8 appears in the centre of the *aitch* (fig. 869) herewith. Under the symbolic picture of Ushas,[1] the dawn, on page 67, fig. 167, vol. i.,

865   866   867

there occurs a combination of two H's. These two *aitches* stand for the Horebs, *i.e.* the Chorebs or Cherubs, or alternatively for the Harits, another name of the Asvins. The word *harits* has survived in Charites, the Greek Graces, and in our word *charity*.

868   869

The inscription under fig. 866 is illegible, but that under fig. 867 is " Adami." The mystics regarded Adam and Eve not as two individuals but as a generic symbol of Humanity. They conceived Everyman as being dual in his character, and as having within himself the masculine

[1] The Hindoo Ushas is said to have sprung from the head of Dyaus in the same way as the Greek Minerva sprang from the head of Zeus.

attributes of Intellect, Science, or Understanding, and the feminine characteristics of Love, Religion, or Will.[1] There has always been a school of Philosophy which has maintained that the story of ADAM and EVE is an extended allegory, and that the " Fall " occurs in every individual who, allowing his " better half " to be seduced by the serpent of sensuality, self-indulgence, or materialism, loses his primitive innocence. It has been said that the *Ave* of Mary reverses the curse of *Eva*, and that Christ, born of the Spirit, is the Saviour and Redeemer of the new Adam. There is no mention in Genesis of Adam having awakened from the deep sleep into which he is recorded to have been thrown. The Cabalists termed the awakened ADAM, *i.e.* the regenerate man " ADAMKAIDMON," and to this term the inscription ADAMI under fig. 866 appears to bear some relation.

The symbolism of the Celestial Twins, the twin dew-drops of the Holy Spirit, the divine duality lurking in the soul of Everyman, the double *you* and the double *me*, may possibly elucidate that enigmatic passage in the Apocrypha, " For the Lord himself, having been asked by someone when his Kingdom should come, said, When the two shall be one, and the outside as the inside, and the male with the female."[2]

---

[1] The names under which these two halves of the soul were designated vary to a certain extent, but the fundamental idea of a hard and a soft side, a worser and a better self, has persisted from time immemorial. Many mystics use the terms *Understanding* for Knowledge or Truth, and *Will* for Love. " There are," says Robert Boyle, " two things which most enable man and make him resemble the Gods—to know the Truth and to do good ; for that diviner part of man—the soul—which alone is capable of wearing the glorious image of its Author, being endowed with *two chief faculties—the understanding and the will*—the former is blest and perfectionated by knowledge, and the latter's loveliest and most improving property is goodness."—*Natural Philosophy*, Robert Boyle, London, 1664. " It is," says an eighteenth-century mystic, " in this double purification of the Understanding and of the Will that the interior life consists."—*Introduction to Fenelon's Works*, vol. i., Antwerp, 1723. [2] 2 Clement xii. 2.

CHAPTER XV

THE WHITE HORSE

*"Nothing is clearer than the marvellous persistence of traditional and immemorial modes of thought, even in the face of conquest and subjugation."—*E. ANWYL (*Celtic Religion*).

THE Welsh chronicles relate of BRITAIN that "the first of the three chieftains who established the colony was HU the Mighty, who came with the original settlers. They came over the hazy sea from the summer country, which is called Deffrobani—that is where Constinoblys now stands."[1]

HU the Mighty, a Sun-god whom Squire equates with the Irish LUG or LUGH and with the Welsh LLEU or LLEW,[2] is said to have obtained his dominion in Britain not by war and bloodshed, but by justice and peace. By the slaying of a Dragon-like monster he caused the cessation of disastrous floods ; then federating his people into tribes as a first step towards civil government, he taught them the art of agriculture, and was the first to draw on British soil a furrow with the plough. He laid the foundations of literature and history by the institution of bardism, and is therefore called the first of the " Three National Pillars of the Isle of Britain."[3]

The Welsh word *llew*, meaning *light* and also *lion*, is probably a corroded form of *el Hu*, "Lord Hu," and may

[1] *Triad*, 4.　　[2] *Mythology of Ancient Britain*, p. 52.　　[3] *Ibid.*

34

certainly be equated with the Irish Sun-god LUGH. At about the period 2000 B.C. ILU was an Assyrian name for the "One Great God."[1] LUG, an alternative title of LUGH, is a contracted form of LUGUS, the Gaulish Sun-god, and the Gaulish LUGUS is what the Greeks called LOGOS, the divine WORD or REASON.

The Celtic for *mind* was *hew*; *hu* in Chinese means *Sir* or *Lord*, and HUGH, the British Christian name, is defined by the authorities as meaning " mind, soul, spirit."[2] In Egypt the word *khu*, i.e. *ak Hu* (?), " Great Hu," meant the " shining, translucent, transparent, intangible essence of a man, and the word is on the whole, perhaps, best rendered by spirit."[3]

HU, the name of the All-pervading, is a root whose ramifications are discernible in many directions. It is apparent in DYHU or DYU, the bright and heavenly divinity of India and Greece; in TAOU, the Chinese Supreme Reason ; and it is again recognisable in HUHI, the Egyptian All-Father. The primitive and elementary HU may be traced not only in the simplicities of such names as the French HUON and the English HEWIN, HUBERT, GOODHEW, etc., but in the intricacies of God-names such as the Mexican HUITZON and HUITZILOPOCHTLI.

The ancient name of MEXICO was ANAHUAC, and the word *huaca* there meant not only *sacred* but also a *tumulus* or artificial *hill*.

The English counties of GLOUCESTERSHIRE, WORCESTERSHIRE, and part of WARWICKSHIRE, were once called HUICCAS, and constituted the territory of a people known as the HUICCII.[4] These HUICCII were presumably worshippers

[1] Pinches (T. G.), *Rel. of Bab. and Ass.*, p. 118.
[2] *New Illus. Dict. of English Language*, p. 446.
[3] *A Guide to the Egyptian Collections in the British Museum*, p. 156.
[4] Wilson, *Imperial Gazetteer*, i. 1032.

of Hu *ik*, the "Great Hu," and may be compared with the QUICHES, *i.e.* the "AK HUISHES" of Central America. HUISH is to this day an English surname ; within the once sacred precincts of AVEBURY there is a HUISH HILL, and elsewhere in BRITAIN are several towns named HUISH or HEWISH.

HUGH TOWN in the Scillies is overlooked by a hill known as the Hu, and *heugh* is an old generic term for *crag* or *cliff.*

Hu the Mighty was seemingly the God of Gentleness ; his name is the root of *humane, winsome, wistful,* and *whisper,* and he is still invoked by children as "Gentle Jes*hu*, meek and mild." The syllables HUISH have coalesced into *hush,* and the modern mother whispering *Hushabye Baby* unconsciously murmurs the benediction, "May the light of Hu be with ye, baby."[1]

In Greek the word *eu* means *good, soft, pleasing,* or *well*— whence such terms as *euphony,* a pleasing sound ; *euphemism,* a soft expression ; and *euphrasia,* delight.

The Wiltshire HUISH is in the PEWSEY district, and the name HUGH is again recognisable in PUGH, a corrosion of AP-HU. The Mighty Hu is also probably responsible for the place-names such as WICK, WICKLOW, WIGTON, and WEXFORD.

Close to HUGH TOWN in the SCILLIES is a place named GUGH, and the surname and place-name KEW may probably be resolved into *ak* Hu.

The patronymic GUY is defined by name dictionaries as meaning *sense,* and in France *gue* or *gui* means *mistletoe.* It

---

[1] Compare the Old Testament injunction, "On this wise ye shall bless the children of Israel, saying unto them, the Lord bless thee and keep thee : *the Lord make His face shine upon thee,* and be gracious unto thee : the Lord lift up his countenance upon thee and give thee peace : and they shall put my name upon *the children* of Israel ; and I will bless them."—Numbers vi. 23– 27. "Hush" is supposed to be a "purely imitative word." Its Danish form is HYSSE and its Swedish HYSSJA. Compare name HUSHAI.

is still a custom in certain parts of FRANCE for children on New Year's Day to run along the streets and rap at all the doors, crying " *Au gui l'an né !* " or " *Au gui l'an neuf !* " In the Island of SEIN in BRITTANY there is an annual mistletoe feast, on which occasion an altar covered with green boughs is erected *in the centre* of a *circular* piece of ground. Thence a procession starts, and thither, having marched round the island, it returns. Musicians form the vanguard, and these are followed by children carrying bill-hooks and oak branches, and leading *an ox* and *a horse* covered with flowers. After them a huge crowd, which stops at intervals, crying " *Gui-na-né, voilà le gui !* " [1]

The flower-laden Horse that figures in this ceremony was the symbol of the Divine Mind or Reason, and *equus*, the Latin for *horse*, resolves into the light of EK HU, *i.e.* the great mind, soul, or spirit.

According to PLATO, the Horse signified in a good sense "reason and opinion coursing about through natural things," and in a bad sense, "a confused fantasy." [2] The Hebrew word for *horse* means also *to explain*. "The signification of a horse as denoting the *intellectual principle* was derived," says Swedenborg, "from the ancient church to the wise round about, even into Greece ; hence it was, that in describing the sun, by which is signified love, they placed therein the god of their wisdom and intelligence, and attributed to him a chariot and four fiery horses ; and in describing the god of the sea, inasmuch as by sea was signified sciences in general, they also allotted horses to him ; hence, too, when they described the birth of the sciences from the intellectual principle, they feigned a flying horse, which with his hoof burst open a fountain, where were virgins who were the sciences ; nor was anything else

[1] Reade, *Veil of Isis*, p. 238.
[2] Madeley, *The Science of Correspondence*, p. 194.

signified by the Trojan horse but an artful contrivance of
the understanding to destroy Walls ; at this day, indeed,
when the intellectual Principle is described, agreeably to
the custom received from the ancients, it is usually described
by a flying horse or Pegasus, and erudition by a fountain ;
but it is known scarcely to anyone that *horse*, in a mystical
sense, signifies the understanding, and that a fountain
signifies truth ; still less is it known that these significations
were derived from the ancient Church to the Gentiles."

TACITUS records that in some parts of Northern Europe
snow-white horses were reared at the public expense in a
sacred grove and never used for service. When the King
as High Priest yoked them to the sacred chariot, their
neighing and snorting were carefully observed and the will
of the Gods therefrom inferred, since it was firmly believed
that these white horses *knew the plans of the heavenly powers*.[1]
The Druids and also the Persian Magi[2] practised divination by means of white horses, and in the Japanese Shinto
Temples there is still maintained a sacred horse—generally
an albino—known as the JIMME. In the temple of NIKKO
there are kept *three* snow-white horses, and in the innermost
shrine of this sacred wonder-spot is nothing but a burnished
disc or *patera* symbol of NIKKO or Father NICHOLAS, the
Unique O.

The colour White has always been accepted as the
symbol of innocence of soul, purity of thought, holiness of
life ; and the words *white* and *wheat* are radically *Huyt* and
Hueet. HU, as the God of Mind, must be responsible for
the words *wot* and *wist*, meaning to *know*—of *wit*, meaning
clever, and also of *humour* or *humeur*. *Wit* is mental *acute-
ness* or *acumen*, and to *whet* means to make *akhute*.

The coin of CUNOBELINUS mentioned *ante* as bearing

[1] *Northern Mythology*, Kauffman, p. 30.
[2] Borlase, *Ant. of Cornwall*, p. 144.

the device of a wheat-spike[1] has on its *verso* a dual-tailed horse. In fig. 870 the Horse is transfixed by a spike, pole, or axis ; in figs. 871 and 873 it is coursing over the Holy Hills, and a three- and seven-fold flaming tree or pillar of

870

light is introduced into the background.[2] In fig. 872 the column or trunk is rooted upon the primal A and the celestial steed is supported by the two C's or crescent moons of the CHARITES. In Sanscrit the word *harit,* meaning *the light of morning, bright,* and *resplendent,* means also *horse.*

871   872   873

Among Oriental nations the White Horse was a symbol of the Sun, and in the Vedas there is an entire hymn addressed to the Sun as a Horse. The English *horse,* akin to *gorse,* is almost identical with the French *ours,* a *bear.*

[1] The Cornish for a beard of wheat was *kulhu*—the Great God HU. The Cornish for corn was *iz* or *izik.*

[2] The emblem of a Horse and Palm-tree is found upon the coinage of CARTHAGE.

Hengist and Horsa mean the *Stallion* and the *Mare*. *Horsa*, a *mare*, may be equated with *ursa*, a *bear*, and may be resolved into Horus, the Ever-established Golden Light. In Icelandic *horse* is *hross*, in Dutch *ros*, in German *ross*, and in Old High German *hros*—all equally resolvable into Horus or Eros.

Ros is the Latin for *dew*, which is symbolically equal to the Sanscrit Dyhu, the French Dieu, and the Cornish *Dew*,[1] meaning *God*. In Cornish *ros* means *mountain*[2] and *wheel*. *Ros* is also the Celtic for *heath*, for which the Latin is *erica*.

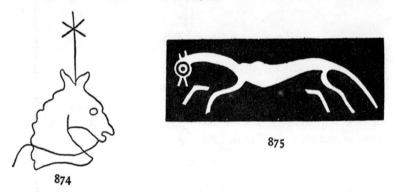

874

875

From this word *erica* it would appear that the poetic ancients regarded the purply-pink globules of the heath blossom as the ambrosia or honey-dew of Great Fire A.

There are still to be seen in Britain certain monumental white horses carved on *Hill*-sides. Most of these figures are in Wiltshire;[3] notably at Pewsey and Cherhill.[4] In Warwickshire[5] there is a red horse, and at Bratton (Buraton) Hill, near Westbury,[6] a white one.

Fig. 875 herewith is a facsimile of the celebrated white horse near Shrivenham[7] in Berkshire.

[1] Compare surnames Dew, Dow, and Daw.
[2] In Cornish *monadh* also means *mountain*.
[3] Willet or Huilletshire?
[4] Ever-existent Fire Hill?
[5] Huarwick?   [6] Huestbury?   [7] Ashurivenham?

The mouth consists of the Two Rays of the Eternal Twins, and the Head and Eye form a point within a circle, the symbol of the Everlasting.[1] This same symbolic horse appearing on a British gold coin of about 150 B.C. is assumed to be "a barbarous copy" of a perfect Greek original, but there are no traces of "barbarism" or copying, and it would rather appear that correctness of drawing has been sacrificed to symbolic purport. Tradition tells us that the White Horse of BERKSHIRE marks the locality of a victory over the Danes, of which the exact site is claimed to be ASHDOWN, anciently known as MONS FRAXINI, the Hill of the Ash-Tree.[2]

The BERK- of BERKSHIRE is from *barruc* or *berroc*, meaning the polled oak[3] under which the shire motes were once held. This sacred tree was, it may be assumed, named *berroc* because it was the symbol of Père OK, the "Great Father."

The Mohammedans tell of a milk-white steed named AL BORAK, each of whose strides was equal to the furthest range of human vision. In Romance one meets with the famous horse BAYARD, the property of the four sons of "AMYON,"[4] evidently AMON or AMMUN.

A magic horse with a mane of gold is a feature of many fairy-tales and it figures with peculiar prominence in the Slav legend entitled NIEZGUINEK. The name NIEZGUINEK means *imperishable*, but primarily it is composed of the syllables *on iz ag Hu in ek*, the "One or Sun light, the mighty HU, the unique." NIEZGUINEK, ELISHA-like, is a plougher with twelve yoke of oxen, and he becomes the possessor of a magic horse, "in truth a most magnificent horse, big and strong,

---

[1] Compare with Serpent's head in fig. 459 (see *ante*, p. 200, vol. i.), and with the altar in a circle of the Breton Mistletoe fête.

[2] *The Scouring of the White Horse*, Hughes, p. 242.

[3] Edmunds, *Traces of History in the Names of Places*, p. 173.

[4] Hulme (F. E.), *Nat. Hist. Lore*, p. 181.

with eyes that flashed like lightning. He leapt up into the air as high as the clouds, and the next moment descended in the middle of a field."[1] This irresistible creature places itself at the service of NIEZGUINEK, who exclaims :

> " Marvel of strength and of beauty so white,
> Horse of my heart, while I sing,
> Rise in the air, like a bird take thy flight,
> Haste to the court of my king."[2]

With each of NIEZGUINEK's tasks this formula is slightly varied, and the descriptions of the horse's behaviour are

876

highly suggestive. " Just as if the horse had seen something in the clouds, he rose swift as an arrow and flew through the air above the fogs."—" The horse arose in the air as if he heard someone calling to him from the clouds."—" The horse rose immediately as if he had been beckoned to by some one in the clouds."—" Then the horse looked up as if there were something he wanted in the clouds."—" Then the horse, as if he saw some strange thing in the clouds, lifted himself up in the air and began to fly."[3]

The Horse also figures largely in the Slav fairy-tale of Prince SLUGOBYL. SLUGOBYL sees a white swan pursued by

---

[1] *Slav Tales*, p. 242.   [2] *Ibid.*, p. 251.   [3] *Ibid.*, pp. 233, 264.

an eagle about to pounce upon it. Seizing a crossbow, he sends an arrow through the eagle, whereupon the grateful swan addresses him : "Valiant Prince Slugobyl, it is not a mere swan who thanks you for your most timely help, but the daughter of the Invisible Knight, who, to escape the pursuit of the giant KOSTEY [the same KOSTEY who annoyed the Princess SUDOLISU], has changed herself into a swan. My father will gladly be of service to you in return for this kindness to me. When in need of his help you have only to say three times, 'Invisible Knight, come to me.'" Having thus spoken, the swan flew away and Prince SLUGOBYL, after watching her for as long as possible, proceeded on his travels. After a while he arrives at the court of a king who is besieged by a large army, and this king promises the hand of his daughter to the man who shall deliver him from his enemies. SLUGOBYL invokes the aid of the Invisible Knight, whereupon he immediately hears a voice at his ear say, "Behold me, Prince, at your service." Upon learning SLUGOBYL's requirement, the Invisible Knight whistles up the magic horse MAGU, whose name is practically the same as *Magus*, *i.e.* a *sage, philosopher, wizard, wiseacre*, or *wiseman*.

> " MAGU, Horse with Golden Mane,
> I want your help yet once again.
> Walk not the earth but fly through space
> As lightnings flash or thunders race.
> Swift as the arrow from the bow
> Come quick, yet so that none can know."

"At that instant a magnificent grey Horse appeared out of a whirlwind of smoke and from his head there hung a golden mane. Swift as the wind was he, flames of fire blazed forth from his nostrils, lightning flashed from his eyes, and volumes of smoke came from his ears." [1]

[1] *Slav Tales*, p. 182.

This popular description of a fairy Horse may be compared with the inquiry in *The Song of Solomon*: "Who is this that cometh out of the wilderness like pillars of smoke?"[1] but more particularly with 2 Samuel xxii.: "In my distress I called upon the Lord, and cried to my God: and he did hear my voice out of his temple, and my cry did enter into his ears. Then the earth shook and trembled; the foundations of heaven moved and shook, because he was wroth. *There went up a smoke out of his nostrils, and fire out of his mouth devoured*: coals were kindled by it. He bowed the heavens also, and came down; and darkness was under his feet. And he rode upon a cherub, and did fly: and he was seen upon the wings of the wind. And he made darkness pavilions round about him, dark waters, and thick clouds of the skies. Through the brightness before him were coals of fire kindled. The Lord thundered from heaven, and the most High uttered his voice."

"I have compared thee, O my Love," says *The Song of Solomon*, "to a company of horses," or, as the literal translation reads, "to my mare." The French word for *mare*, *jument*, is obviously *ju-ment*, the Ever-Existing *Mens* or *Mind*; the English *mare* is the French *mère*, meaning *mother*: in French *mer*, and in Latin *mare*, means the sea. Radically the word *mare* may be resolved into MA RE, the mother of RA or RE, a derivation which may be accounted for mystically; or poetically, on the grounds that RA, the Sun, must daily have been seen to emerge at dawn from the Sea and to sink again at nightfall into her bosom. One of the Greek terms for *dawn* was *akra nux*, i.e. *akra*, the Great UR-A, *onux*,[2] the one great Fire. The Greek for *day* is *nuera*, which may be anglicised into *new era*. The Illyrian for *dawn* was *zora* = *iz* or *a*, the Sanscrit is *agnya* = AGNI-A, and

[1] iii. 6.   [2] Compare the precious stone *onyx*.

the Sanscrit for day is *ahan* or *ahar*, the "one A" or "A fire."
The English *east* = *izt* is "light resplendent," the Mayan
for *west* was *ix*, and in the word *occident* we may recognise *ok se den*, the "resplendent den of OKSE," the mighty
Fire.

In BABYLON the horse was described as "the god ZU," [1]
and in Gypsy language the word *zi* means *mind*. [2] The
Greek for *horse* was *ikkos*, the "great light," and the Saxon
was *ehu*, probably pronounced AYHU.

In Saxon times *mare* was written *mere*, which now means
not only *pure*, *true*, and *simple*, but also a *lake*. Lakes, *lacs*,
or *lochs*, were once held sacred, and Lake-names, from the
radical Loch EWE, in many directions perpetuate the memory
of their original sanctity. [3] A *ewer* is a vessel for carrying
water, and *aqua* is the Latin for *water*. [4]

In Egyptian *mer* meant *to love* ; the Dutch for *mare* is
merrie, which in English means *gay*, and the Old German
for a war-horse was *marah*.

The Horse, or *hack* (Spanish *hacka*), or *nag* is said to
whinny, [5] and *winne* is Celtic for *white*. *Pony* must be related
to EPONA the Gaulish Horse-Goddess, and *hippa*, the Greek
for horse—from the Phœnician HIP, signifying the *Parent of
All*—may be compared with the English synonyms *hobby* and
hobin. [6] A Goddess named HIPPA, represented with the head
of a horse, was said to have been the nurse of BACCHUS, and
a round or circle for horse exercises is named *hippodrome*,

---

[1] Pinches. *Religion of Babylonia*, p. 103.

[2] Borrow (G.), *Romano Lavo-Lil*, p. 67.

[3] At the time of writing an English syndicate is dredging a South
American lake for sacrificial offerings. It has already recovered a considerable amount of treasure.

[4] The zodiacal sign of AQUARIUS, the water-carrier, is the hieroglyph ♒.

[5] To *whine* or *pule* meant perhaps to cry for one's mother.

[6] Payne-Knight. *Symbol. Lang. of Ancient Art*, p. 79.

i.e. the hippa *drum*.[1]   The French for *stable* is *écurie*, Great
Fire Eye, and the English word *mews* means not only a
home for horses, but also a cage for hawks.   To *muse* means
to *think* or *meditate*, and *amusing* is akin to *merrie*, *gay*, and
humorous.   *Mus* is Latin for *mouse*, an animal which, as
already noted, was sacred to APOLLO,[2] and *souris*, the French
for *mouse*, is akin to *sourire*, a smile.   *Smile* is connected with
smintheus, the Greek for *mouse*, and SMINTHEUS was one
of the titles of APOLLO.   The name resolves into *theos*,
God, and *smin*—originally *simon*—the sole fire, or *semen*,
the seed.

> " That Light whose *smile* kindles the universe,
>   That Beauty in which all things work and move." [3]

In Egypt the Shrew mouse was held sacred, and the
word *shrew* by the addition of a *d* becomes *shrewd*, *i.e.*
acute, *witty*, *clever*.   Cinderella's coach was drawn by mice [4]
which turned magically into white horses, *i.e.* the golden-
footed steeds or harits of the Morning.

The White Lady of nursery rhyme who rides upon a
White Horse and whose bells make music wherever she goes
is obviously our Lady of Wisdom.[5]   Popular tradition has
many legends about white ladies who usually dwell in forts
and mountains as enchanted maidens waiting for deliverance.
They delight to appear in warm sunshine to poor shepherds

---

[1] The *drom*edary has *twin* hills on its back.   The *twin* DROMIOS introduced into Shakespeare's "Comedy of Errors" makes me suspect that *drom*
somewhere meant *twin*.

[2] Near Penzance and NEWLYN are the towns of PAUL and MOUSEHOLE
(pronounced " Mousel ").

[3] Shelley, *Adonais*.

[4] Æsop represents a mouse as nibbling a netted lion free.

[5] " Ride a cock-horse to Banbury Cross
        To see a White Lady ride on a White Horse ;
     Rings on her fingers and bells on her toes,
     And so she makes music wherever she goes."
                    Mother Goose's Book of Nursery Rhymes.

or herd-boys. They are either combing their long hair,
or washing themselves, drying wheat, beating flax, or spinning ; they also point out treasures and beg for deliverance,
offering as reward flowers, corn, or chaff, which gifts turn
immediately into gold or silver. They wear snow-white or
half-white, half-black garments and yellow or green shoes.
In GERMANY the White Lady is generally called BERTHA,
which was a name of the Great Goddess of Nature.[1]

A mare is one of the possessions of Cinderella, and she
addresses it :

> " Bow to me, Blank,[2] my steed,
> The last maid that rode thee
> Was I indeed." [3]

" Hail beauteous mares ! " cries CINDERELLA to the six
wonderful white animals that draw her crystal chariot, " fair
are ye all, ye that were bred in my father's stall." [4] According to another version, CINDERELLA is set free from her
seven years' imprisonment by a horse, PEGASUS-like, kicking
a hole through the roof of her cave. She exclaims :

> " Here in the mound full seven years long
> Did no one ask me for a song,
> And then a horse I found above."

Sometimes CINDERELLA is described as acquiring her
steed from a marvellous oak-tree. Whenever hungry, she
cries :

> " Little Bull come to me,
> Open ! Oak-tree,
> On a hinge of gold." [5]

Whereupon a young bull rushes to the oak-tree and buts
it until the tree opens, and Cinderella finds within every-

[1] *Chambers's Encyclopædia*, x. 643.   [2] *Blank=blanc=white*.
[3] *Cinderella*, p. 231.   [4] *Ibid.*, p. 190.   [5] *Ibid.*, p. 278.

thing she wants. Her magic horse is described in very curious terms as "partly gold and partly silver," sometimes as "tricoloured—the first gold, the second silver, the third inestimable," and occasionally as "a horse with hair partly of gold, silver, and something better." [1]

The music made by the White Lady of the White Horse was symbolised by a Harp or a Lyre. The Irish Harp that sounded once in TARA's halls has still the figure of WISDOM as its pillar, and is the same instrument as the Harp of DAVID, the Son of JESSE.

877

In fig. 877 the twin *gees* or *sees* of the CHARITES appear under a seven-jewelled Harp. The Druidic harps were made in the form of a *tri*angle, their strings were *three* in number and their turning-keys had each *three* arms. It was believed that the soul of a dead man lingered by the body until such time as the music of the sacred harp released and sped it on its way to heaven. If a man's career had been honourable and he had obeyed the "three grand articles of religion," the Bards sang a Requiem or Death Song, and the strains of this Requiem served as a passport to the Soul's ascent.

In the emblem herewith the Goddess of Light is urging her *gee-gees* upward. The *Art* of ARTEMIS is Welsh for

[1] *Cinderella*, pp. 361, 363, 383.

bear, and the cult of ARTEMIS was associated with the worship of a She-*bear*. *Artemes* is Greek for *perfect*.

Artemis, ('Diana), goddess of the Moon. (Gorii, Mus. Flor., vol. 2, tav. 88.)

878

In the Vedic Hymn quoted on p. 2 the TWINS were invoked "like two horns come to us," and in the figures herewith CINDERELLA'S steeds are combined with the two

879   880   881

horns of the Crescent Moon. In fig. 881 the steeds and the horns are supporting the King or Queen of Universal Justice.

It was an ancient custom to hold the Courts of Justice upon natural hill-tops or upon artificial mounds, and these sites were known in Scotland as MOAT HILLS or Hills of Justice. The word *moat* is evidently the Egyptian MAAT, MAHT, MUT, or MAUT, Goddess of Truth and Justice, and the Scotch *moat* cannot differ from the English *moot*. Within historic times there was a *folkmoot* held in the churchyard of St Paul's Cathedral,[1] and there can be little doubt that Ludgate Hill was once dedicated to the God of Justice. At the base of the Hill is the Church of ST MARTIN, and at the top the parish of ST MARTIN le Grand : within a stone's-throw stood at one time the Church of ST EWINE.[2] EWINE, a Saint of whom I can trace nothing, is HEWIN[3] or HEWONE, and MARTIN was seemingly once MAATIN or

882   883

MAAT, the ONE. The Bird herewith represents either a Martlet or a Martin, both of which appear to owe their nomenclature to the Great MAAT. It is recorded that ISIS assumed the form of a swallow when searching for OSIRIS, and ISIS is also said to have assumed the form of a mare under the name CERES.

CERES was the reputed Giver to the Greeks of most salutary laws. The Latin for *law* is *lex*, "Lord Great Fire," and it is from the source of *equus*, the Latin for *horse*, that are derived the terms *equal, equity,* and *equitable. Ulex,* the Latin for *gorse,* may be compared with *ilex,* the Evergreen *Oak.*

The Sanscrit for *Right* is *rigu* and the Zend *erezu* ; the

---

[1] Wheatley (H. B.), *London,* p. 10.

[2] Stow, Everyman's Library, p. 307.

[3] Compare surnames GODWIN or GOODWIN. A *whin*-bush is a gorse or mighty fire bush.

Latin for *law* is *judex*; the Zend and Sanscrit is *dis*. Dis,[1] one of the names of the Celtic PLUTO, is probably the root of *dzhyrna*, a *day*, whence presumably the word *discern*.

English judges wear a *horse-hair* wig that is almost identical in form with the *Klaft* or head-dress worn by Isis, as shown in fig. 884, and this head-gear was supposed to endow its wearer with divine wisdom and discernment.[2] HU, the mighty Mind, is not only responsible for the words *wise*, *wiseacre*, and *wisdom*, but apparently also for the word *wig*[3] or HUIG.[4] Other terms for *wig* are *peruke* or *perruque*,

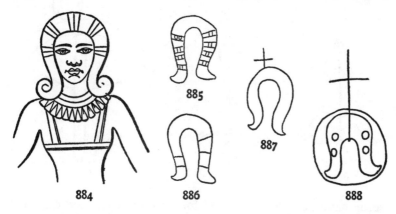

884   885   886   887   888

and *periwig* resolves into either *peri*, *all pervading*, or *pere*, Father HUIG. In Cornish the word *hueg* meant *sweet*, *dear*, *delicious*; and *dedwh*, the Cornish for *law*, may probably be equated with "Dad HU."[5] *Peruez*, the Cornish for *learned*,

[1] Compare place-name DISS.

[2] The Cornish for *reason* was *kaz*, the Great light. *Mind* was *brez*.

[3] Wig-making flourished in Egypt, and the kings of Persia wore wigs. —Layard, *Nineveh*, p. 97.

[4] Compare GREAT WIGBOROUGH.

[5] The French for *wisdom* is *sagesse*, *i.e.* the light of the A, the ever-existent *esse*, and the English *sage* and *sagacious* are similarly derived. "Quick in the *uptake*" means swift of apprehension. A *swift* is a large black *swallow*, and *quick* as well as *swift* means also, as in "quick and the dead," *alive* or *being*.

resolves into *Pere hu ez*, the "light or essence of Father Hu." *Prudence* is a form of *wisdom*.

The word *law* in Old Saxon was *lag*, and in Icelandic it is *log*; the Celtic Sun-god Lug was entitled Lamfada, meaning "of the Long Hand," and Llew, his Welsh equivalent, bore the epithet Llaw Gyffes, *i.e.* "of the Firm Hand."[1] We have here an ancient form of the word *gyves* (fetters) and of the phrase, "The Long Hand of the Law."

Among the marvellous *tumuli* of the Mississippi valley

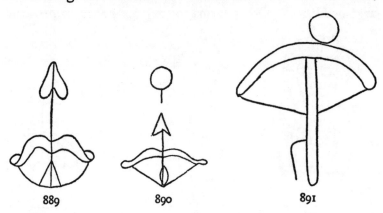

889   890   891

some have been found in the form of a buffalo, some in that of a bear, and some in that of a man. "The human figure," says Squier, "is not uncommon among the effigies, and is always characterised by *the extraordinary and unnatural length of its arms.*"[2]

It is possible that the expression "hue and cry" is due to Hu, the Law or Witness, and that to be "accused" was to be brought into the Great Light or Court of Akhu.

The central criminal court of this country is situated in Ludgate Hill, and is known as the Old Bailey. The *bailey* of a castle was the main tower, the donjon or keep;

[1] Squire, *Mythology of Ancient Britain*, p. 25.
[2] Quoted from Buckley (T. A.), *Great Cities of Ancient World*, p. 268.

bail means security, and the word *bali*, "Father Everlasting," is the same as BEULAH, as the Irish "land of fay, the beautiful land of BALOW," and as "the honey isle of BELI," a bardic term for Britain. That BA is the same as Bo is evident from the alternative use of the terms *Bay* window or *Bow* window. There is a place named Bow near OKEHAMPTON, and another near London on the River LEA. Near ASKRIGG in Yorkshire is a BOWBRIDGE, and in London there is a Church of ST MARY LE Bow.

The symbolic Bows illustrated in figs. 889 and 890 are designed like the horns of an Ox, Bull, or Buffalo. The

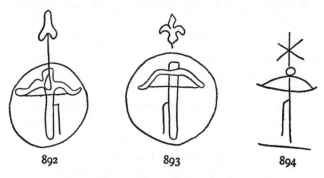

892   893   894

Latin *apis*, meaning a *bow*, is identical with APIS, the sacred Egyptian *Bull*, and the word is again traceable in *apse*, *i.e.* the *bow* of the chancel. *Bo*, the root of *bous* and *bos*, is the Irish and Gaelic for *ox*; *bu* was Cornish for *ox*, and *beu* was Cornish for *alive*; *beo* is Irish, and *byw* is Welsh, for *living* or *being*. The Latin for *bee*, the insect that gives honey, is *apis*, and a large bee is called a *bumble*. An under-bailiff is known as a *bum-bailiff*; *bumble* means *beadle*, and the German for *beadle* is *betel*, which cannot differ from *beetle*. ST BEES Head in Yorkshire is said to be named after a certain ST BEE associated with WHITBY ABBEY. ST BEE was alternatively known as ST BEGA, which may be anglicised into "Big A."

The Church of St Mary le Bow was known alternatively as St Mary Arcubus, and the *Arquebuse,* Crossbow, or *arcubalista* was, as illustrated in the emblems herewith, evidently the symbol of Arcubalista, the Sovereign Archer.

The Babylonians represented the Supreme Deity as an Archer shooting a *three*-headed arrow,[1] and one of the Signs of the Zodiac is Sagittarius the Archer. The Saxon for a *bay* was *wich*; the Latin for a *bow* is *arcus*; the Greek is *toxon*—and the Greek for *life, being,* and also a *bowstring* is *bios.* English Bows were almost invariably cut from Yew trees, and that the evergreen Yew (Greek, *taxos*) was a sacred tree is evident from its appearance, generally as twins, in Churchyards.

A Bow is represented as the weapon of Diana and of Apollo, and the Arrows of Apollo symbolised the lightning of the Supreme Power.

> "The sunbeams are my shafts, with which I kill
>   Deceit, that loves the night and fears the day :
> All men who do or even imagine ill
>   Fly me, and from the glory of my ray
> Good minds and open actions take new might,
> Until diminished by the reign of night."[2]

The English *arrow* was originally *arewe,*[3] the light of Ewe ; in Sanscrit and Zend *arrow* is *ishu,* again the light of Hu ; the Greek terms for *arrow* were *ios* = the light of the One, *belos* = the light of Bel, and *toxeuma* = the resplendent great light of the Solar A. Compare "Yea, he sent out his *arrows,* and scattered them ; and he shot out *lightnings,* and discomfited them."[4]

In the emblems herewith the arrows form the cross of Lux, and most of them are tipped with the heart of Eros

---

[1] Layard, p. 211.   [2] Shelley, *Hymn of Apollo.*
[3] Skeat.   [4] Psalm xviii. 14.

or *Erezu*, the Right. "For *Love* is strong as death, its passion unappeasable as the grave, its shafts are *arrows of fire*, the *lightnings* of a God."[1]

The weapon of EROS or CUPID is always represented as a Bow, and the personal application of the Bow and Arrow

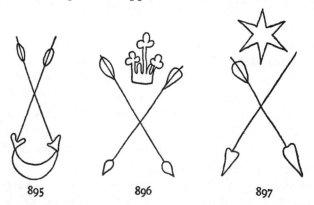

895   896   897

emblems herewith may be understood from Blake's well-known lines :

> "Bring me my Bow of burning gold !
> Bring me my Arrows of desire !
> Bring me my Spear !   O clouds, unfold !
> Bring me my Chariot of fire !
>
> I will not cease from mental Fight,
> Nor shall my Sword sleep in my hand,
> Till we have built Jerusalem
> In England's green and pleasant land."

The primitive word *bow* implies that the weapon derived its name from similarity in form to the rainbow, a radiant seven-hued symbol of the Great Bow or Father. The seven elementary *Hues* of the spectrum when blended into ONE form *white*, which is a combination of all colours.

Within the Church of St Mary *Arcubus* or *le Bow* there

[1] *Song of Solomon.*

used to be held a Judicial Court, and opposite to Bow Church is OLD JEWRY. The English jury consists of *twelve* picked men ; in Old French *ajuirie* meant *aid* or *succour*, and *jury-mast* is presumably used in this sense.

In OLD JEWRY there is a church of ST OVARY UPWELL and the *Up* of this UPWELL occurs persistently in the proper names and place-names of this district. Close by is ABCHURCH Lane, called, according to Stow, after " ST MARIE ABCHURCH, APECHURCH, or UPCHURCH as I have read it." [1] In connection with Bow CHURCH which stands in CHEAPSIDE, Stow mentions a tradesman named GOOD-CHEPE ; what is now Leadenhall Street was known at one time as BLANCK CHEPESTON,[2] and there is little doubt that EAST CHEAP, WEST CHEAP, and the central district or Ward of CHEAPE, are verbally identical with CHEAP or CHEOP, the Ever-existent Eye. There is thus a curiously unexpected propriety in Mr Wheatley's remark : " Other cities have shifted their centres, but London remains as it always was. The Bank, the Royal Exchange, and the Mansion House, occupy ground which has been the *Eye of London* since Roman times." [3]

CHEAPSIDE almost borders on the Old BAILEY and may be said to have been on one side of the *bailey*, *tower* or *keep*. That *keep* and *cheap* are variants of the same idea is evident from the fact that in Anglo-Saxon *ceap* meant *price* and in Dutch *koopen* means to *buy*. In Anglo-Saxon *copa* meant a *tub*, *coop*, or *vat*, and in CHEAPSIDE there stood a famous prison-house known as the *Tun*, where malefactors having been *copped* or *cap*tured were *cooped* up and *kept* in safe *keep*ing.

It would appear—among other reasons from the name

---

[1] *Survey*, p. 196.
[2] See the ancient map in the porch of the Church of St. Martin's in the Fields.　　　　　　　　　　　　　　　　[3] *London*, p. viii.

LUDWIG [1] = LUD, the Mighty Mind—that at one period of British History CHEOP, CHEAPE, or CHEPE was known under the name of LUD. London was known to the Welsh as CAERLUD, the Seat of LUD, and on LUDGATE HILL where now stands the Cathedral of PAUL or POWLE as it used to be called, seemingly once stood a shrine of LUD. Near CHEPSTOW is LUD's town of LYDNEY; the Eastern LYDIA was also known as LUD, and in CORNWALL is LUDGAN, pronounced LUDGEON. KING LUD of LUDGATE HILL was known alternatively as KING BROWN,[2] *i.e.* "King Bruin," and also as IMMANUENCE [3]—the later name being obviously

898   899   900

akin to IMMANUEL, "God with us," one of the prophetic titles applied by Christianity to JESHU.

It is customary for English judges to be addressed in court as "M'LUD," and it may be that LUD was originally a generic term of *judge*. The French for *judge* is *juge*, the same as the English *geegee*; and a synonym for the word *judgment* is *doom*. In Teutonic *dom* means *law*, and neither *dom* or *doom* differ from *dome*. At the recent Durbar in India King GEORGE and Queen MARY were seated under a golden dome, the symbol of *d'ome*, the Resplendent Sun, of Dominion, and of *Dominus*, the Lord. The chief

---

[1] LUDWIG=LUDOVICUS=LOUIS or LEWIS=LEW.

[2] *Bron* was Cornish for *breast* and *pap*. *Bryn* was Cornish for a *hill*.

[3] Wilson, *Imperial Gazetteer*, ii. 136. Compare adjectives *immense* and *huge*.

magistrate in the Isle of MAN is called the "Deemster," and in fig. 898 the Ox or Steer of Day is represented *domed*. The mouths are formed respectively like the M of Maat or the waves of *aqua* and the SS of *Sanctus Spiritus*. *Dam* was Irish for *ox*, and the Gaulish Goddess of Cattle was known as *Damona*. *Damn* means *condemn* ; *dam* also means *mother*, and this syllable is no doubt the root of *dame* and *madam*. The Dome of St Paul's may be described as the very apple of the Eye of London, and surmounting the Dome of the new OLD BAILEY is a *five*-rayed figure of MAAT or, as she is now named, JUSTICE.[1]

To be tried by a Magistrate (*i.e. Magustrate*) or a Mayor = *mare*, is described as being brought before the BEAK. The old Bow Street[2] Runners used to carry with them as a symbol of authority a small tipstaff, and a precisely similar custom prevails among the Yezidis of PERSIA. LAYARD states that they carried for this purpose the bird-tipped staff that symbolised the HOLY ONE. The modern truncheon borne by the English constable is not so much a weapon of offence as a symbol of Authority or TURUNCHEON.[3]

The word *police* originally meant "civil government" ; in Brittany *poelluz* or *poellek* means *judicious*, and the root of all these words is Great PAUL or APOLLO.

In the Greek alphabet our letter Q is represented by *kappa* or *koppa*. Q is *ak Hu*, and the London police are called coppers, *i.e.* those who "cop," a word evidently allied to *coppes*, the Old English for the stocks. The Greek *kappa* is the English *k*, i.e. *ak a*, and in fig. 901 this *k* surmounts the *P* of PAUL. In fig. 902 it is ingeniously con-

---

[1] Beneath this figure is the inscription, "DEFEND THE CHILDREN OF THE POOR AND PUNISH THE WRONGDOER."

[2] Bow Street was so called because when built it was bow-shaped.

[3] *Tir* is Persian for arrow.

structed to form I C, the initials of IESOUS CHRISTOS. In Sanscrit the word *ki* means *punish*, and in England *punishment* is popularly known as a *whopping, wigging, walloping,* or *whacking.*

It was sometimes customary to build Christian churches in the circular form of APAK or AKOP, the Great Eye, and of this a good example exists in the TEMPLE or TEMPOL Church near LUDGATE. The Badge of the Inner Temple is PEGASUS, the flying horse.

Coptis is the name of a genus of the Buttercup or golden-eye family. The Eastern people called the COPTS or KUBTS, descendants of the old Egyptians, were presumably followers

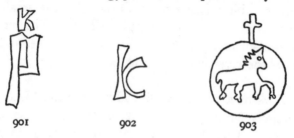

901   902   903

of *ak op te.* Their present religion, a form of Christianity, is described as " JACOBITE," and they assign their conversion from paganism to ST MARK. The word *mark* is Irish, Gaelic, Welsh, and Cornish, for *horse.*

An *apt* remark is one well aimed and which hits the *mark* or *bull's-eye.* ABDY or ABDE is an English surname, and in Egyptian the word *abti* meant *east.*

The Gaulish word for *horse* was *epos,* the " Eye of Light " ; the Greek is *hippos,* and the German is *pferd,* i.e. *opferde,* the Eye of Fire Resplendent. The parish church of HORSHAM in Sussex is dedicated to ST MARK ; the parish of HORSLEYDOWN in East London is divided into HORSLEYDOWN ST MARK and HORSLEYDOWN ST JOHN. In KENT, the county of " INVICTA," the invincible and

incorruptible White Horse, is a place named HORSE-
MONDEN.

Near CANTERBURY, whose oldest church is said to be
that of St Martin, is a place named LYDD, and within the
precincts of CANTERBURY is still standing a great *tumulus*
known as "the DANE JOHN." Philologically this may be
equated with *donjon* or *dungeon*, *i.e.* the central tower or
Main KEEP of a castle, and its meaning may be understood
as *don* or *dun*, a *hill, fort*, or *stronghold* of JON or GEON, the
Existent Sun or ONE.

A White Horse was the emblem of HANOVER[1] or HAN-
NOVER, and the Egyptian AUNEFER was an alternative name
for HORUS. Near LISKEARD in Cornwall is the small port of
LOOE or, as it was sometimes called, BIAN. The main quay
and market-place of LOOE is called HANNAFORE, and at the
mouth of the river is an islet named LOOE or ST GEORGE'S
Island.

In HANOVER of the White Horse are the HARZ Moun-
tains, largely famous on account of their topmost peak, the
BROCKEN.[2] The Fire Festivals once held there were
regarded by Christianity as diabolical, and the *Walpurgis*
Night—the Night of the Strong Father, the Ever-Existent
Light—has become a synonym for Hell. But the cry
of *ooroorake !* with which the fiends are said to have hailed
LUCIFER is seemingly cognate with the Greek *eureka !* and
like *hurrah* or *hurray* may be resolved into the Fire of the
Great A. Surmounting the emblem herewith is a *five-
pronged rake*—a variant of the more customary three-
pronged spear or trident. The Latin for anything sharply-
rayed or toothed is *broccus*, i.e. *bur ok us*, the "Light of the
Great Father," and this word is evidently cognate to
BROCKEN, and to its alternative name BRUCTERUS. The

---

[1] Hanover is on the River LEINE.
[2] Known also as BLOCKSBERG and MONS BRUCTERUS.

Bull of fig. 904 suggests that BRUCTERUS might be rendered BARUC TAUROS, and that the synonymous BLOCKSBERG might be understood as BULLOCK'S BERG.

Near COLOGNE is the Mountain known as the HORSEL-BERG or BERG of URSULA. The HORSELBERG, like the BROCKEN, fell into evil repute, and is now regarded as the *locale* of TANNHAUSER'S adventure with VENUS. The

904

Goddess HORSEL,[1] the Swabian VENUS, is identical with URSULA, the Everlasting *Bear*, or HORUS ; and the story of ST URSULA and the eleven thousand virgins is obviously the debris of some fairy-tale anent the Great Bear and the myriad stars of her train.

Heureuse is the French for *happy*, and RUSSE or RUSSIA is symbolised by *ours* or HORUS, the Great Bear.

In BRITTANY, where the cult of a stone mare still

[1] Traces of *Horse* or HORSEL worship are probably to be found in the place-names HORSELYDOWN and HORSENDEN HILL, near HARROW.

flourishes to this day,[1] the word for *light* is *goulou*, the Mighty Hu Everlasting; and the same Hu is perhaps the radical of *lumière* and *lumen*, i.e. *el Hu mon*, the Sole Lord Hu, the Illuminator.

The Arabs connect the word *Wisdom* with a horse's Bridle,[2] and in the emblems herewith the Bridles are unmistakably identified as Wisdom by the pearl and the Fleur-de-lys. In Hindoo philosophy *Manas* the *Mind* is compared to a *bridle*, and, as has been seen, the constituents of I O were regarded as I = the Author, and O = "the regulator" or *bridle* of Time and Motion.

905

906

907

In solar heads the emanating rays are almost invariably represented as flaming hair, and Wisdom, the Fairy Queen, like Apollo, the golden-tressed, is conventionally described as having locks like a waterfall of golden light. The *hair* of the Princess (*ante*, p. 185, vol. i.) is said to have lighted up the sky every morning and evening. The Gnostics are said to have seen in the shaggy hairs of the goat-footed PAN mystic allusions to the solar rays,[3] and that the English *hair* is simply *ar*, the light, may be confirmed by a comparison with words like *locks* or *tresses* and with their equivalents in other

[1] Le Braz, A., *Land of Pardons*, p. 235.
[2] Introduction to *Proverbs*, Temple Bible, p. 19.
[3] C. W. King, *The Gnostics*, p. 446.

languages. The *locks* of fig. 33 (*ante* ,p. 27, vol. i.) were marked with the sign of *lux*. The French *cheveux* [1] resolves itself into Ever-existing *feux*, *fires*. *Feax*, *i.e.* the "fire of the Great Fire," was the Anglo-Saxon for *hair*; *auburn* means hair like the burning Au or A; and *shaggy* means *great light*-y. The Waldensian pastors, proverbially "shining lights," were known as *barbes*, and *barbe* is French for *beard*.

THOR was usually represented as *red*-bearded; I have already suggested that the flowing *blue* beard of SIN, the Assyrian God of Wisdom, typified the light of descending Truth, and a similar idea evidently underlay the golden mane of the Horse of Wonder. According to the Slav peasants and herdsmen, "His mane was like a cloud of gold"; and the word *mane* (Anglo-Saxon *manu*, Old High German *mana*) is obviously allied to the Sanscrit *manas*—mind.

Irish Mythology relates that the radiance of LUG's face was such that it seemed like the Sun, and none was able to gaze steadily at it. LUG, the acknowledged Master of all Arts, was the possessor of a magic spear; his sling was seen in Heaven as the Rainbow, and the Milky Way was called "LUG's Chain." [2] The Greeks conceived this glittering starway as the track to the palaces of the Gods, [3] and the Red Indians of North America still term it the "Ashen Path" or the "Path of Souls." [4] LUG's Chain may be identified with the chain tied to the foot of the Olympian Throne by which ZEUS drew men up to Heaven, and it was probably symbolised by the chain hung occasionally from the roof of pagan shrines. At the Great Temple of UPSALA, which is described by contemporaries as being "all of gold,"

---

[1] The French for *horses* is *chevaux*.
[2] C. Squire, *Mythology of Ancient Britain*, p. 26.
[3] Bulfinch, *Age of Fable*, p. 16.
[4] A. Lang, *Custom and Myth*, p. 122.

there was "a golden chain hanging on the pinnacles of the building, and seen glittering afar by those who approach the place." [1]

Lug's Chain may no doubt be equated with the Masonic "Cable tow," and with the threefold cord worn by the priests in East and West. The tassels at the extremities of the cable tow, judging from the symbol herewith, typified *t-ass-el*, the resplendent Light God. The Italian for *tassel* is *frangia*, and the German *quaste*, *i.e.* "Great Hu, the shining Light." Lug's Chain may also be met with under different imagery in the fairy-tale of Jack and the Beanstalk. The

908

stalks of this magic plant were, it is said, "of an immense thickness, and had so entwined that they formed a ladder nearly like a chain in appearance." [2] Looking upwards, Jack was unable to discern the top, as "it appeared to be lost in the clouds." Nevertheless, he started the ascent, and after an arduous climb reached a strange country, where there met him "a handsome young woman," who was not only "beautiful and lively," but was "dressed in the most elegant manner, and had a small white wand in her hand, on the top of which was a peacock of pure gold." She informs Jack that it was she who had secretly prompted him to exchange his cow for the magic beans. "By my power the

[1] W. A. Craigie, *Religion of Ancient Scandinavia*, p. 39.
[2] *English Folk-lore and Legends*, anonymous, 1880, p. 131.

beanstalk grew to so great a height and formed a ladder. I need not add I inspired you with a strong desire to ascend the ladder." Aided by her instructions, Jack recovers from the malevolent ogre three treasures—a golden harp, a hen that lays golden eggs, and bags of gold and silver. Upon the giant pursuing Jack down the beanstalk, the magic plant twines him into an entangled knot, and the villagers kill him at their leisure.

The word *bean*—in mediæval English *bene*—is cognate to the Dutch *boon* and Old High German *bona*.[1] It thus radically means *good*, and the beneficent stalk of Goodness may be equated with the stalk or stem of JESSE, the ladder of JACOB, and the chain of LUG. We speak unwittingly nowadays of an "extraordinary chain of Good Luck," but the word *luck* implies that our ancestors regarded "luck" as something other than a blind and unseeing chance. *Chance* is the root of CHANCERY, and the Lord CHANCELLOR represents Supreme LAW.

The Chain of *Luck* or *Lux* figures frequently in Mythology, notably as the thread bestowed by ARIADNE on THESEUS, by which he succeeded in escaping from the Labyrinth. The Fairy Godmother gives CINDERELLA a ball of thread by means of which "she can find her way home when mother deserts her." On another occasion Two Pigeons appear, bestow upon Cinderella a ball of thread that unwinds of itself, and conduct her to an oak-tree. Sometimes CINDERELLA's enchanted thread consists of three balls of different colours.[2] Into the Chains of Good Luck here illustrated have been interwoven a manifold variety of emblems, including the letter L of LUCK, LUG, or LUX.

The symbol of ST LUKE or LUCAS was an Ox. In HORSLEYDOWN, near the hospice of ST THOMAS, which is

---

[1] Skeat.　　　　[2] *Cinderella*, pp. 275, 277, 352

in the parish of St George, was once a lazar-house, known as the *Loke*,[1] and *lock-up* is a synonym for *prison*.

In Western Georgia—where St George was regarded as the god of "good fortune"—there is a so-called "Monastery of the Chain," wherein are preserved an iron Bow, an iron Chain, and an iron Arrow. This church is dedicated to "St George of Many Forces."[2]

In Egypt the symbol of *Mind, Reason,* or *Understanding*

908a

909   908b

was the Crocodile. "It is said," says Plutarch, "to have been made an emblem of the Deity, as being the sole animal destitute of a tongue. For the Divine Reason stands not in need of voice, but walking along a silent path and rule, guides mortal affairs according to justice, and the crocodile alone, of things living in liquid, veils its eyes with a thin transparent membrane which it draws down from the upper lid, so as to see without being seen, which is the attribute of the Supreme Deity."[3]

[1] See Stow.
[2] See article "St George the Moon God" in *The Quest*, vol. iii. No. 3.
[3] *Isis and Osiris.*

In EGYPT this great symbol of CHEOP, the "Ever-existent Eye," was particularly worshipped at ONUPHIS, *i.e.* *on up is*, the One Eye of Light. At NUBTI ("One Resplendent Orb") or OMBOS ("Sun Bull") the crocodile was identified with SET or SUT. The God SEBEK was figured as a crocodile-headed man, and *sebek*, which was the generic term for *crocodile*, resolves into either *is eb ek* or *se bek*, the Fire of the Great Father.

Among BENT's discoveries in MASHONALAND was a wooden platter decorated in the centre with a crocodile or lizard, around which appear certain zodiacal signs.[1] Speaking of the Ba-quaina, or children of the *quaina* or crocodile, BENT says : "Their *siboko* [compare SEBEK], or tribal object of veneration, is the crocodile, which animal they will not kill or touch under any provocation whatsoever. The Ba-quaina are one of the most powerful of the Bechuana-land feud tribes, and it often occurred to me, Can the name Bechuanaland, for which nobody can give a satisfactory derivation, and of which the natives themselves are entirely ignorant, be a corruption of this name ?"[2]

The *huana* of BECHUANA may, no doubt, be equated with *yuana*, the West Indian word for *lizard*. There is a South American giant lizard called *iguana*,[3] and the African BECHUANALAND may perhaps be understood as the Land of "Buck Lizard," or *Obek*, the Great Eye, or *Bauk*, Father Great HU, the one A.[4]

The Giant Lizard or Alligator was the object of profound veneration in Mexico ; HUANA CAPAC was a famous Peruvian monarch, and the word *alligator* is said to be an Anglicised corruption of the Spanish-American *El lagarto*, *i.e.* the Great

---

[1] See frontispiece, *Ruined Cities of Mashonaland.*
[2] *The Ruined Cities of Mashonaland*, p. 15.
[3] ST IGUINOU is a Breton Saint.
[4] The Sanscrit for mother is *ana* ; for son, *oghlu* ; for Lord, *agha*.

Lizard.   The Italian for *lizard* is *lucerta*, the " shining light," and our *lizard*[1] is closely akin to *wizard*.

The Lizard figures upon the breast of certain figures of the wise MINERVA, and in Europe it was worshipped among the Slav nations as late as the sixteenth century.[2]   There was a popular superstition that the Lizard conceived through the ear and brought forth through the mouth, whence it was regarded as "a type of the generation of the Word, that is, the Logos or Divine Wisdom."[3]   Pope Felix believed that the Virgin MARY conceived of the Holy Ghost through her ear, and a lizard is figured over the door of SEVILLE Cathedral.

There is a LIZARD Point in the Scilly Isles, where possibly was a primitive Beacon-fire.[4]   At the more famous LIZARD near HELSTON and CAERLEON,[5] in Cornwall, is now a revolving Light of one million candle-power.

In ENGLAND we call the little water-lizard a *newt*, or, as it ought to be, *an ewt*.   The word was originally spelt

---

[1] Compare surnames IZARD and TIZZARD.

[2] Morfill (W. R.), *Rel. Sys. of the World*, p. 272.

[3] King (C. W.), *The Gnostics*, p. 107.

[4] I suspect, however, that many of these Cornish headlands were named after the Sun.   The Celtic temperament is expressed by the Breton poet, Anatole le Braz : " Notice the great solemn promontories where the Sun, the Breton HEOL, own brother to HELIOS, the Greek, walks every summer morning, wrapped in the first pure shimmerings of his delicate light, and at evening leaves his long rays of sumptuous purple trailing behind him.   Is it surprising that generations of Celts have looked upon this place as his sanctuary, an open temple dedicated to him whom still they call ' the King of Stars,' the god whose radiant presence is all the sweeter to them, from being so rarely vouchsafed in their sombre climate ?"—*The Land of Pardons*, p. 134.

[5] Next SIERRA LEONE in West Africa is LAGOS, which neighbours on to ASHANTI, capital town ACCRA.   The place- and river-names hereabout are curious, *e.g.* ELMINA, BENIN, PRAH, BONNY, OPOBO, ABRAKAMPA, TIMBUCTOO, TOMBO, TAO, TUMMO, etc.   Sir Evelyn Wood mentions two chiefs named QUAMINA ESSEVIE and QUACOE ANDOO.   The HAUSSAS are now excellent British soldiers.   *Kshanti* is Sanscrit for *patient*.   *Antipater* was a Gnostic term for God.

ewte, and may be resolved into "resplendent HEW," *i.e.*
"resplendent *Mind*." The tails of the *ewts* here illustrated
are formed into the Hebrew character *yod*. This was a
symbol under which the Jews expressed the Ever Being
JAH or JEHOVAH.

910   911

The Cornish for *ewt* or lizard was *pedrevan* ; and as *padar*
in Cornish meant *father*, and *pedar* meant four, the word
pedrevan may be resolved into either Four or Fire Father
Evan, *i.e.* BACCHUS.

The old naturalists mention "the Stellion, which is a
beast like a Lyzard," [1] and the word *stellion* cannot differ from

912   913

stallion, a horse. The imaginary Salamander, a lizard born
of and dwelling in fire, must obviously have had a symbolic
origin.

At the foot of the Fire Tree illustrated on p. 271 there
appears not only a lizard, but also a snail. The French for
snail [2] is *limace*, and the Italian *lumaca*. The sea-snail is termed
a *winkle*, [3] and *periwinkle* resolves, like *periwig*, into the "All-
pervading HU, the one Great God."

Isaiah likens the Daughter of Zion to "a cottage in a
vineyard " and "a *lodge* in a garden of cucumbers." [4] The

---

[1] Hulme (F. E.), *Natural History Lore*, p. 154.
[2] *Sunail*, or Sun-god ?
[3] Compare place-name WINKELBURY.
[4] i. 8.

Masonic *Lodge*, and *Logic*, a synonym for *Reason*, contain the same idea as the word *Wisdom*, *i.e.* the *domus* or domicile of HUIZ.

The snail is a *slug* with a little house on its back; it leaves a glittering track or trail, which I suggest was identified with LUG's Chain or the silvery smear of the Milky Way, the Ashen Path, the Track of Souls. Silver was the emblem of Knowledge; and the Snail-men of the dark ages were they who left bright tracks behind them in the form of books. The snail, when he emerges from his shell, is seen to be exquisitely horned, but more often he remains invisible within his little house, a symbol of the idea, "Verily Thou art a God that hidest Thyself." The name AMMON was

914   915

interpreted by the Greeks to mean "concealment" or "something which is hidden," and in Egyptian AMEN meant "the hidden God."[1]

It is not impossible that the House-*Martin* was so named because she is the builder of a little round house with a door, and it was perhaps for the same reason that the Jenny-*Wren*—"God Almighty's little hen"—was once esteemed to be so sacred. The Druids used to draw auguries not from her flight, but from her chirpings,[2] *i.e.* her *speech* or wisdom (?). The "jocund lyttel fowle" shown in figs. 914 and 915 is presumably a wren—the builder of a round nest with a circular side door, the symbol of the Point within a Circle.

LUG is reputed to have put an end to the rule of the giants by blinding their terrible leader with a carefully

[1] Budge (W.), *Legends of the Gods*, p. 211.
[2] Squire, *Mythology of Babylonia*, i. p. 417.

prepared slingstone. This battle, suggestive of the fight between DAVID and GOLIATH, is said to have taken place at SLIGO. The "*five* smooth stones from the brook" with which DAVID defeated his opponent were probably symbolic of the five powers of perfections of LUX. They are comparable to the *five* beans from which the magic beanstalk grew, and the *five* stones tossed up and caught on the back of the hand for purposes of augury by British and Irish priestesses.

Slug, "the light of LUG," is akin to the place SLIGO, to the name SLUGOBYL, and to the word *Slughorn* or *Slogan*. According to Skeat, this expression means "cry of the

916

host," and it may thus seemingly be equated with BANZI ! HOSANNA ! HURRAH ! etc. Primarily the shout resolves into *is el og an*, the "light of our Lord the Great One."

The doctrine of an incarnate *Logos, Word, Mind*, or *Reason* was prominent in Chaldean, Egyptian, Persian, and Greek philosophy, but it was not incorporated into Christian teaching until the middle of the second century. In fig. 916 Christ the LOGOS surmounted by the cross of ST GEORGE is represented as the Lion of JUDAH. "He shall roar like a lion," says HOSEA, "After two days will he revive us : in the third day will he raise us up and we shall live in his sight."[1] It is a Christian tenet that JESU descended into hell "and the third day he rose again from

[1] xi. 10 ; vi. 2.

the dead."[1]　The old naturalists used to believe that the lion was always born dead or in a state of stupor, but that in the space of three days "it became endowed with life by the breath or the roaring voice of its sire."[2]

The forms under which the Sire of Life has from time to time been fabled to overshadow the virgin soul are multifarious.　In addition to his transformations into a Swan, a Flame of Fire, a Pigeon, and a Bull, ZEUS is related to have reached the imprisoned DANAË[3] in the guise of a golden shower.　At the present day the Bridal veil of Roumanian girls is composed of a shower of loose golden threads, and according to an Indian version of Cinderella, showers of golden dew fell periodically upon her bridegroom.

The Chinese variant of the Immaculate Conception relates that the Virgin having "trod *in a footprint of God's*," her divine child HOU CHI was born *like a lamb*.　"He was exposed in a narrow lane, but sheep and oxen protected and suckled him ; he was exposed in a wide forest, but

---

[1] ZOROASTER, OSIRIS, HORUS, ADONIS, DIONYSOS, HERCULES, HERMES, BALDUR, and QUETZALCOATL (the Mexican crucified Saviour) are all recorded to have descended into Hell and to have risen again on the third day.—See Doane (A. W.), *Bible Myths*, p. 213.

[2] Heath (S.), *Romance of Symbolism*, p. 153.

[3] In the *Assumpta Maria* of Francis Thompson, the Virgin Mary is identified with Danaë :

> " I am Daniel's mystic Mountain,
> 　Whence the mighty stone was rolled ;
> I am the four Rivers' fountain,
> 　Watering Paradise of old ;
> Cloud down-raining the Just One am,
> 　*Danaë of the Shower of Gold ;*
> I the Hostel of the Sun am ;
> 　He the Lamb, and I the Fold.
> He the Anteros and Eros,
> 　I the body, He the Cross ;
> He is fast to me, *Ischyros,*
> 　*Agios Athanatos !* "

wood-cutters found him ; he was exposed on cold ice, but birds covered him with their wings." [1] The similarities here to JESHU, born amid the sheep and oxen of a Bethlehem stable, extend even to the name, and Hou CHI—HU, the Ever-Existent—is essentially identical with JESHU.

In the emblems herewith the Lion of Lord HU is holding up the Sword of Justice—the same weapon as in combination with the cross of ST GEORGE constitutes the arms of the City of London. [2]

" We wrestle not," said PAUL, " against flesh and blood,

917   918

but against principalities, against powers, against the rulers of the darkness of this world, against spiritual wickedness in high places. Wherefore take unto you the whole armour of God, that ye may be able to withstand in the evil day, and having done all, to stand. Stand therefore, having your loins girt about with truth, and having on the breast-plate of righteousness ; And your feet shod with the preparation of the gospel of peace ; Above all, taking the shield of faith, wherewith ye shall be able to quench all the fiery darts of the wicked. And take the helmet of salva-tion, and the sword of the Spirit, which is *the word of God* : Praying always with all prayer and supplication in the

[1] Giles (H. A.), *Religion of Ancient China*, p. 22.
[2] These arms were originally supported by twin *lions*. See Stow.

Spirit, and watching thereunto with all perseverance and supplication for all saints." [1]

The symbolism of the sword as the *word* of God is enshrined in the word *Sword*, i.e. *se-word* [2] or *is-word*, the Fire or Light of the *Word*. The Anglo-Saxon for a sword was *seax*, "the Fire of the great Fire." Similarly the Italian *spada* resolves into *sepada*, the Fire of the Shining Father, and the German *sabel* into Fire of BEL. A certain kind of sword was known in England as a *whin*yard, and a heavy sword was termed a *brand*.

The Great Sword of Justice has at times been reverenced as the symbol of God Himself, and HENLEY thus treats it in his well-known *Song of the Sword* :

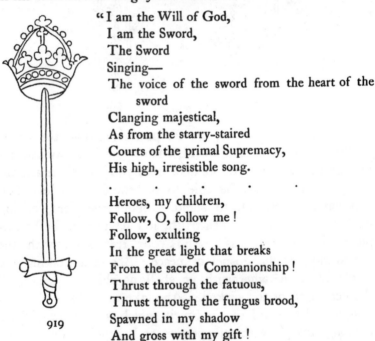

919

"I am the Will of God,
I am the Sword,
The Sword
Singing—
The voice of the sword from the heart of the
    sword
Clanging majestical,
As from the starry-staired
Courts of the primal Supremacy,
His high, irresistible song.

.   .   .   .   .

Heroes, my children,
Follow, O, follow me !
Follow, exulting
In the great light that breaks
From the sacred Companionship !
Thrust through the fatuous,
Thrust through the fungus brood,
Spawned in my shadow
And gross with my gift !

---

[1] Ephesians vi. 12–18.
[2] Compare surname SEWARD.

Thrust through, and hearken
O, hark, to the Trumpet,
The Virgin of Battles,
Calling, still calling you
Into the Presence,
Sons of the Judgment,
Pure wafts of the Will !
Edged to annihilate,
Hilted with government,
Follow, O, follow me
Till the waste places
All the grey globe over
Ooze, as the honeycomb
Drips, with the sweetness
Distilled of my strength."

Every Mythology of any consequence includes a dazzling and resistless sword of Light. The Japanese know it as "the cloud assembling sword of Heaven," and in Aryan Mythology its wielder is named CHRYSAOR, the golden Light. There is an Eastern kind of sword termed a *krees*, and this weapon is waved like a tongue of flame.

King ARTHUR's magic sword was named MIRANDOISA, a word resolving into *miranda*, wonderful, *is A*, "light of the A." According to some versions, ARTHUR's sword was called EXCALIBUR [1] or ESSICALIBUR : in both cases the -LIBUR resolves into "Everlasting Father," and *exika-* or *essika-* yields "great fire or spirit of the Great A."

King ARTHUR, like BEL, HORUS, and GEORGE, was the slayer of an infesting dragon. It was the avowed mission of King Arthur's Knights of the *Round Table*, i.e. *Perfection* or the Circle of the Sun, to fare forth into all countries for the protection of women, the chastisement of oppressors,

[1] Mexican Mythology mentions a dauntless and ambitious XELHUA. This name is seemingly an earlier form of EXCELSIOR.

the liberation of the enchanted, the enchainment of giants, and the slaying of malicious dwarfs.[1]

Arthur's first weapon was extracted from an anvil: "There was seen," says MALORY, "in the Churchyard at the east end by the High Altar, a great stone foursquare, like unto a marble stone, and in midst thereof was like an anvil of steel a foot on high, and therein stuck a fair sword."

The anvil[2] represented herewith with a cross or sword sticking from it, was the emblem of the primal Furnace, the spark-whirling Forge or Force of the Universe.

"EXCALIBUR," King ARTHUR's second sword, was bestowed upon him by the lone Lady of the Lake:

> " Nine years she wrought it, sitting in the deeps
> Upon the hidden bases of the hills."

TENNYSON describes her as :

> " Clothed in white samite, mystic, wonderful,
> She gave the King his huge cross-hilted sword,
> Whereby to drive the heathen out : a mist
> Of incense curl'd about her, and her face
> Wellnigh was hidden in the minster gloom ;
> But there was heard among the holy hymns
> A voice as of the waters, for she dwells
> Down in a deep ; calm, whatsoever storms
> May shake the world, and when the surface rolls,
> Hath power to walk the waters like our Lord."

---

[1] Apropos the recent silly exhibition of sham Chivalry, *i.e. Chevalerie*, at Earl's Court, *Punch* says :
> " Ah, Sirs, if I may change at will
> From chaff to earnest in a breath,
> Wrongs unredressed are with us still—
> Hunger and want, disease and death ;
> Powers of the dark o'errun these Christian realms
> For lack of knightly service. Come, let's see, then,
> How, wearing England's favour on your helms,
> Ye, too, can ride abroad to 'break the heathen.'"

[2] Greek *anafalz, an-a-fal-z,* the one A, the Strong Fire.

In heraldry the Sword is frequently hilted with the three perfect circles of Good Thought, Good Deed, and Good Word.

In the emblems herewith the divine Hand holds a thunderbolt, mace, sceptre, or truncheon. The Mace is still the customary symbol of the Mayor's office.

The Egyptians conceived KNEPH, the Father of PTAH, as a man of *blue* colour with a girdle round his loins, a sceptre in his hand, and crowned with a plume of feathers. PORPHYRIUS, speaking of ZEUS the Creator, says : " The philosophers—that is the initiated—represented Him as a

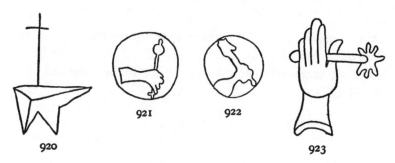

920 · 921 · 922 · 923

man *seated,* alluding to His immutable essence ; *the upper part of his body naked,* because it is in its upper portions (in the skies) that the universe is seen most uncovered ; *clothed from the waist below,* because the terrestrial things are those most hidden from view. *He holds a sceptre in His left hand,* because the heart is on that side, and the heart is the seat of understanding that regulates all the actions of man." [1] In the emblem herewith (fig. 924) the figure is holding a sceptre or thunderbolt in the *left* hand, and his loins are girt about with Truth. In fig. 925 a two-peaked mountain-top is surmounted by the holy Four or Fire of the Divine Equity, and attached to this small emblem is a feathered or rayed

[1] Le Plongeon, *Sacred Mysticism,* pp. 72, 73.

figure seated upon a five-pointed cockscomb, saw,[1] or *broccus*. The figure is wearing what is seemingly a gauntlet or glove, and in figs. 926 to 928 this object serves as a separate and

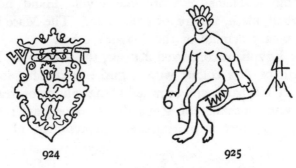

924   925

distinct emblem. It is a poetic commonplace that the Dawn is rosy-*fingered*, and the five fingers of the glove, rayed out dawnwise, seemingly caused this article to be regarded as a symbol of *ag love*, the great LOVER. Of a statue of the

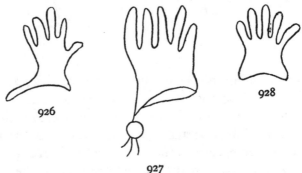

926

928

927

Mayan THAAH, found by her husband in MEXICO, Mrs LE PLONGEON states : " The backs of the hands appeared as if covered with mittens."[2]

ODIN or WOTAN (HU-OTAN) is said to have worn a *blue* coat ; the Druidic High Priests and the Jewish High

[1] Compare *saw*, meaning a *wise saying*. *Saw* = Is-AW, the light of the Aw.
[2] *London Magazine*, April 1910, p. 129.

Priests alike wore *blue* robes, and, according to PLATO's relation, the priests of lost ATLANTIS wore " most beautiful azure robes." At the time of the Roman invasion CÆSAR found the Britons arrayed against him tattooed like the MAORIS of to-day, in *blue* paint. Each tribe was distinctively marked with the device of its symbolic animal, totem, or mascot, and the blue paint used for this purpose was called *Woad*. *Woad*, a Gallic herb yielding a blue dye, was probably named after Woden. It is also the word under which *blue*-green glass was known, and the British habit of daubing oneself with *blue* war-paint may be contrasted with the similar sacrificial ceremony among the MAYAS. It points to the probability that when the ancient Briton went into battle he did so with the full intention of sacrificing himself *pro deo* or *pro patria*.

The expression " blue-blooded" probably originated from the symbolic idea that the Divine blood was blue, and that the nearer one's kinship to the Divine, the bluer the blood ; hence the more perfect the *aristocracy*, *i.e.* the Order of EROS or HORUS or IRIS.

The Greek for *blue*—bel HU, beautiful HU, or BEL hue, the hue of BEL—is *glaukos*. The Breton for *blue* is *perse*, the French is *vrai*, and the Italian *vero* or *excellente*. Blue is indeed so widely the symbol of *la verité*, the Truth or the True, *i.e. tur Hu*, the Enduring HU, that *true blue* is a proverbial saw.

Into the chalk side of WADEN HILL near AVEBURY there has been cut the figure of a *white horse*. WADEN is the All-Father WODEN or WOTAN, and in Anglo-Saxon *witan* meant *to know*. WOTAN cannot but be related to the VOTAN of South America, and among the most ancient of the Mayan tribes, as also in Hebrew, *votan* means *to give* — an idea which we English have retained in the words *vote* and *votive*. As *tan* meant *fire* the name VOTAN resolves into VO-TAN,

"The Giver of Fire." In Gypsy language *potan* means
tinder,[1] and *tinder* does not differ from the adjective *tender*.
Fire was originally obtained by the friction of *tinder*-wood
or *timber*. *Timber* may be equated with *tambour*, a drum,
and the words *wood* and *wooden*, as also *Wednesday*, may be
traced to WODEN or HU, the giver of Fire. The Greek for
wood is *xylon* (*ek zi lone*), the French is *bois*, and the Latin
for a board or plank is *axis*.

The word *vote* is derived by Skeat from the Latin
votum, a *wish*, i.e. HUISH. "The word WISH," says Sir
George Dasent, "originally meant the perfect ideal, the
actual fruition of all joy and desire, and not, as now, the
empty longing for the object of our desires. From this
original abstract meaning it was but a step to pass to the
concrete, to personify the idea, to make it an immortal
essence and attribute of the Divinity, another name for the
greatest of all Gods Himself. And so we find a host of
passages in early writers, in every one of which 'God' or
'Odin' might be substituted for 'Wish' with perfect
propriety. Here we read how 'The Wish' has hands,
feet, power, sight, toil, and art ; how he works and
labours, shapes and masters, inclines his ear, thinks, swears,
curses and rejoices, adopts children, and takes men into his
house ; behaves, in short, as a Being of boundless power
and infinite free-will. Still more, he rejoices in his own
works as in a child, and thus appears in a thoroughly
patriarchal point of view as the Lord of Creation, glorying
in his handiwork, as the father of a family in early times
was glad at heart when he reckoned his children as arrows
in his quiver, and beheld his house full of a long line of
retainers and dependents." [2]

The memory of Great WISH is possibly preserved in the

---

[1] Compare Scandinavian *tandstickor* = tinder-sticks = matches.
[2] *Popular Tales from the Norse*, p. 47.

place-name GREAT WISHFORD [1] on Salisbury Plain, and in the common words *wish* and *will*. *Wish* or *huish* is equivalent to *desire*, i.e. *de sire*, the shining Sire ; the French for *desire* is *volonté*, i.e. *vol on te*, the "strong resplendent one." The word *will* is radically the same as *well*, *weal*,[2] and *wheel*. *Owel* was Cornish for *hill* and survives in BROWN WILLY, WILLY PARK, etc. ; HOWEL was the last King of Cornwall, and HOWELL is a modern surname.[3] The plural of *œil*, the French for *eye*, is *yeux*, and the Lord HU is probably also responsible for the word *wool*. Baskets of carded *wool* were carried in procession at the Eleusinian Festivals.[4] *Huil* is Cornish for *to do* or *to make*, and *huilan* Cornish for a *beetle*. The name WILL is a contracted form of WILLIAM, of which the French form is GUILLAUME, *i.e. ag huilaume*, the Mighty HU, our Lord the Sun ; and BILL, an alternative form of WILL, is presumably BEL.

The letters W and V are often interchangeable, and it will be remembered that Mr Samuel Weller, senior, preferred to spell WELLER with a V. In other countries the same interchangeability is apparent, and the Indian VISHNU is alternatively referred to as WISHNU. [5] The *chakra, disc*, or *patara*, which WISHNU is usually represented as holding, may be equated with the Wheel of the Sun or Circle of Perfection, and the word *chakra* resolves into "ever-existent great RA" or *ur A*, "Fire A." The caste mark worn by

[1] *Ford = fort = strong.* Compare ROMFORD, originally ROMFORT, in ESSEX.

[2] The range of hills constituting the backbone of KENT is called the WEALD OF KENT.

[3] Compare also WALLACE and WALLIS. Near BIRKENHEAD are WALLASEY, WILLASTON, HOOLE, HOOSE, HOOTON, POOLTON, LISCARD, BROMBOROUGH, BURTON, UPTON, HOPTON, and BOOTLE.

[4] The Irish bagpipes were known as *uilleans* or *woollens*, also as *unions*.

[5] In the ancient Sanscrit alphabet there was no W, and V occupied its place.

the followers of VISHNU is a white, or it may be red, circular
spot on their foreheads.   The name VISHNU is from the
root *Vish*, "to pervade"; it means "The all-pervading,
penetrating, and encompassing One," and stands for Divine
Intelligence or Wisdom.   VISHNU, under the guise of a
Fish, is said to have led the ark of mankind to safety in
the same way as APOLLO guided the vessel of the Cretan
mariners to KRISA.   According to the Hindoos, it was in the
form of VISHNU that the Supreme Spirit "without beginning
or end, omniscient and omnipresent, eternal, unchangeable,
and supremely happy," exhibited his sympathy with human
trials and his love for the human race.   In the *Bhagavad
Gita* (The Song of the Most High) VISHNU is represented
as saying : "Every time that religion is in danger and that
iniquity triumphs I issue forth for the defence of the good
and the suppression of the wicked; for the establishment of
justice I manifest myself from age to age."

Nine principal occasions are said to have already
occurred on which VISHNU, whose initial surmounts fig. 929,
has thus interposed for the benefit of humanity.   The first
was in the form of a Fish, and the word *fish* (Dutch *vische*)
may be equated with the first syllable of VISHNU, a name
which is sometimes translated to mean " born of a fish."

The identification of a Saviour with a fish was common
in ancient theosophies ; in the *Talmud* the Messiah is called
DAG, which also means *fish* and *preserver*, and it is supposed
to have been for this reason that the primitive Christians
adopted the Fish as a sign of Christ.

The Fish was sacred among the Babylonians, Phœnicians,
and Assyrians, and seems to have been regarded as an
emblem of fecundity.   But, according to Swedenborg, fish
were the symbols of "scientifics"[1] or knowledge, presumably because they were able to explore the uttermost

[1] See *Concordance*.

depths of the sea.[1]   MANU, the ancestor of all humanity, is represented in Indian legend as being instructed in all kinds of *knowledge* by a fish, and the "Salmon of *Knowledge*" is a familiar feature in fairy-tale.

According to the Irish Legend of FUIN MAC CUMHAL, "there was a Salmon which, if caught and eaten, would communicate such *wisdom*, prowess, and good fortune to the

929

eater, that from that day both fame and prosperity would attend him in all his wars."   This wonderful fish is secured by FUIN MAC CUMHAL, and on the instant that it came between his teeth "he felt as *wise* and *prudent* as if he were a hundred years old."   The tale concludes : "Thus it was that FUIN MAC CUMHAL happened on the Salmon of *Knowledge*, and time and your patience would fail me to recount all his succeeding renowned deeds."[2]

[1] This idea is strengthened by the facts narrated by Dr Eisler in "John-Jonah-Oannes"?   See *The Quest*, vol. iii. No. 3.

[2] *Folk-Lore and Legends*, Ireland, p. 5.

The word *salmon* is related to SOLOMON, the proverbial *wise* king, and that *Fish* were regarded as the symbolic equivalents to the *Horse* may be further inferred from the existence of a THRACIAN coin, whereon the Deity is represented as a human figure armed with a bow, riding a winged horse which terminates in a fish.[1] The idea here seems to be that the rider upon the combination Horse-Fish is Lord of all Knowledge on Land and Sea.

It is a curious fact that Jesus Christ was represented in the Catacombs by *two* fishes, which are the zodiacal sign

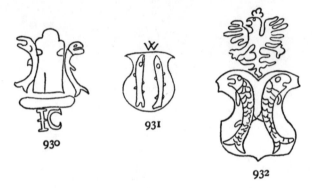

930   931   932

PISCES. In fig. 930 these two fishes are identified with Jesus Christ, the Tower of Salvation; in fig. 931 they are surmounted with the twin V's or double HU, and in fig. 932 with an *aquila*.

TERTULLIAN termed Christians "fishes bred in the water and saved by one great Fish"; PAULINUS alludes to Jesu as "the Fish of the living water"; and PROSPER refers to Him as "the Fish dressed at His death—the great Fish Who satisfied for Himself the disciples on the shore and offered Himself as a fish to the whole world."

The tail feathers of fig. 933 form the Root or Stem of Jesse, to which are attached the twin circles in con-

[1] Payne-Knight, p. 78.

junction with what apparently is a bow, a crescent moon, or a cresset.

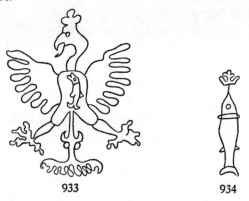

933   934

In Old Irish the word *ischa*, which is the Eastern form of J ESUS, means a *fish*, and the Greek *ichtheus* may be resolved into *ik theos*, the Great God.

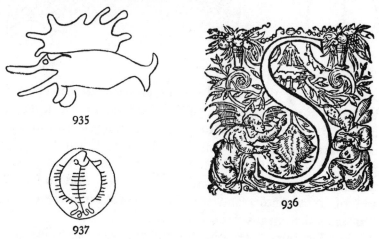

935

937

936

Fig. 934 is a nondescript kind of fish formed like a column or tower, passing, Maypole-like, through the ring or O of I O. Fig. 935 is presumably a " John Dory." This name as it stands resolves into the Existent One, the Golden or Enduring Unit. In French *jaune* means yellow, a *hue* the colour of the Sun, and one in which VISHNU is always represented as being clad.

In fig. 936 two *genii* are represented as adoring a *Sole*, and in fig. 937 this fish appears in the centre of the Solar eye. It may be understood to symbolise the "*Soul* of the World," or Solmona, the "Sole lone A."

Within the Eye of fig. 938 is a *Jack, Pike,* or *Luce*. In EGYPT special reverence was paid to a fish which PLUTARCH refers to as the *oxyrhyncus,* and which Dr BUDGE considers

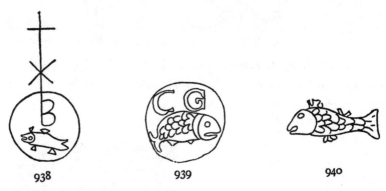

938   939   940

was "probably the pike."[1]   Another peculiarly sacred fish was the Egyptian *an,* which is described as "a kind of bream."[2]   The sturdy fish represented in figs. 939 and 940 is perhaps this sacred *bream, i.e.* a BRAHM (Cornish *ziu*), or perhaps a *carp*. Carp is the root of *carpo,* a seed-vessel, and of *carpentarius,* a carpenter : Christ was said to be the son of a carpenter, and the Zend word for carpenter is *Tashan,* which means "the Creator."

The Dolphins herewith, crowned with the varied insignia of divinity, are like those illustrated *ante,* p. 28—evidently emblems of the Saviour and Creator. *Delphis,* the Greek

[1] *Legends of the Gods,* p. 206.
[2] *Ibid.,* p. 207.

for *dolphin*, may be compared with *delphus*, the Greek for *womb*.

According to Greek legend, the great Temple at DELPHI was founded by APOLLO, who, in the guise of a Dolphin, led thither a crew of Cretan mariners. Upon reaching the sands

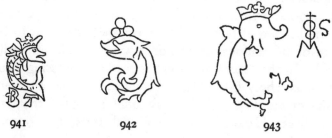

941   942   943

of KRISA, APOLLO leapt from the vessel like a star, whilst sparks of light streamed from him till their radiance reached the heavens. Hastening to his Sanctuary, he lighted a fire and returned to the astonished mariners in his proper form of a beautiful youth, who informed them that if they would avoid falsehood in words and violence in deed, their name

944   945

would be known throughout the world as the guardians of APOLLO's shrine and the interpreters of his will. So they followed him to PYTHO, while the heavenly Being led the way, filling the air with melody.

The English *well*, meaning *good*, is phonetically *huel*,[1] and this same term denotes also a spring or fountain. The original sanctity of wells is well known; the worship of

[1] Compare place-name EWELL.

wells [1] was nowhere more prominent than in WALES ; [2] and at the town of WELLS there is still standing a majestic shrine.

Sacred Wells were believed to cure sore eyes, and were generally said to possess a guardian spirit. At BALLY-MOREREIGH in IRELAND is a holy well called TOBER MONACHAN, where the Spirit is believed to be a Salmon. At the bottom of one of the SLIGO wells are said to be " a brace of miraculous trout not always visible to ordinary eyes.[3]   In the Island of SKYE [4] is a well possessing two fish known as " holy fish," black in colour and never augmenting in size or number.[5]   It is a frequent metaphor that JESU is a Well, *the* HUEL or WATER of Salvation, the opener of blind eyes.

One of the incarnations of VISHNU is fabled to have been in the form of a Boar which destroyed a demon and raised the submerged Earth from the Sea.   The wild boar was sacred in Babylonia and among other Semitic nations ; [6] it was also a favourite Gaulish emblem, and there is extant a Celtic figure of DIANA riding on a boar's back.[7]   In BRITAIN the boar occurs frequently on the coins of the ICENI and other tribes,[8] and in the legends of all Celtic races the boar occupies an honoured place.   In Northern Mythology the Sun-God FREY is represented as riding on a boar called GULLINBURSTI (Golden-Bristle).   FREY had great personal beauty in addition to his divine powers : " He rules over rain and sunshine, and it is good to call on

[1] The Hebrew for a well is *beer*, and the Arabian *bir*.   The Anglo-Saxon for "a place where water flows forth" was *kell, i.e.* "Great God."

[2] The patron saint of WALES is ST DAVID or DEWI=d'HUHI (?).

[3] *Isikeye*, the light of the Great Eye (?).

[4] Gomme (G. L.), *Ethnology in Folk-Lore*, p. 93.

[5] *Ibid.*, p. 103.

[6] *Religion of Babylonia and Assyria*, M. Jastrow, p. 92.

[7] *Celtic Religion*, E. Anwyl, p. 30.

[8] *Ibid.*

him for peace and plenty; he also has power over the prosperity of men."[1] The souls of departed heroes are represented as feasting in VALHALLA on boar's meat, the supply of which was inexhaustible. At Yuletide it was

946   947

customary to lead a boar into the Hall of the King, whereupon men laid their hands upon its bristles and thus made their vows upon important matters; the sacred boar was then sacrificed by way of atonement.

VISHNU in his form of a boar is described as "vast as a

948   949

mountain; his tusks were white, sharp, and fearful; fire flashed from his eyes like lightning; and he was radiant as the Sun."[2]

The tail of fig. 947 is formed like a cross, and surmounting figs. 948 and 949 is the K, KAY, or KAPPA, which may here stand for "KESAVA," the name under which VISHNU is hailed in his boar form. A Vedic hymn invokes him as "KESAVA, Sovereign of the earth, Cause of production, destruction, and existence." "*Thou art*, O God! there is none other supreme condition than Thou. Thou, Lord,

---

[1] *Religion of Ancient Scandinavia*, W. A. Craigie, p. 28.
[2] *Hindoo Mythology*, W. J. Wilkins, p. 123.

art the person of the sacrifice ; Thy feet are the Vedas ; Thy
tusks are the stake to which the victim is bound ; Thy
teeth are the offerings ; Thy mouth is the altar ; Thy tongue
is the fire ; and the hairs of Thy body are the sacrificial
grass. *Thy eyes*, O Omnipotent ! *are day and night;* thy
head is the seat of all. . . . Do Thou, who art eternal, who
art in size a mountain, be propitious." [1]

The word *boar* does not differ from *bear* ; the Zend for
boar is *hu* ; and the Cornish for sow was *baneu, i.e.* the good
Hu. *Hog* means the Mighty One, and *pig* the Mighty Hoop.
That *hog* and *pig* had once pleasant associations may be
assumed from the surname Pegg, and from the City Church
near London Stone known as St Bennet's *Sherehog. Ehog*
was the Cornish word for *salmon*, and *pig* is Welsh for *pike*,
the fish. *Twrch*, the ancient British for *hog*, probably does not
differ from *torch*, meaning a blazing light, and resolving into
t-or-che, " resplendent fire, ever-existent."

Sanglier, the French for boar, resolves into *san ag li er*,
the Holy, Mighty, Everlasting Fire, and the boar must, I
think, have been adopted as a symbol of Fire on account
of its bristly and prickly hide. It was popularly supposed
that the " *ireful* boar " was so hot that its tusks scorched
hounds and hunters. The Welsh for *boar* is *moch*, the
Gaulish was *moccus, i.e. om ok us*, the Sun, the Great Light,
and Moccus was a Gaulish term for Mercury.[2]

In close proximity to Cheapside and St Paul's there
used to stand a famous Blue Boar Inn. As boars are not
naturally *blue*, one may surmise that this impressionist sign
of the Blue Boar was reproduced from some old symbolic
painting.

The two animals here illustrated having no tusks, must
be assumed to be female pigs. In Egypt the Sow was held

---

[1] *Hindoo Mythology*, W. J. Wilkins, p. 124.
[2] Anwyl (Ed.), *Celtic Religion*, p. 30.

sacred to Isis, and small figures of sows were there worn as amulets attached to necklaces.[1] Judging from the word *sus*, a sow,[2] the female pig symbolised the SUSTAINER, and that this characteristic should have been seized upon by the

950   951

symbolists is not surprising when one contemplates upwards of twenty little sucking pigs being simultaneously nourished. Under fig. 950 is the I C of JESUS, the Everlasting Sustainer, and under fig. 951, the clover leaf and C R of CHRISTUS REDEMPTOR. The English *sow* may be equated with the Greek

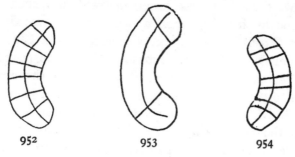

952   953   954

zoo, as in *zoologv*, meaning *Life*. The Welsh for *sow* is *hwch*, the Dutch is *zog*, and the Icelandic is *syr*. In French *sœur* means *sister*, a word that varies into *suster* and *soster*. The root *sos* in Cornish, meaning *Friend* and *Comforter*, reappears in the name JESUS, the Ever-Existent Sos or Sus.

At the Feast of MARTIN-, MARTLE-, or MARTILMAS, it was customary to lay in sustenance for the long winter months

---

[1] *A Guide to the Egyptian Collections in the British Museum*, p. 96.
[2] *Sow*=the *sou* of *soutenir*, to *sustain*.

by smoking or salting a sufficient supply of provisions. In GERMANY part of the Martelmas festivities used to consist of the Feast of Sausages. The French word *saucisse* and the English *sausage* are both radically *sos*, as in *sostenuto* and *sustainer*.

In PERU the potato and the maize were both "adored as symbols of sustenance."[1] The former was known as *acsumama*, which may be Anglicised into "Great Sow Mamma" or "Great Life Mother," and the golden *maize* was known as *Saramama*, the "Fire RA Mamma." Our English *bacon* is probably the same word as *boucan*, a kind of preserved meat used by the native Caribs, and said to be the origin of the term *buccaneer*.[2] The words *bacon*, *sausage*, *ham*, *brawn*, and *pork* all contain the implication that these foods or *progs* were once viewed as gifts or symbols of Père og, the Mighty Father.

St Martin's Day was commemorated in certain parts of Europe by feasting upon a *goose*, and it was also the Feast of *Wine*. The ancient Calendar of the Church of Rome remarks upon Martinmas: "Wines are tasted and drawn from the lees. The Vinalia, a feast of the ancients removed to this day. Bacchus in the figure of Martin."[3]

On St Martin's Eve boys used to expose vessels of water in the belief that it would be converted into wine, and, Santa Claus-like, the parents humoured and deceived them by substituting wine.[4] The first miracle recorded of JESUS CHRIST was the conversion of water into wine, and the Christian Eucharist, which in primitive days was celebrated by the eating of a Fish,[5] is now celebrated by the

---

[1] Spence (L.), *Mythology of Mexico and Peru*, p. 54.
[2] Anderson (R. A.), *Extinct Civ. of the West*, p. 174.
[3] Brand, p. 218.   [4] *Ibid.*
[5] Julius Africanus (an early Christian writer) says: "Christ is the great Fish taken by the fish-hook of God, and whose flesh nourishes the whole world."

eating of bread and the drinking of wine. The word *wine* may be traced to EWINE, and the term *eucharist* must be

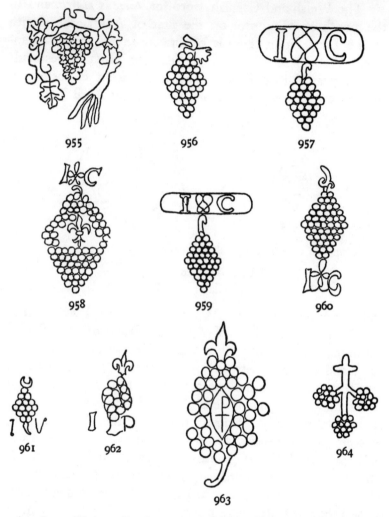

related to *Christ*. In fig. 965 the True Vine is represented as an acorn, in fig. 966 the tail is formed like an *iris*, and the mane is designed like a bunch of raisins. The word *raison* must be cognate to *reason*, and the word *grape* to *agapemone*, the Greek for Love Feast.

The Welsh and Cornish word for *horse* is *march*, and in the month of MARCH or on the first of APRIL, the month of the Lord Apur, there is celebrated in the East the so-called Festival of Huli. The Feast of HULI corresponds to European All Fools' Day, and in France it is customary to term the victim not an April Fool but an April Fish.

965   966

There is an old English couplet—

> " The fish fried
> Was Christ that died,"

and it appears probable that the Indian word *huli* is HU Everlasting. The first of April or Feast of the Vernal Equinox, was anciently observed in Britain and India as a High and General Festival. At that period the Sun entered into the sign ARIES and with it there returned a spirit of Awakening, of rejuvenescence, and of unbounded hilarity. It may perhaps be assumed that HU, the Lord of *wit*, *humour*, and *amusement*, was in his alternative title of LUD, the root of *ludi*, *i.e.* games and sports, and likewise of *ludicrous*. From the word *wag* one must conclude either that HU the Mighty was regarded as the Supreme Humorist, or else that *wag* originally meant one with *hu ag*, a mighty mind.[1] At the festivities of Whitsuntide—and the *Whitsun*

---

[1] Compare surnames WAGG, WAGSTAFFE, and WEGG. Also place-name WIGAN.

of this word is probably related to Huitzon, the Mexican Divinity—the ancient Britons abandoned themselves to a Festival called Wakes. That this word meant Hu akse, Hu, the Great Fire and Light, is probable from the fact that multitudes of both old and young "used to meet *about break of day*, shouting *Holy Wakes! Holy Wakes!*"[1]

The Lancashire Wakes last seven or ten days, and this *holyday, beano,* or *wayzgoose* is in some towns termed the *Fair, i.e.* the *Fire* or *Furry* Festival, the Feast in honour of Bean or Bene.

In his *Anatomy of Abuses* Stubbes alludes to "Feastes and Wakesses," wherefrom it would appear that the modern term *wake* is a corruption of wakes. The festivities of Hu ake, the great Awakener, are now chiefly maintained at Irish funerals, and the existence of this word in this connection implies that our ancestors regarded death not as sleep, still less as extinction, but as the Great Awakening.

The Bridegroom of *The Song of Solomon* is described as leaping and dancing upon the hills. In Northern England *wakes* were known as *hoppings*, a word said to be derived from *hoppan*, the Anglo-Saxon for *leap* or *dance*, and *hop* is often now used to mean a dance. Dancing is still a religious function among primitive peoples, and that modern dances once similarly had a sacred significance is to be inferred from names such as *mazurka, polonaise, polacca, polka,* and *valse.*

The *valse* or *waltz* would appear to have been a *whorl* or *whirl* in honour of *hu ol tz*, Hu, the God resplendent, or *val se*, the Mighty Fire. The French *can-can* was originally, no doubt, a frenzied Sun-dance, and the British *Hey* was once probably a jig in honour of the A.

In olden time when a church was about to be built, " they watched and prayed on the vigil of the dedication

[1] Brand, p. 291.

and took that point of the horizon where the Sun arose for the East."[1]   The word *Easter*[2] or EOSTRE, meaning the Enduring Eos, the Dawn or the Enduring Light, does not differ from ISTAR, the Goddess who descended to and arose from the under-world.   The name ISTAR is the source of our *star*,[3] and Christ the "Dayspring," who is said to have ascended on Easter Day, is described as the Bright and *Morning* Star.   The French for *morning* is *matin*, *i.e.* MARTIN or MAATIN, the unique TRUTH, the unique JUSTICE.

In the north of England YULE-tide was sometimes called *Zule*,[4] a fact seemingly equating HU with ZU, the Solar Horse, and *zoo*, the Greek for *life*.   At the sanctuary of

967   968

ZEUS at DODONA (i.e. *Dad one*, the One Father ?), the Song of the Priestesses was "Zeus was, Zeus is, Zeus will be; a Great Zeus."[5]

It is supposed that there is one more final manifestation of VISHNU yet to come, in which he will appear on a *white horse* with a drawn sword to restore the order of righteousness.   This event is probably the subject of the equestrian figures herewith.

It was believed that THOR was not really slain at the twilight of the Gods, but merely blighted and rendered insensible for a while by the poisonous breath of his

[1] See Brand, p. 294.
[2] Easter is preceded by SHERE or MAUNDY Thursday.
[3] Latin, *aster*.   [4] Brand, p. 217.
[5] Müller, *Science of Language*, ii. p. 458.

adversary, the World Snake. BALDUR was expected to come again, and King Arthur, the Celtic Messiah, was believed to be nowise dead, but merely to have retired temporarily in order at some future day to emerge from his mysterious retreat. Until quite recently Welsh shepherds regaled one another with stories, describing how one of their number found his way into the presence of King ARTHUR and his men, asleep in a cave resplendent with untold wealth of gold.[1] It was supposed that the King and his Knights were only awaiting the destined signal in order to return and take once more an active part in the affairs of the world. The inscription upon his tomb was reported as, "Here Arthur lies, King once and King to be," and the poets have persistently and consistently glorified King Arthur into a Messiah.[2] The gradual and for a time imperceptible character of this return is pointed by MERLIN in his prophecy, "like *the dawn* will he arise from his mysterious retreat," and this return, "like the Dawn" from a *cave*, may be compared with the story of CINDERELLA's imprisonment in a cave and her liberation by the *kick of a horse's hoof* through the roof.

ST GEORGE is always represented as riding on a *white* horse ; the heavenly Twins with stars upon their brows were said to ride upon *white* horses ; and the second coming of JESUS CHRIST will, it is believed, like the return of VISHNU, be upon a *white* horse : "And I saw heaven opened, and behold a *white* horse ; and he that sat upon him was called

---

[1] Rhys (Sir J.), Introduction to *La Morte d'Arthur*. This cave was located on Snowdon, and the spiritual significance with which Snowdon was once regarded is indicated by its ancient and poetic name Y-WYDDEA, *i.e.* "THE PRESENCE." There is a hill in Berkshire called SINODUN.

[2] *E.g.*, "This Great deliverer shall Europe save,
Which haughty monarchs labour to enslave ;
Then shall Religion rear her starry head,
And light divine through all the nations spread."
(Blackmore, R. B., 1695. *Prince Arthur*, Book I.)

Faithful and True, and in righteousness he doth judge and make war. His eyes were as a flame of fire, and on his head were many crowns ; and he had a name written, that no man knew, but he himself. And he was clothed with a vesture dipped in blood : and his name is called The Word

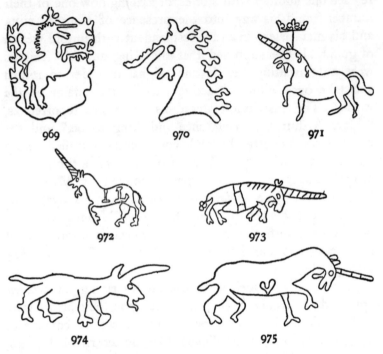

of God. And the armies which were in heaven followed him upon white horses." [1]

A white horse — the symbol of Innocent and Pure Intellect or Reason—when equipped with a horn becomes the Unicorn of Fable and Mythology. Some writers describe the Unicorn's horn as being movable at will, "a kind of small sword, in short, with which no hunter who was not exceeding cunning in fence could have a chance."

[1] Revelation xix, 11–14.

The Unicorns here illustrated are clearly emblematic of the Great Spirit of Pure Reason, and the butting attitude of figs. 973 to 975 is suggestive of Joseph's benediction, "his horns are like the horns of unicorns : with them he shall push the people together to the ends of the earth." [1]

According to the authors of *The Perfect Way*, "The act of butting with the horns typifies the employment of the intellect, whether for attack or defence," and this curious statement is somewhat verified by modern metaphors such as "rebutting," an argument, or "ramming" it well home.

That the Unicorn's horn typified the Sword or Word of

976   977

God is supported by the fact that the weapon of fig. 976 is formed like the wavy line of the Spirit or the soft flowing waters of AQUA. Over fig. 977 is the I of IESOUS or the Holy and Incomprehensible ONE.

The Chinese have a tradition that the Unicorn, or, as they term it, the *Lin*—i.e. *el un*, the Alone, the "powerful One," or the "One God" ?—is so holy and harmless that it will not tread even upon an insect. The *Lin*, described by Oriental authorities as "a spiritual beast," an "auspicious and perfect beast" which "appears when sages are born," is said to be *twelve* feet in height and of *five* colours. Its horn is "an emblem of goodness," [2] and in CHINA it is believed that, Messiah-like, the *Lin* is yet "to come in the

---

[1] Deuteronomy xxxiii. 17.
[2] Gould, C., *Mythical Monsters*, pp. 351, 352.

shape of an incomparable man, a revealer of mysteries super-natural and divine, and a great lover of all mankind."[1]

The Unicorn is the ancient crest of the Kings of Israel, and is still retained by the Mikado of Japan. The Japanese for *unicorn* is " *Sin You*, or divine sheep," i.e. *ewe* (?), and in Japanese tradition *Sin You* exercises the role of Judge, spar-ing the innocent and sentencing the guilty. In CHINA the *Lin* is sometimes called the *Lu*, which may, perhaps, be resolved into *el Hu*.

In the Old Testament the Unicorn is termed *reem*, i.e. *ur eem*, the Sun Light. In KORDOFAN it is known as the *arase*—evidently the final syllables of *arucharis*, its Ethiopian name. The heart of *love* on figs. 973 and 975 justify the inflection of *arase* into EROS, and of *arucharis* into *charis* or CHRIST. In TIBET the *arucharis* is known as *Serou*, i.e. " Sire HU " (?), also as *kere*, the Great Fire (?), and as *tsopo*, " resplendent Fire Father." In some parts of CHINA the Unicorn is known as *Poh* and in others as *Piao*,[2] i.e. *Pa Ao* or " Father First and Last."

---

[1] M'Leod, N., *Epitome of the Ancient History of Japan*, p. 116.
[2] Gould, C., *Mythical Monsters*, pp. 342, 346, 347, 355, 359.

CHAPTER XVI

THE SIGN OF THE CROSS

"The roses of Greece have shed their petals; Imperial Rome has seen corruption. But the holy spirit of Man has risen, reappearing in each age of faith, arising as each Eastertide the Soul of the world appears in resurrection. Youth and age in eternal recurrence keep the spiritual lamps aflame upon the altars that we raise to life. The same Death guards his portals, the same Love sets the bell of morning ringing the carillon, as the horses of Aurora leap into the light of day. Tithonus, the weary one, reminds us for ever of our mortality, while every grove is full of fauns and dryads. And Pan but sleeps. Those of us who look for the union of Christianity with the beauty of Hellas, feel that the hour draws nearer wherein men and women will live a fuller life, wherein all that is pale and mean in modern times will sink into nothing, and the full sunlight of a new day will flood the Soul of Man, waking daily to the far call of an ever clearer Destiny."

REGINALD R. BUCKLEY.

THERE is a Slav fairy-tale entitled OHNIVAK, the Bird of Fire, which tells how a certain young and inexperienced Prince acquired a feather from the wing of OHNIVAK; "so lovely and bright was it that it illumined all the galleries of the palace and they needed no other light."[1] One of the Sufi poets in a mystical poem called *The Language of the Birds*, tells how the mysterious SIMURGH (which in his allegory typifies God) passed over the land of CHINA and let fall thereon one of its feathers. This single feather filled CHINA with wonder and delight, and everyone who saw it sought to preserve for himself, in a sketch or painting, some semblance of its beauty. "Therefore," says a tradition

[1] *Slav Tales*, p. 269.

attributed to MAHOMET, "'seek knowledge even unto China,' for there, as in every land, be it never so remote or uncouth, shall traces of that for which you seek be found."[1]

The story of OHNIVAK recounts that the King could think upon naught else than how this beautiful and miraculous Bird of Fire might be acquired. One day, summoning his three sons, he said : " My dear children, you see the sad state I am in. If I could but hear the bird OHNIVAK sing just once, I should be cured of this disease of the heart ; otherwise, it will be my death." Whereupon the three sons dutifully set forth in quest of the Bird of Wonder, and their first adventure is to meet a famished Fox who begs for food. The two elder brothers maliciously ill-treat this creature, but the youngest compassionately gives it his food. The Fox says : "You have fed *me* well ; in return I will serve *you* well ; mount your horse and follow me. If you do everything I tell you, the Bird of Fire shall be yours." Then he set off at a run before the horseman, clearing the road for him with his bushy tail. By this marvellous means mountains were cut down, ravines filled up, and rivers bridged over.[2]

The Fox of Europe corresponds to the Jackal or Fox of Egypt, which was reverenced as the maker of tracks in the desert. "The Jackal paths," says Professor PETRIE, "are the best guides to practicable courses, avoiding the valleys and precipices : and so the animal was known as UP-UAT, 'the opener of ways,' who showed the way for the dead across the Western desert."[3] It is clear that one may equate the road-levelling Fox of European fairy-tale with

---

[1] *Religious Systems of the World*, p. 325. Compare Ecclesiasticus : "In every people and nation I (Wisdom) got a possession ; with all these I sought rest."

[2] *Slav Tales*, p. 274.   [3] *Religion of Ancient Egypt*, p. 24.

Up-uat, the Egyptian "opener of the ways"; and from the emblems herewith it would appear that their designers, supposing themselves to be Up-uats, self-applied the injunction of Isaiah, "Prepare ye the way of the people; cast up, cast up the highway; gather out the stones; lift up a standard for the people."[1]

Fig. 978 is intently nosing along the ground, and in fig. 979 the parched and thirsty wilderness is ingeniously implied by the lolling tongue, "The wilderness and the solitary place shall be glad for them; and the desert shall rejoice, and blossom as the rose . . . for in the wilderness

978 979 980 981

shall waters break out, and streams in the desert. And the parched ground shall become a pool, and the thirsty land springs of water: in the habitation of dragons, where each lay, shall be grass with reeds and rushes. And an highway shall be there, and a way, and it shall be called the way of holiness."[2]

The Egyptians hailed Osiris as the "opener of ways to the Gods"; also as He who "bringeth three to the mountains";[3] and they represented Anubis, whose office in the Pantheon was that of the pathfinder, with the head of a jackal.

The word Anubis is an alternative name for Anpu, the

[1] lxii. 10.   [2] Isaiah xxxv.
[3] *The Burden of Isis*, J. T. Dennis, pp. 41, 48.

"one Father," and in EGYPT *anpu* was the generic term for *jackal*. In fig. 982 the jackal-headed ANUBIS, the "one orb of Light," is apparently blessing a candidate, over whom hovers the Dove of the Spirit.

The Fox was the symbol of *wiliness*, quick-wittedness, and wisdom, and in the Gnostic monument already referred

982

to, the eager recipient of the mystic blood is represented as a fox.

The Gnostics were exceptionally great artists in dissimulation, and to contemplate them at work one must observe the admonition of SOLON : " Fools, ye are treading in the footsteps of the fox ; can ye not read the hidden meaning of these winning words ? "

In fig. 985 a Fox—the symbol of the pathfinder, of

wisdom, of subtlety, and of pious fraud[1]—is finding Honey in a Tree which doubtless represents the Tree of Life; and in fig. 986 a Marigold or Sunflower Tree is being supported by Foxes cloaked.

983   984

It was a persistent complaint against the Gnostics that they cloaked their real tenets by conforming outwardly with the established worship of any state or city they inhabited, thus maintaining their secret ideas without notice or molestation. Their policy was, "Learn to know all, but

985

986[2]

keep thyself unknown," and as the Son of God lived unknown in the world, so they conducted themselves as beings invisible and unknown.[3]

---

[1] "The prudence of the ancients," said Richard de Bury, "discovered a remedy by which the wanton part of mankind might in a manner be taken in *by a pious fraud,* and the delicate Minerva lie hid under the dissembling mask of pleasure."—*Philobiblon.*

[2] Reduced from *Printers' Marks,* W. Roberts.

[3] IRENÆUS complained: "Neither can they be detected as Christian heretics, because they assimilate themselves to all sects." Their method was to form esoteric schools, which in many cases endangered the organisa-

By the Gnostics Hermes and also Osiris were identified with Christ, the Guider of Souls, and a jackal-headed figure was sometimes portrayed upon a cross.[1]

Not only was there a certain amount of confusion between the Fox and the Jackal, but in Egypt certain species of dogs were also held sacred and mummified on merely the general ground of similarity with the Jackal.

By the Persians the Dog was regarded as the special animal of ORMUZ, and it is still held in peculiar reverence by the Parsees. SIRIUS, the brightest star in the Sky, forms part of a constellation termed "The Great Dog," and the name SIRIUS cannot but be related to OSIRIS. The so-called Dog days were reckoned by the old astronomers from the rising of this sacred star.

In India the Dog SARAMA figures as a symbol of the Dawn and as the forerunner of INDRA, the "one enduring A," "He as whose Messenger I came hither from afar."[2] "This myth," says MAX MÜLLER, "is clear enough. It is a reproduction of the old story of the break of day. The bright cows, the rays of the sun, or the rain-clouds—for both go by the same name—have been stolen by the powers of darkness, by the Night and her manifold progeny. Gods and men are anxious for their return. But where are they to be found? They are hidden in a dark and strong stable or scattered along the ends of the sky, and the robbers will not restore them. At last in the farthest distance the first signs of the Dawn appear; she peeps

tion of the Christian communities. TERTULLIAN complained, doubtless with good reason, "They undermine ours in order to build up their own."

[1] This innocent and pious emblem was often misconstrued by the clergy into a blasphemous jibe at the Christian religion.

[2] CALEB, the Israelite who with JOSHUA spied out the promised land, was evidently a personification of the Heavenly Dog. The word *caleb* means dog, and according to the authors of *The Perfect Way*, "implies the necessity of intelligence to the successful quest of Salvation."

about, and runs with lightning quickness, it may be, like a hound after a scent, across the darkness of the sky. She is looking for something, and, following the right path, she has found it. She has heard the lowing of the cows, and she returns to her starting-place with more intense splendour. After her return there rises *Indra*, the god of light, ready to do battle in good earnest against the gloomy powers, to break open the strong stable in which the bright cows were kept, and to bring light and strength and life back to his pious worshippers. This is the simple myth of *Sarama* ; composed originally of a few fragments of ancient speech, such as 'the Panis stole the cows,' *i.e.* the light of day is gone ; 'Sarama looks for the cows,' *i.e.* the Dawn is spreading ; 'Indra has burst the dark stable,' *i.e.* the sun has risen." [1]

SARAMA, the Dawn Dog, is said to have been a greyhound, and is obviously the same as the mysterious *veltro* or greyhound-Messiah mentioned several times by DANTE. In *Hell* the poet alludes to a ruthless monster that blocked his way and continued her accursed depredations :

"Until that *greyhound* come who shall destroy
Her with sharp pain. He will not life support
By earth or its base metals, but by love,
Wisdom and Virtue. . . .
He with incessant chase, through every town,
Shall worry, until he to Hell at length
Restore her, thence by Envy first let loose."

In Icelandic *grey* means *dog*. The word *greyhound* is a form of the Anglo-Saxon *grighund*, the hound of *ag ur ay*, the "mighty fire A," or *ag ur ig*, the "mighty, mighty Fire." SARAMA may be resolved into *se*, the Fire, and *rama*, the Sanscrit for *Sun*.

[1] *Science of Language*, ii. pp. 488–489.

Celtic Mythology assigns a fiery omnipotent Hound to Lug :

> " That hound of mightiest deeds,
> Which was irresistible in hardness of combat,
> Was better than wealth ever known,
> A ball of fire every night.

987

988   989

990   991

> Other virtues had that beautiful hound
> (Better this property than any other property);
> Mead or wine would grow of it,
> Should it bathe in spring water." [1]

---

[1] Quoted in *Mythology of Br. Isles*, Squire, i. p. 63.

In addition to its symbolism of *intelligence*—the *smeller-out*, the *courser*—the dog served also as the emblem of the Guardian, the Watcher, and the Barker. He is conceived in India as watching unseen at the doors of heaven during the night and giving his first bark in the morning.[1] "Guardian of the house, destroyer of evil who assumest all forms, be to us a helpful friend. . . . Bark at the thief, O restless one." The term *bark*—Anglo-Saxon *beorcan*, Icelandic *berkja*—presumably arose from the conception that the watchdog's bark was the voice of the protecting *berkja* or "great Father, ever-existent." The Spanish for *dog* is *perro*, which may be equated with the Old German

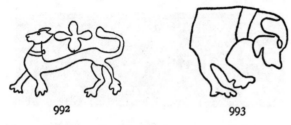

992   993

pero or *bero*, a *bear*. In Gypsy language *chok* means *watch*, *watching*; and *chukkal*—which may be equated with *jackal*, the "ever-existent, great God"—means a *dog*.

An English name for dogs—a name so common as almost to be generic—is GYP, the Ever-Existent Eye. The Greek for *dog* is *kuon*, the "one great Hu," and the Latin is *canis*, the "one great Light." In Greek mythology IKARIUS—identified with the Great Bear—has a dog named MAIRA ; the hound of King ARTHUR was named CABAL ; and in Japanese Temples there is generally to be seen the image of AMA-INU, the "Heavenly Dog," who is credited with a power of driving away demons.[2]

The word *dog* is used as a verb to *track* or hang per-

[1] Müller, *Science of Language*, ii. p. 492.
[2] Chamberlain (B. H.), *Japan*, p. 38.

sistently on to, and the *dignified* mien of fig. 992 is curiously suggestive of Thompson's "Hound of Heaven" :

> Still with unhurrying chase
> And imperturbed pace
> Deliberate speed, majestic instancy
> Came on the following feet.

The word *dog* is allied to the Greek words *dogma* and *doxy*, meaning strong thought or opinion. *Education* is now understood to mean *knowledge*; but radically it means a leading or bringing out. *Duke* or *dux* means a leader, and the Duke of VENICE was termed the *Doge*.[1] The root *dog*

994

is also, no doubt, the base of DAGON, the Solar-fish-god of the PHILISTINES. DAGON was known sometimes as ODAKON, sometimes as ON, and sometimes as OANNES or IANNES, the last being evidently the same as JOHANNES, the Ever-Existent One-Light. *Daghan*[2] in Hebrew means *corn*; *dagh* is Hebrew for *fish*; and *tag* is German for *day*.

In GREECE the Twins were known as POLYDEUCES, a word which as it stands means *many dukes* or *many leaders*. The word *deuce*, used to-day as an ejaculation, may be equated with the first syllable of *disheal!*—an exclamation which is made in the Highlands on any sudden peril or emergency.

Among the Greeks the God of good luck and of *dice* or

---

[1] *Dug* was Cornish for a *general*.
[2] Compare place-name DAGENHAM, near BARKING.

the *cubes* was HERMES. HERMES, the Greek LOGOS, the golden-shod Emissary and Herald of Heaven—like ANUBIS—was regarded as the Conductor of Souls ; and in LEIGHTON'S familiar picture, " The Return of Persephone," it is HERMES who is depicted leading PERSEPHONE from the realms of Darkness into Daylight.

HERMES, entitled TRISMEGISTUS, " thrice greatest," was invoked as " the *Eye* of *Mind*," [1] as Mind itself, [2] and as the altogether Good or God. [3]

The magic instrument with which HERMES, the Good Shepherd, either lulled the tired to slumber or roused the sleeping into wakefulness, was the white-ribboned staff or wand *caduceus*—a word suggesting *duce*, the leading light, and *ca*, the Great A.

Among the Latins HERMES the Guide—i.e. *Guy de*, the shining Sense or Mistletoe—was known as MERCURY, *i.e.* the " Fire of *merak*," the Great Mare. In the emblem herewith the *caduceus* is spanned by an encompassing winged horse or mare.

The symbols of MERCURY, the great Mind or Mare, were a *lizard* and a *cock*, and among the animals sacrificed to him was a pregnant *sow*.

The writer of St John's Gospel attributes to JESUS CHRIST the words, " I am the *way*, the truth, and the life." [4] In the emblem herewith the initials of JESU the LOGOS are posed on either side of a Signpost—a cross-like symbol of the Living HUAY. The Anglo-Saxon for a *way* was *wag*, whence place-names such as WAKEFIELD, WAKERING, etc.

---

[1] "'Tis He who is the Eye of Mind ; may He accept the praise of these my Powers."

[2] " I, Mind, Myself, am present with holy men and good, the pure and merciful, men who live piously."

[3] " Thee I invoke ! Come unto me, O Good, Thou altogether good, come to the Good."—See *Hymns of Hermes*, Mead, pp. 13, 15, 17.

[4] xiv. 6.

The pagan god of ways was MERCURY, to whom numerous statues were erected at the roadsides and at the cross-roads. These so-called *herms* or *hermæ* were particularly placed at *three*-road-junctions, and so numerous

995

996

were these holy three-ways or *trivia* that the word *trivial* came to denote something commonplace and negligible. Under the name TERMINUS, HERMES was the God of boundaries, and the name TERMINUS cannot but be related to the British ERMINE Street.

There is a second very famous prehistoric Way, of which the remains crop up in various parts of England under the

name of "The Ichnield Way." This is supposed to have
derived its name from Boadicea's tribe, the Iceni, but the
origin is probably older. In Greek *ichnos* means a *track*,
and *ichneia* a tracking. A certain kind of *lizard* is termed
ichneumon, because, says Skeat, "it tracks out and devours
crocodiles' eggs." The name *ichneumon* may be resolved
into *ik en Hu mon*, the "Great One, the Solitary Hu."

A third great ancient British main road is known as
London Stone, and elsewhere as Watling Street. The Wat
of this name may be compared with the uat of Up-uat, the
Egyptian opener of the ways.

In Tudor England *wat* was a colloquial name for the
hare or *coney*,[1] and in the design herewith hares are associated with twin bowmen and with *horned* or *intelligent*
hounds which are nosing along the ground towards the
central figure of Eros or Cupid, the five-rayed unaging
Child.

The name *wat* suggests that the hare or rabbit may
have been thus named because it is one of this animal's
characteristics to make well-defined runs or tracks across
the meadows ; and this idea is somewhat strengthened by
the fact that the method of a hare's *running* was used by
the Druids for divination. The course of a hare set free
from the bosom of Boadicea, persuaded that unfortunate
Queen of the Iceni to her disastrous action.

It was customary in Britain to place crosses at the cross-
roads, and thousands of these "Celtic" monuments are
still in existence. It was also customary to sanctify market-
places by a cross, and the words *market, merchandise,
merchant,*[2] *commerce,*[3] are all traceable to the *merciful*[4]

---

[1] See Shakespeare's *Venus and Adonis.*
[2] Compare Channel Islands, Marchant and Herm.
[3] Compare Mercia or Meorcland.
[4] Compare River Mersey.

MERCURY who was the God of Merchants. *Mart*, a synonym for *market*, may be equated with the North of England word *mart*, meaning an *ox* or *cow*.

997

In Greece MERCURY, the God of commerce and good luck, was alternatively known under the names CAMILLUS, ARCAS, and AGONEUS. He was represented with a cock upon his wrist, and was offered sacrifices of honey because he was the God of sweetness, eloquence, and persuasiveness.[1] In Egypt he was represented with the head of a dog, and identified with THOTH, THOT, or THAUT.

THAUT was alternatively known in Egypt as TEHUTI and TECHU. The former resolves into *te-Hu-ti*, shining, resplendent HU; the latter into *t-ek-Hu*, the resplendent, great

998   999

Mind; and it may be that the name THAUT is the origin of the Anglo-Saxon *thoht*, modern English *thought*.

In Egyptian the word *techu* meant not only the bird we call an *ibis*, the symbol of THAUT, but also the instrument which corresponds to the needle of the Balance of Scales.[2] The name TECHU must be allied to *tuche*, the Greek for *Fortune* or *good luck*, and perhaps also to the English *tike*, a *dog*.[3]

The import of the workman hammering herewith upon his anvil is doubtless expressed in the following passage from *The Romance of the Rose*:

[1] Compare *wheedle*.

[2] Renouf, *Hibbert Lectures*, p. 116.

[3] Danish *tiig*, a dog; Swedish *tik*, a bitch dog. TICKELL is a surname; *tickle* means "to touch lightly," also to *amuse*.

> " Be not dismayed,
> But set you boldly to your trade,
> Your arms unto the shoulders bare,
> And all your energies prepare
> To hammer, forge, and blow the fire.
>
>   .   .   .   .
>
> Well may those hang their heads for shame
> Whose thriftless sloth my words proclaim,
> Who wilfully the trouble spare
> Themselves upon the tablets fair
> To write their names, or to achieve
> Such work as may hereafter leave
> Their stamp upon the world."

But in addition to the personal application of this emblem the ancients conceived God Himself to be the Master Workman, the mighty Artisan, the Forger of the Universe, and the Out-showerer of living Sparks. The Egyptian PTAH—" I am all that has been, is, or shall be "— was known as the Artificer in Metals, the Caster, the Sculptor, and the Great Architect of the Universe. The word *thah* in Maya means the *worker*, hence the *maker* and *creator*,[1] and the name THAH, like THAU, the Supreme Deity of Druidism, probably meant "The A " or AWE.

The Latin for a smith is *faber*, i.e. "*feu* or Fire Father," and the English word *labour*, pronounced *liber* in London dialect, may be equated with LIBER, the giver of all *goods* and *huelth* (wealth). The word *work* is related to HU, who, under the name HERMES, was hymned as He " who made the Fire to shine " ; " who fixed the Earth and hung up Heaven, and gave command that Ocean should afford sweet water[2] to the Earth."

In Egypt there were two theories as to the creation of

---

[1] Le Plongeon, *Sacred Mysticism*, p. 73.

[2] The Greek for *water* is *udor*, and the Sun of MERCURY is fabled to have been EUDORUS. Compare also *sudor=sweat*, and *humidity*.

the world—(1) that it was the work of PTAH, the Great Artificer ; (2) that it had been brought into being by the *word* of THAUT, who, when he uttered any name, caused the object thereby to exist.[1] The Egyptian word for *will* or intention was *ab*, and for *intelligence* it was *khu*,[2] *i.e.* AK HU ? The *khu* or intelligent portion of the soul was figured as a crested bird, perhaps the crested bird known nowadays as a *hoopoo* or *pupu* ; KHU was the God of Light, and in ordinary use the word *khu* meant *glorious* and *shining*.

In SOUTH AMERICA the natives pictured the Souls in Paradise as birds, and it is not improbable that the exquisite parrakeet-like *quezal*[3] was named after *ak Hu ez al*, Great Hu, the Light God.

The Egyptians personified the primeval, illimitable, and incomprehensible Ocean under the name NU, and one of their accounts of the Creation relates that the Creator raised Himself out of NU, *i.e. on Hu*, the "One MIND" (?).

The Ancients seem to have pictured to themselves the Primal Cause as boundless, impassive, and quiescent Mind, and this Mind or Brain when active, energetic, or creative, they conceived as THOUGHT.

The physical basis upon which materialism has been wont to rest has of late years been split into electric fragments by the discovery that the material atom is no longer strong in its solid singleness, but consists of a whirling system of electrons. "Endless evolutionary processes in the physical world, beginning," says Professor Barrett, "no one knows how, and blindly going on, no one knows whither, cannot explain the visible universe. For behind—and the source of all tangible matter—lies the unseen, intangible, incomprehensible Ether ; and behind—

---

[1] Petrie, *Religion of Ancient Egypt*, p. 67.
[2] *Ibid.*, pp. 7, 8.
[3] The *quezal* figures on the postage stamps of GUATEMALA.

and the source of all physical energy—lies an unseen, all-pervasive, and incomprehensible *Force*. The progress of science is in fact steadily pushing back the boundaries of the seen, and compelling us to believe, as we were told long ago, 'that what is seen hath not been made out of things which do appear,' but is the offspring of an unseen universe, and an unseen, indwelling, and transcendent Power. . . . Whatever be the unseen, unknown, and immanent Power behind, it presents all the characteristics of purposive guidance, having a definite aim, and therefore I prefer to call this inscrutable factor 'Thought.'"[1] The works of the savant, the musician, the engineer, the architect, the poet, and the painter, are all equally the fabrications of the Great Workman THOUGHT, "our thoughts are greater than ourselves, our dreams ofttimes more solid than our acts."[2] The familiar legend of PYGMALION, the sculptor, and of the vivifying of his ideal GALATEA, is closely related to the Persian idea that after death there comes to every pure man the figure of a maiden, "beautiful, shining, and with shining arms." "What maiden art thou?" asks the soul. "I am," she replies, "thy good thoughts, words, and works, thy good law."[3] Conversely the soul of an unclean thinker is frighted in the next world by the appearance of a very loathly lady.

The Egyptians represented THAUT as the weigher of men's souls. That the soul is condemned or rewarded by its own *thought*—an idea once very current—is reflected in the words of WOTAN, "I sentence thee not, thou thyself thy sentence hast shaped."[4]

In the Egyptian *Book of the Dead* THAUT is hailed as

---

[1] "Creative Thought," *The Quest*, vol. i. p. 601.
[2] F. W. Faber.
[3] *The Teachings of Zoroaster*, S. A. Kapadia, p. 62.
[4] Wagner, *The Valkyre*.

the " Everlasting King," the " Lord of Justice who giveth
victory to him who is injured, and who taketh the defence
of the oppressed." The 95th chapter ends with the words,
" I am the protection of the Great One against assault, and
I give vigour to the sword which is in the hand of THOTH
in the storm." It was the sword of THAUT that effected
the triumph of OSIRIS over his enemies, and it was also
THAUT who assisted ISIS in her distress. THAUT, as we
have seen, was regarded as the Moon-god and the Marshal
of the Starry Hosts. In the emblems herewith the T of
THAUT is associated not only with the crescent moon, but
also with the Great Bear of ARTHUR, the " Director of

1000   1001   1002

Toil."[1] The Lapps of the present day worship the Bear,
" along with THOR, CHRIST, the Sun, and the Serpent."[2]

In Latin mythology the great artist of the Smithy and
the builder not only of the Solar palaces but also of the
furniture and of the Solar chariots was VULCAN. The first
syllable of this name (whence VOLCANO) would appear to
have been derived from the same source as *volo*, meaning
the will. In Northern mythology VULCAN figures as
FOLAND, PHALAND, and VALLAND, and in England as
WAYLAND SMITH.

Near LOOE in CORNWALL is a place named WAYLAND
CROSS, close to ASHEN CROSS, and in the Vale of the White
Horse at ASHDOWN in BERKSHIRE there is a cromlech known
traditionally as the Cave of WAYLAND, the Invisible Smith.

[1] Rhys (Sir J.), Intro., *Morte d'Arthur.*
[2] Lang (A.), *Custom and Myth*, p. 176.

Christian missionaries degraded HUAYLAND[1] into a demon ;
but there is little doubt that he was originally, like the
Invisible Knight of the Slavs, a personification of Good
Thought and Good-WILL.

It is a metaphoric commonplace to liken the Brain to a
Forge, and Thought to a hammering blacksmith. SHAKE-
SPEARE refers to "the quick forge and working house of
thought,"[2] and at the present moment one of our popular
magazines heads its monthly editorial matter, " Sparks from
our anvil."[3] The prevalence of this simile between Thought
and the Smithy is perpetuated in the metaphorical manner
in which we nowadays refer to a *striking* thought, a *brilliant*
idea, a *flash* of genius, a *scorching* wit, and a *sparkling* repartee.

The Greeks made CHARIS the wife of HEPHAISTOS,[4] the
Heavenly Smith ; of *Wisdom* SOLOMON inquires : " Who of
all that are is a more cunning workman than she ?"[5] and
he enlarges his idea in the passage, " Reason is a spark
struck by the beating of our heart."

In fig. 1003 the anvil of the Great Artisan is associated
with a hammer ; in fig. 1004 this hammer surmounts the
Solar wheel, sunflower, or chrysanthemum ; and in fig. 1005
it is associated with the B of LA BOUR. The Egyptians
worshipped a God of the Beautiful Face, who was called
" Great Chief of the Hammer " ; one of the Mexican
divinities was entitled " Great Seer of the Hammer " ;[6] and
the Slavs assigned a hammer to PERUN.

---

[1] There is a tradition at Ashdown that
> " King Gaarge did here the Dragon slay,
> And down below on yonder hill
> They buried him, as I heard tell."
> *The Scouring of the White Horse*, Hughes, p. 242.

[2] *Henry V.*, Prologue.   [3] *The Royal Magazine.*

[4] Hephaistos, like Vulcan, was *lame* ; the Egyptians represented PTAH
as limping.

[5] Wisdom of Solomon viii. 6.

[6] Churchward, *Signs and Symbols*, p. 34.

The sign of THOR was the Solar Wheel,[1] and his weapon, a short-handled hammer named MIOLNIR ("the smasher"), which he used both in peace and war either to bless or to shatter. When THOR donned his belt of strength and his gloves of iron there was no monster that the hammer would not crush, and after being thrown it always returned of itself into the hand of its Master. The *Svastika*—a symbol of "good luck," known in Japan as *manji*[2]—was in Europe termed as "Thor's Hammer,"[3] and the Hammer of THOR

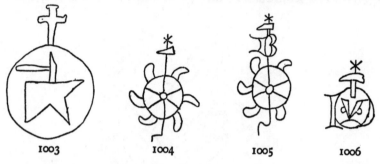

1003   1004   1005   1006

was equivalent to the Cross of CHRIST. Thus of King Olaf Longfellow writes :.

> " O'er his drinking horn, the sign
> He made of the Cross Divine,
> And he drank and mutter'd his prayers ;
> But the Berserks evermore
> Made the sign of *the Hammer of Thor*
> Over theirs."

The word cross in its various forms, *crux, cruz, crowz, croaz, krois, krouz,* etc., resolves into *ak ur os,* the light of the

---

[1] *Vide* the THOR cross at Kirk Bride, Isle of Man.

[2] The Japanese God MONJU is the personification and apotheosis of transcendental *Wisdom*.

[3] Thor was the guardian and defender of the Home, and in Icelandic Sagas is hailed as the Protector of the Earth and Friend of Man. From the name THOR we derive THURSDAY, upon which day the folk met to consult about the commonweal, and for the maintenance of peace and concord.

Great Fire. The same root is the base of CHRIST, KRISTNA, *crystal*, *chrysanthemum*, *crest*, and of *cresset*,[1] *i.e.* a light in a cup at the top of a pole. In Cornish *kerrys* meant *loved* or *beloved*, and in fig. 1007 CERES or the *Magna Mater* is upholding a cresset : the Lion of Judah, marked with a T, is grasping the arrows of Light and the sword or truncheon of dominion.

The word *hammer* was in Anglo-Saxon *hamor*, the " fire or gold of the Immutable Sun " ;[2] in Cornish it was *orz*, again

ProPatria

1007

yielding "golden fire." *Hamor* is cognate with *amor*, *love* (see fig. 1010) ; the Latin for a *hammer* is *marcus*, the French is *martel* or *marteau*, and in England a heavy hammer used to be known as a *beetle*. The African DINKAS of the present day have a " Great Chief of the Hammer," and also the " House of the Axe " in the form of a " Sacred Spear," which their tradition states " came down from heaven or the clouds in a thunderstorm."[3] In fig. 1013 the crossed hammers are

---

[1] In Cornish *kryssat* means a *hawk*.

[2] This etymology is strengthened by a consideration of the golden-yellow little bird called a yellow *hammer*.

[3] Churchward, *Signs and Symbols*, p. 37.

pointed like spears or arrows, and in figs. 1014 and 1015 there is an intentional combination of hammer and axe.

1008   1009   1010

The Axe as a symbol of the power of Light, originated presumably from the fact that primitive men saw with their

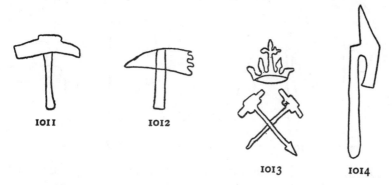

1011   1012   1013   1014

own eyes giant trees cleft from top to bottom by the axe-like stroke of Lightning.[1] Among the Mayas the "Great

[1] The power of the magic weapon of romance, whether it be Roland's Horn, Arthur's Sword, Poseidon's Trident, or Thor's Hammer, is such that it shatters and overturns even the granite rocks. This traditional effect may be compared with the statement of the unromantic Swedenborg: "The power of angels in the spiritual world is so great that if I were to make known all that I have seen of this power it would appear incredible. Any obstacle there, which ought to be removed because it is contrary to Divine Order, they cast down and overturn merely by an effort of the will and by a look. Thus I have seen mountains, which were inhabited by the wicked, cast down and overthrown, and sometimes shaken from end to end as though by an earthquake. Thus also I have seen rocks cleft asunder down to the abyss, and the wicked who were upon them swallowed up. I have also seen

Seer of the Hammer" was known likewise as " God of the Axe"; PTAH represented by an Axe was entitled in Egypt the "Cleaver of the Way";[1] a Cretan vase painting of the MINOAN period represents a fish and a double axe; and an Assyrian cylinder in the British Museum[2] illustrates the sacrifice of a fish to a divinity represented by the symbol of an erected axe.

In fig. 1019 the head of an Axe is identified with AKSE[3] by the circle of the Perfect One, and in fig. 1017 by the three Circles of Good Thought, Good Word, and Good

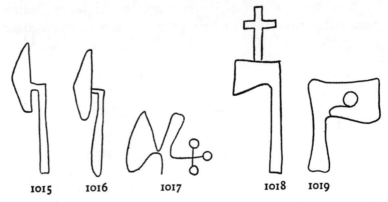

1015   1016   1017   1018 1019

Deed. The French for *axe* is *hache*, and in fig. 1020 the Tree of Life, equivalent to the Mighty *Ash* or *fraxinus*, is

some hundreds of thousands of evil spirits dispersed by angels and cast into hell. Numbers are of no avail against them, nor are cunning devices and confederacies. . . . It must be understood, however, that the angels have no power of themselves, but that all their power is from the Lord; and that they are powers only so far as they acknowledge this. If any angel supposes that he possesses power from himself, he instantly becomes so weak that he cannot even resist one evil spirit; therefore the angels attribute no merit to themselves, and refuse all praise and glory for their deeds, ascribing all praise and glory to the Lord."—*Heaven and Hell*, 229–230.

[1] Churchward, *Signs and Symbols*, p. 37.

[2] No. 89, 470.

[3] To mark a track with an axe is described as *blazing* a trail. The Supreme God is known to the Zulus as TIXE, *i.e.* "resplendent axe" (?).

associated with an *hache*. The Cornish for *axe* was *bul,* the Icelandic for *axe* is *ox,* and in Anglo-Saxon the word was spelled *acus, i.e.* "the Great Light." In BRITTANY the natives—originally, perhaps, with the idea of "diamond cut diamond "—still build stone axes into their chimneys "to ward off lightning." [1] The Breton name for axe is *bouc'hal* or *boc'hal,* and as LE ROUZIC observes : "undoubtedly these stone implements played a great rôle in the minds of these

1020

primitive people. There is therefore nothing surprising in the fact that they transformed them into symbolic and religious emblems, probably of a phallic kind." [2]

Traces of the Axe as a religious symbol used within churches exist in the street name familiar to Londoners, ST MARY AXE. "In ST MARIE Street," says STOW, "had ye of old time a parish church of ST MARIE the Virgin ; ST URSULA and the eleven thousand Virgins, which church

[1] Johnson (W.), *Byeways in British Archæology,* p. 80.
[2] LE ROUZIC (Z.), *The Megalithic Monuments of Carnac,* p. 28.

was commonly called ST MARIE at the AXE—*of the sign of an axe over against the east end thereof.*"[1]

The Battle-axe was similarly a symbol equivalent to the Sword, Hammer, or Cross, and it is thus treated by TENNYSON in *The Coming of Arthur* :

> " Blow trumpet, for the world is white with May ;
> Blow trumpet, the long night hath roll'd away !
> Blow thro' the living world—' Let the King reign.'

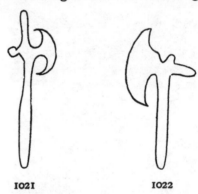

1021   1022

> Strike for the King and live ! his knights have heard
> That God hath told the King a secret word.
> Fall battleaxe, and flash brand !   Let the King reign.
>
> Strike for the King and die ! and if thou diest,
> The King is King, and ever wills the highest.
> Clang battleaxe, and clash brand !   Let the King reign.
>
> Blow, for our Sun is mighty in his May !
> Blow, for our Sun is mightier day by day !
> Clang battleaxe, and clash brand !   Let the King reign."

By some writers the symbolism of the Fish is believed to be based upon the " very natural comparison between a *fish tail* and the sacred *double axe*."[2]   In all probability the

---

[1] Everyman's Library, p. 145. (Italics mine.)
[2] See "Orpheus the Fisher," Dr Robert Eisler, *The Quest*, vol. i. No. 2.

double axe is a more ancient symbol than the single axe, as the earliest axes must have been double-edged stones tied to the end of a stock.

The T or *Thau mysticum* is said to have derived its form from two axes placed back to back, in which case the crossed axes herewith are a variant of this symbol. Fig. 1026 evidently represents the " Cleaver of the Way " or *Clever* One, but whether the object in his hand is a cleaver, a hammer, or a T, it is difficult to say. In fig. 1027 the Lion is obviously armed with a T, and in fig. 1028 four *Thaus* point, like the flaming sword that guarded EDEN, to all four

1023   1024   1025

quarters of the Universe. In German the word *thau* means *dew* ; in Cornish *ta* or *da* meant *good*.[1]

Just as the Egyptians assumed the earth to have been created by the word of THAUT, so in the Psalms of DAVID the " Word " is identified as the Artisan of the Universe : " By the *word* of the Lord were the heavens made ; and all the host of them by the breath of his mouth." [2]

There is a vision recorded in Revelation of a Rider upon a White Horse whose name was " The Word of God." " And out of his mouth went a sharp two-edged sword : and his countenance was as the sun shineth in his strength." [3] In the symbolism of the face, the mouth, as has been mentioned, stood for the " Word," and the hammer-shaped T forming the mouth of the Lion-face herewith therefore

---

[1] Compare surnames TYE, TOYE, DAY, DEW, etc.
[2] xxxiii. 6.   [3] i. 16 ; xix. 13, 15.

answers to the passage, " Is not my *word* like as a fire ? saith
the Lord ; and like a hammer that breaketh the rock in

1026   1027

pieces ?"[1]   The T-shaped mouth presents an appearance of
putting out the tongue, and it is highly remarkable that in
MEXICO the tongue protruding from the mouth was the

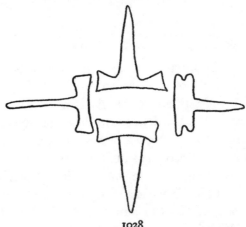

1028

symbol of *Wisdom*. It is often thus found in the portraits
of priests, kings, and other exalted personages supposed to
be endowed with Great Wisdom.[2] The putting out of the

[1] Jeremiah xxiii. 29.   [2] *Queen Moo*, p. 158.

tongue was also a symbol of great Wisdom in INDIA, and at the present day in THIBET a respectful salutation consists of uncovering the head and lolling out the tongue.[1]

In the emblem herewith the world-wide symbol of the Cross is being worshipped by a kneeling figure, and from the base of figure 1031 there blazes a *five*fold splendour.

On Celtic crosses *five* knobs or bosses, erroneously supposed to represent the "five wounds of Christ," are of frequent occurrence.

Referring to the builders of CARNAC and the neighbour-

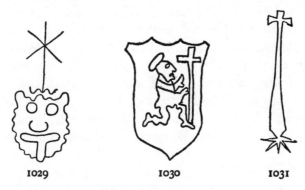

1029   1030   1031

ing monuments, LE ROUZIC writes : "The cross, the symbol adopted by the Christians, is found on their tombs—some of which were placed on the roadsides, and especially at cross-roads—and everywhere the cross symbolises the Son of God."[2]

Among the Egyptians, Phœnicians, and Chaldees, the solar cross—originally perhaps the two crossed fire-making sticks—typified the life to come, and it has also been found adorning the breasts of statues and statuettes in the ancient cities of Central AMERICA. In BABYLON it was associated with water deities, and in ASSYRIA and BRITAIN was the

[1] *Queen Moo*, p. 265.
[2] *The Megalithic Monuments of Carnac*, p. 28.

emblem of creative power and eternity. In INDIA, CHINA, and SCANDINAVIA, it represented heaven and immortality, and among the Mayas, rejuvenescence and freedom from physical suffering. It was placed as a symbol on the breast of the initiate after his " new birth " was accomplished in the Dionysiac and Eleusinian mysteries, and it seems universally to have been the sign not of tragedy or failure, but of power, happiness, and everlasting love. The island of KRISA was the chief seat of APOLLO-worship ; in Russian the word *krasa* means *beauty*. *Ak er os*, the " great Fire Light," or " great EROS," is the root also responsible for the Indian KRISTNA and the English proper names CRISPIAN, CRISPIN, CHRISTOPHER, CHRISTINE, CHRISTABEL, and CROSBY.

The word *cross* is seemingly identical with the Zulu *kaross*—a term applied to the luck-bringing, leopard-skin cloak or mantle. The Leopard or Panther, symbolising the many-eyed WATCHER, has already been considered. The Chariot of BACCHUS or DIONYSOS is always represented as being drawn by Leopards, Panthers, Tigers, or Lynxes, and the whole of the Pard tribe seem to have been sacred to the watchful God of Fire. The white variety of Leopard is termed an *ounce* or *once*, *i.e.* the " One Fire." The *Lynx*, a proverbially keen-sighted quadruped, was known to the Anglo-Saxons as *lox*. In Swedish it is called *lo*, in Russian *ruise*, and in Persian *rus*, to which is no doubt allied our word *ruse*, a synonym for *wile* or *guile*, *i.e.* mighty *wile* ?

The animal called a *cheetah* might perhaps be spelt *cheater*, and it is sometimes difficult to draw the line between *wile*, *guile*, and *cheating*. Originally the *cheetah* seems to have symbolised the " Ever-existent, Brilliant A."

The blazing stripes of the tiger's skin are obviously responsible for its name *tig ur*, the " resplendent mighty Fire."

" Tyger ! Tyger ! burning bright,
In the forests of the night :
What immortal hand or eye,
Could frame thy fearful symmetry ?

In what distant deeps or skies
Burnt the fire of thine eyes ?
On what wings dare we aspire ?
What the hand dare seize the fire ?

What the hammer ? what the chain ?
In what furnace was thy brain ?
What the anvil ? what dread grasp
Dare its deadly terrors clasp ? " [1]

The Shrine at NIKKO includes a Monastery and a Mount dedicated to the four good spirits, *White Tiger, Azure Dragon, Vermilion Bird*, and *Sombre Warrior*.

In Zend *tighri* means an arrow, and *tighra* sharp. The word *tigress* may be equated with the River TIGRIS, and the term *tiger* is closely related to *jaguar* [2] or *yagoar*. In BRAZIL *jagua* [3] is a common term for tigers and also for dogs.

The flash-like, black and white stripes of the African horse known as a *quagga* or *zebra* are doubtless responsible for its symbolism of *ze bur a*, " Fire Father A," or *quagga*, the " Great HU, the Mighty A." The lustrous black and white markings of the magpie's plumage were also probably responsible for this bird being regarded as the favourite of BACCHUS.

The North American Indians used to dance a dance called BELLOHCK-NA-PIE, for which ceremony some were painted perfectly black, some partially black, and some a vermilion colour. [4] During this dance they wore horns on

---

[1] William Blake.   [2] Compare surname JAGGARD.
[3] The chief city in URUGUAY is JAGUARDO.
[4] G. Catling, "North American Indians," quoted in *Atlantis*, p. 113.

their head like those used in Europe as symbolical of BEL or BAL. All over the world the rays of the sun and the crescent of the moon seem to have suggested horns. PAN is said to have had pyramidal horns tapering from earth to Heaven, and the poetic idea that horns symbolised *light* has lingered into prosaic Christianity, where we find MOSES represented sometimes as horned and sometimes with two shafts of fire or light springing from his forehead.

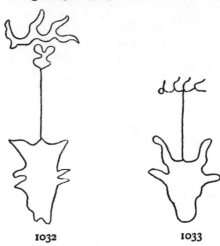

1032   1033

The *asp* or sacred horned serpent was known alternatively as the *cerastes*. The *ceras* of this word is equivalent to *cross*, and in Greek *keras* means a *horn*. The term *cerastes* may thus be considered as *keras tes*, the horned, shining light or Essence, and the word *tes* or *tez*[1] occurs again very significantly in TEZPI,[2] a Mexican title for Coxcox, their Great Ancestor. The word *asp* or *aspe*, a synonym for *cerastes*, resolves as it stands into "Light Father": in Hebrew *erastus* means *beloved*, and *cerastes* might thus be rendered "Great Beloved."

Surmounting the head of an ox herewith are *four*fold

[1] Compare English River TEES.   [2] See *Atlantis*, p. 99.

pieces of buck or stag horn, and precisely similar symbols are often represented on Chinese pottery in conjunction with the Dragon of the Infinite.

The branching antlers of the buck have apparently universally and from time immemorial been likened to the rising of the Sun, and as late as the sixteenth century a procession, headed by the antlers of a stag, formed part of the ritual of St Paul's Cathedral. This ceremony was thus described by Stow : " Now what I have heard by report and have partly seen, it followeth : On the feast day of the commemoration of St Paul, the buck being brought up to the steps of the high altar in Paul's Church, at the hour of procession, the dean and chapter being apparelled in copes and vestments, with garlands of roses on their heads, they sent the body of the buck to baking, and had the head fixed on a pole, borne before the cross in their procession, until they issued out of the west door, where the keeper that brought it blowed the death of the buck, and then the horners that were about the city presently answered him in like manner." [1] This blowing of horns all about the city may be compared with the similar heralding of the elevation of the Mistletoe at YORK Minster. The garlands of *roses* were clearly symbolic of EROS, and it is also noteworthy that the dean and chapter of St Paul's wore on this occasion special vestments, " the one embroidered with *bucks*, the other with *does*." [2]

In the year 1316, when digging the foundation of a new chapel at St Paul's, there was uncovered a large deposit of oxen skulls, " which thing," says Stow, " confirmed greatly the opinion of those which have reported that of old time there had been a temple of JUPITER and that there was daily sacrifice of beasts." [3]

In fig. 1034 the head of an Ox or Bugle is surmounted by a

[1] *The Survey of London*, p. 299. [2] *Ibid.*, p. 299. [3] *Ibid.*, p. 298.

bugle or horn, which may no doubt be equated with the " horn of salvation " mentioned so frequently in the Old Testament. *Corne*, a *horn*, is responsible for the place-name CORNWALL or CORNOUAILLE, and probably also for ST CORNELY in BRITTANY. LE ROUZIC observes that the worship of ST CORNELY " replaced the worship of the ox of which M. MILNE and I found a statue in the ruins of the Gallo-Roman villa of BOSSENO." [1] The place-name BOSSENO, which may be compared with BOSSINEY, BOSCASTLE,[2] etc., in CORN-WALL, is probably derived from *bos*, an *ox*. The French for

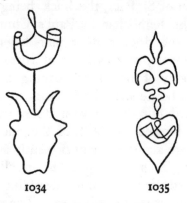

1034   1035

horn is *cor*, which does not differ from *core*, a centre, from *cur*, meaning originally a *house dog*, nor from *cœur*, the French for *heart*. In fig. 1035 the *cor*, *cœur*, and *iris* are all combined into one. In English a *hart* is equivalent to a *hind*, and ESTHER, the star-like " hind of the dawn," might just as appropriately be termed the *Hound* of Heaven. The word *hart* does not differ from *harit*, and the Old German for *hart* was *hiruz*, i.e. *iris* or EROS. The immaculate ARTEMIS or DIANA, to whom the stag was sacred, was some-times represented in statuary with three heads, that of a

---

[1] *The Megalithic Monuments of Carnac*, p. 31.

[2] The fiction that BOSCASTLE is a contraction of BOTTREAUX CASTLE need not be considered.

horse, a dog, and a boar. Because she was worshipped at the cross-ways, one of her names was TRIVIA, and in Art she is represented as being drawn along sometimes by two white harts and sometimes by four stags with golden antlers. In the emblem herewith the advance of Art is accompanied by the Charites or Graces,[1] and by the Hounds of Heaven.

In *The Song of Solomon* CHRIST, the Morning Star and *Dayspring* from on high, is likened several times to a swift roe and a young hart. In INDIA there is a genus of deer known as the *axis, cheetal,* or *chittra.*

The Greek for stag is *elaphos,* a word allied to *elephant* and resolving into *elaph os,* the light of Alif. The giant

1036

deer named *elk*[2] was probably once *el ek,* the Great God, and may be compared with EL-UK, an Egyptian and Babylonian title for the Sun.[3] The word *moose* may be equated with the English *mouse,* and with the nine resplendent *Muses.*

In the Middle Ages there was believed to be an animal known as the *yale.* It was described by naturalists as a composition of horse, elephant, boar, unicorn, and stag, and was known alternatively as a *bagwyn.* The word *yale* is evidently related to *yael,* the Hebrew for a wild goat, and to *ayyal,* which is translated in the Bible as *hart.* The *Yale*

[1] Near St Mary Axe was GRACE, *i.e.* AGEROS Church. In Cornwall is a shrine to ST GRACE.

[2] Compare place-names ELKSTON and ELKINGTON.

[3] See Payne-Knight, p. 69.

was obviously a symbol of the ALL or the WHOLE, and its alternative Welsh name *bagwyn* may be Anglicised into BIG ONE, or the Holy BUCK.[1]

In China and Japan the mythic beast corresponding to the BAGWYN is known as the BAKU. The protecting, evil-averting BAKU (BUCK HU ?) is described as resembling a goat, "it has nine tails, four ears, and its eyes are on its back." According to another authority, it has the trunk of an elephant, the eyes of a rhinoceros, the tail of a bull, and the legs of a tiger." [2]

The ancients appear to have deliberately modified material animals to suit their symbolic conceptions. The Egyptians artificially caused the two horns of cattle and rams to point respectively fore and aft, an idea which the Latins preserved in the belief that JANUS, the opener of the Gates of Day, faced in two directions—front and rear. At the present day the African DINKAS who occupy a great territory in the BAHR-EL-GHAZAL south of the White Nile, train the horns of certain cattle fore and aft. Dr SHIPLEY, writing in *Country Life*, observes : " All the Dinka cattle, which belong to the African variety of *Bos indicus*, are not treated in this way, only the leader of the herd, who is always an ox and never a bull. This leader is called a ' majok,' and there is never more than one majok in each herd at one time. Rarely cows act as leaders, and though they may be highly trained, the term ' majok ' is never applied to them. The herdsmen have a deep affection for their majoks, and it is a compliment to the Dinka young men to apply the term ' majok ' to them. It seems to be applied much as we used to use the term ' buck.' " [3]

The *maj* of majok is probably *mage*, " a wise one," and the *ok* is the *ok* of *ox*.

---

[1] *Wyn* is Irish for *holy*.   [2] See Murray's *Japan*, p. 196.
[3] March 23, 1912.

The Kaffirs have, like the Dinkas, preserved what must obviously be a custom of fabulous antiquity. They train the horns of their cattle sometimes into a perfect *circle*, sometimes into the one horn of the *unicorn, einhorn,* or *monoceros,* and at others into bizarre spikes and firelike spirals. In the illustration herewith, taken from Wood's *Natural History*,[1] the horns have in two instances been trained to imitate the antlers of a stag.

In Irish the word *dawen* means *sacred cow,* and it would appear that the Egyptians identified some of their cows with

1037

the *dawn* by decorating their horns with the gloves, digits, or fingers of the dawn. I again quote Dr SHIPLEY, who, commenting upon the design herewith (1038), observes : " It is incomplete, and in some ways inexplicable. There is the outline of a human head with a somewhat elaborate head-dress emerging between the base of the two horns. The extremity of the left horn ends in what seems to be a hand ; that of the right has been cut away. It may, of course, be argued that these processes represent arms only, and not horns ; but the absence of any indication of shoulder, elbow, and wrist, and, above all, the relative proportions of these parts to the human head, and to the ox's head, encourage

[1] 1868, vol. i. 67.

me in the belief that the artist meant them to represent horns, and for some mysterious purpose let them end in hands or perhaps in gloves. It is possible that these animals are merely fantastically-decorated animal tributes brought to the King of Egypt as offerings to the god Amon. No one who has studied Egyptian drawings can fail to be impressed by the sense of proportion and of the value of relative size that the artists of those times showed. It is not without significance that this ox just mentioned is

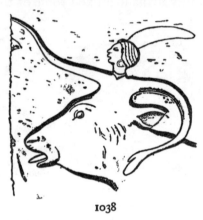

1038

being led by a company of Ethiopians, among whom, according to Pliny, the yale is bred. Mr F. W. Green tells me the 'hands' are probably gloves, and that he knows of another instance where the tips of horns were ensheathed in gloves." [1]

It is noteworthy that the Druidic term for the sacred cow was *mona*, a transposition of AMON, the Sole A.

Fig. 1039 represents a Yale as it was conceived in A.D. 1200. It has a tail of fire, the snout of a boar, the flexible horns of a unicorn, and is leaping hart-like over a *five*fold mountain. By Christian mystics the Lover of

[1] *Country Life*, March 23, 1912.

The Song of Solomon, leaping upon the mountains of Bether, is identified with Christ. At CHRIST's College, Cambridge, according to Dr Shipley, who writes without any suspicion of the animal's symbolism, "by some lucky chance the yale has been preserved pure and undefiled."[1] It appears upon the gateways, and a single yale occurs as the seal of the Master of Christ's.

There is a kind of deer known as the *urial* or *gad : urial*

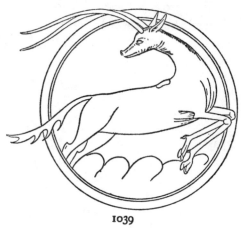

1039

may be resolved into *ur yale*, the "fiery, ever-existent God," and *gad* may be equated with *God*.[2]

The word *gazelle* means "mighty blazing God"; the Persian *nilgau*—an antelope whose name means in Persian "blue cow"—may be resolved into *un il ag au*, "the one God, the mighty A"; and the French *cerf* may be equated with the English *seraph*. The African *gnu*, like AGNEW, the English surname, resolves into the mighty, unique HU, who is everlastingly *new*. The Sanscrit for an antelope is *harina*, which is evidently allied to *hran*, the Anglo-Saxon, and *hreinn*, the Icelandic, for *deer*. In fig. 1040 the symbol

[1] *Country Life*, March 23, 1912.
[2] Compare GAD'S HILL near ROCHESTER, etc.

of *Zora*, the Dawn, is branded with the Z R of Zeus, the generative *dew, doe,* or *hreinn (rain ?)*.[1]

The twin[2] fires of fig. 1043 are designed like wings or, as the word was originally written, *winge, i.e.* Hu, the one Existent. According to Shakespeare, "Ignorance is the curse of God, *Knowledge* the wing whereby we fly to Heaven": the word *pinion* may be equated with *opinion*, and opinions are the *thoughts* and ideas whereby we rise, or otherwise. The cross between the horns of figs. 1042 and 1043 suggests the legend of St Hubert. The same legend is related of St Eustace, *i.e.* Heu, the Essence, the

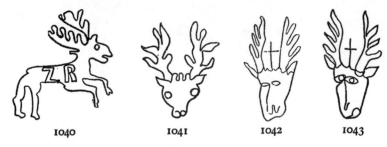

| 1040 | 1041 | 1042 | 1043 |

resplendent Fire. In each case the stag is said to have turned upon its hunter with the inquiry : "Why persecutest thou me ? I am Jesus Christ."

St Hubert is the patron saint of hunting, and his far-famed horn is preserved in the Church of St Hubert at Liège. This horn may be equated with the horn of Oberon and with the horn of the mythic Huon, one blast upon which was sufficient to bring 100,000 warriors to the rescue in the hour of need.

The English word *deer* resolves as it stands into *di ur*,

---

[1] The Japanese mystics maintain that "God is like water in respect to his purity and liquidness, because water pervades into the bottom of the earth and spreads throughout the sky ; moreover, it washes away all dirts." "Therefore man must be also like water, by imitating God." "God is in the world, especially in our minds."   [2] Twin = *t'Huin* (?).

the Shining Fire. That *deer* may be equated with *dear*, meaning *beloved*, is evident from the fact that *carou* or *karo*, the Cornish for a stag or *deer*, is clearly the same word as the Italian *caro*=*dear* or *beloved*. The Greek for a *deer* is *dorcas*; DORCAS is a Christian name; and DORCAS has become a synonym for *charity*. The district lying between the Rivers TYNE and HUMBER was originally called DEIRA, and the county of CORNWALL, anciently CORINEA, is supposed to have been thus named because its indented coastline is like a horn or antler. The Hebrew for a horn is *keren*; and *corne*, the French for *horn*, is the same word as the English *corn* or *wheat*. The Gauls worshipped a deity named CERNUNNOS, who was represented as an old man from whose head branched the horns of a stag.[1]

In the DEIRA district the name HUMBER reoccurs in the forms NORTHUMBERLAND and CUMBER- or AC UMBERLAND. The same root is also apparent in UMBRIA, in CAMBRIA, an alternative name for Wales, and in CAMBERWELL, a still existing WELL near BROCKWELL and BRIXTON. AMBRES was a name of the Celtic JUPITER; *embers* are burning ashes; and the *Ember* Days and *Ember* Week are supposed to be traceable to *ymbryne*, the Anglo-Saxon for a *circuit*. The word *umber* is evidently identical with *amber* or, as it was originally spelled, *aumbre*. Amber was supposed to shield the living from evil and to speed the dead, and charms or amulets of amber are of frequent occurrence in prehistoric tombs. In Scandinavian barrows small axes made of amber have been uncovered; in British barrows amber beads are common. The golden transparency of amber doubtless will account for its adoption as a symbol of *am ber*, the Sun Father. In Greek *ambrotos* means *immortal*, and *ambrosia* was fabled to be the drink of Immortality. As a symbol of immortality, the Egyptians placed within their

[1] See Borlase, *Ant. of Cornwall*, p. 107.

tombs the *crux ansata* ; it was doubtless with the same idea that Scandinavia used the amber axe. In British graves one finds sometimes a small hammer *banded alternatively black and white*, sometimes a piece of stag-horn, sometimes a "crystal ball," and sometimes a boar's tusk.[1] Each of these objects was seemingly a prehistoric sign or symbol of "the cross."

The word CUMBER is clearly related to ST UNCUMBER, who was known alternatively as WILGEFORTIS, *i.e.* HU, the Lord ever-existent, the strong light.

When His Majesty King GEORGE V. was in INDIA for

1044	1045	1046	1047

the Coronation Durbar, the daily papers reported the prime ceremony as follows : "Hand in hand the Emperor and Empress descended from their thrones and walked in stately procession to the Central Pavilion beneath the golden dome. Their diadems blazed in the sun. Over their heads were the shimmering symbols of their imperial estate —the *Umbrella*, the Fan, and the Mace."

The word *umbrella* (Italian *ombrella*) points to the probability that this article—an emblem of royalty in nearly all parts of the globe—was once regarded as a symbol of the radiant Solar wheel. *Umbella*, the Latin for *umbrella*,[2] is derived from *umbel*, "an umbrella-like inflorescence," and in

---

[1] Johnson (W.), *Byeways in Brit. Arch.*, pp. 297, 302, 305.

[2] *A* often means *without*; thus *umbra*=shade may once have implied *umbera* or *without umber*.

fig. 1044 the *umbel* or Sun of BEL surmounts a bullock or *monox*.[1]

In the Old Testament the Deity is hymned as "the horn of my salvation, my high tower, and my refuge."[2] "Thou hast also given me the shield of thy salvation, and thy *gentleness* hath made me great."

The twin fishes and I C of fig. 930 (*ante*, p. 84) identified the tower there illustrated with the gentle JESUS; the coping-stone of fig. 1045 is an IRIS and the pinnacle of fig. 1046 a CLOVER.

The word *tower* is the same as the French *tour*, which also means a *wheel*, and it may be equated with the Gaelic *torr*, meaning a conical hill and a castle. The Egyptian for fortress was *t'ra*, and one of the surnames of APOLLO was TORTOR, *i.e. Tower of Towers* (?).

The Cornish name for *tower* is *lug*. In Scotland— particularly in the county of Ross — are the plentiful remains of round towers which are there known as *brochs*. The word *broch* is the same as the Saxon *burg* and as the BERK- or BARK- of English place-names. The arms of BERKSHIRE are the Dragon or Great Serpent, and in fig. 1047 this emblem appears upon the *berk* or *burok*. *Brock* is the ancient name for a badger, because, it is supposed, of his white-streaked face; *brocket* means a red deer two years' old; and *broche* means a stag's horn.

Sometimes circular towers were called *peels* = Pauls, and sometimes *duns*. The fabled stronghold of King ARTHUR, now called TINTAGEL, was alternatively known as DUNDAGEL. Allowing for the interchangeability of T and D, both names resolve into *dun d ag el*, the Stronghold of the Resplendent, Mighty God.

The Scotch *broch* or *peel* served as a sanctuary from wandering marauders and materially justified its title BUROK

---

[1] In Stow's time MONOX was an English surname.　　[2] 2 Samuel xxii. 3.

or PEEL as "a high tower and a refuge." But in IRELAND, NEW MEXICO, COLORADO, SARDINIA, INDIA, and elsewhere, there exist round towers of which the inside dimensions are too small to shelter more than a very few people, and which apparently were erected solely as religious symbols. One of the most remarkable of the Irish Round Towers is divided into *three* stages by *external bands* (note fig. 1048) corresponding to the levels of three floors within. At KELLS and DRUMLANE part of the building is constructed from a material called *ashlar*, *i.e.* "a facing of squared

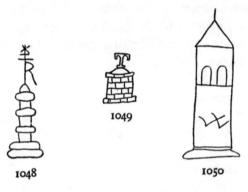

1048   1049   1050

stones," and the T-surmounted tower herewith appears to be constructed either of *ashlar* or brick. As a rule, the Celtic Round Towers were built without mortar, and one of these mortarless erections has been found within the ruined temple of ZIMBABWE.

Two round towers similar to the Irish type are to be seen in the yet extant plan of the monastery of ST GALL in SWITZERLAND, and in the Latin inscription attached to the plan these are said to be *Ad Universa Superspicienda*, *i.e.* "To the universal Over-Seer."[1] In the emblem herewith a tower capped with the customary conical roof is marked with the double HU and surmounted with the spire or spike

[1] *Chambers's Encyclopædia*, ix. 2.

of the One. In Ireland the burgs are known as Bell
Towers; in China the sacred towers or *pagodas* are hung
with bells; and in Italy the watch-towers were termed

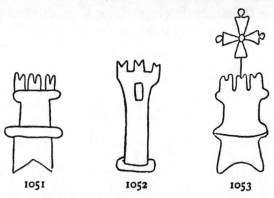

1051   1052   1053

martellos for the supposed reason that the watchman gave
the alarm by striking a bell with a *martello* or *hammer*.

The battlements of the Martellos herewith are formed
like M's, the three M-like turrets doubtless standing for the
Three Queens of the Trinity or Truth—Maat, Mary, or

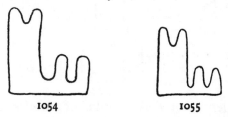

1054   1055

Martin, in the three aspects of Good Thought, Good
Deed, Good Word.

One of the most famous Irish towers is that of
Monasterboise, a name resolving into Mon aster, the lone
Star, and Boice, the Father of Light.

Figs. 1054 and 1055 are something like castles and something like mountains, or they might be called " monasteries."
The outstanding M is presumably Maat, and the two

smaller mounts a variant of the twins. It is not unlikely that in Christian Cathedrals the great central spire was understood to symbolise the Holy One and the smaller towers the Celestial offspring. The Cornish word for *spire* was *peal* or *pel*, and it is indubitable that a *spire*[1] or *pinnacle*

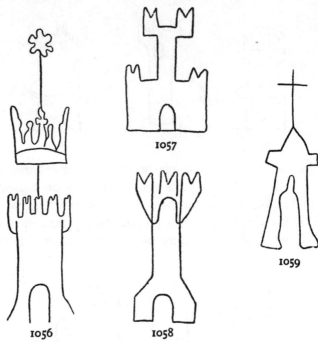

1057

1059

1056   1058

was once widely revered as a symbol of *pan ak el*, the universal Great God pointing to the stars. Mr COWAN quotes a MAORI lullaby in which the Sky Father is thus associated with a pinnacle :

> " From Heaven's *pinnacle* thou comest,
>   O my Son,
>   Born of the very Sky
>   Of Heaven—that—Stands—Alone." [2]

---

[1] *Spire* may be equated with *spear, spore* (a *seed* and also a *track*), *espoir* (*hope*), and *aspire*.   [2] *The Maoris*, p. 107.

Fig. 1057 is designed like the letter Y—emblem of the Three-in-One; and if fig. 1058 be turned upside down, it forms a Y-shaped tree trunk or pillar rooted in and springing from a mountain cleft.[1]   The Cornish word for Yew-tree was *broch*.

Fig. 1059 is something like a Tower and something like a Tent or Tabernacle, *i.e. taberna ac el,* the "booth or tent of Great God."   The Tabernacle or Tent of Tetragrammaton is said by the author of *The Canon* to have been a "mystical image of the universe intended for a shrine for the pantheistic Deity whose nature is enigmatically shadowed forth in the Law."[2]

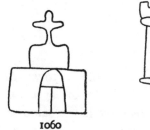

1060   1061   1062

The Tabernacle faced the East so that when the Sun arose it might send its first rays upon it, and this symbolism corresponds to that surrounding the "small, white spire" reverenced by the Arabian YEZIDIS.   This spire, "kept as pure as repeated coats of whitewash can make it," is called, says LAYARD, "the Sanctuary of SHEIK SHEMS or the Sun; it is so placed that the first rays of that luminary should as frequently as possible fall upon it."[3]   Attached to the Yezidi sanctuary of the small, white spike or spire was a drove of white oxen dedicated to the Sun.   The Latin for *spike* is *broca*.

The gate of fig. 1060 is formed of T, and the entire emblem is either a Tower, or the oblong square of a

---

[1] There is a famous round tower at CASHEL in Ireland.
[2] P. 160.   [3] *Nineveh,* p. 183.

Masonic "Lodge," [1] or a pilgrim's water-bottle. These bottles used to be called water-bugs or "bugs," and the word *bottle* cannot differ from *beetle*,[2] nor from the place-name BOOTLE.

The letter T appears under the Twin *bergs* of fig. 1061. The twin minarets of fig. 1062 are marked C C, and they surmount an inscription reading Dɪ Io. The lettering

1063

1064

around this Eye reads GRUNEBERG, probably a town of which the name may be resolved into the Berg of *ag ur un*, the mighty, unique Fire. The word *minaret* is the same as *manaret*, the Arabian for a *lamp* or *lighthouse*, and it is allied to *manorah*, the Hebrew for a *candlestick*.

The Twin towers of fig. 1063 form an *aitch*, and the

[1] "A Mason's lodge . . . is a microcosm or picture of the universe."
 "What is the form of the lodge?"
 "A long square."
 "How long?"
 "From east to west."
 "How broad?"
 "Between north and south."
 "How deep?"
 "From the surface of the earth to the centre."
 "How high?"
 "Even as high as the Heavens." (See *The Canon*, anon. p. 238.)

[2] BUGGE seems to have been once a very popular name in London, and the arms of the family were "three water-bugs." The city church of ST DIONYS was alternatively known as "BACKE" Church, and JOHN BUGGE, Esquire, was a great benefactor to that work.

moon-face of HERMES [1] surmounts an H. Underneath the triple-domed gateway of fig. 1064 is the H of HERMES and the holy figure 4, a number which among the Greeks was sacred to MERCURY. The portals of fig. 1065 are apparently being thrown open by a two-headed eagle, and the double-Hu towers of fig. 1066 are surmounted by a standard of which the trails form the C R of CHRISTUS REDEMPTOR.

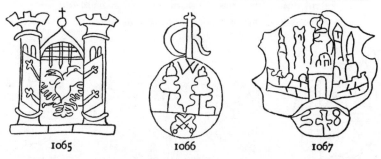

1065   1066   1067

The flame-like towers, pinnacles, and minarets of fig. 1067 are suggestive of the City of the Sun, which may be equated with CAMELOT, the wonder city of King ARTHUR.

> " Camelot, a city of shadowy palaces
> And stately, rich in emblem and the work
> Of ancient kings who did their days in stone ;
> Which Merlin's hand, the Mage at Arthur's court,
> Knowing all arts, had touch'd, and everywhere
> At Arthur's ordinance, tipt with lessening peak
> And pinnacle, and had made it spire to heaven."

One of the great features of this fairy city was its magic portal.[2] "There was," says TENNYSON, " no gate like it under heaven."

---

[1] In GEORGIA the worship of ST GEORGE is associated with remains of Moon-worship. See article "St George, the Moon-God" in *The Quest*, vol. iii. No. 3.

[2] This magic gateway was reproduced upon the English shilling of 1648. The design upon this coin has hitherto been assumed to represent Pontefract Castle, but Pontefract Castle never exhibited from its gate-tower an arm extending a sword as high and as upright as the castle itself.

" For barefoot on the keystone, which was lined
And rippled like an ever-fleeting wave,
The Lady of the Lake stood : all her dress
Swept from her sides as water flowing away ;
But like the cross her great and goodly arms
Stretch'd under all the cornice and upheld ;
And drops of water fell from either hand ;
And down from one a sword was hung, from one
A censer, either worn with wind and storm ;

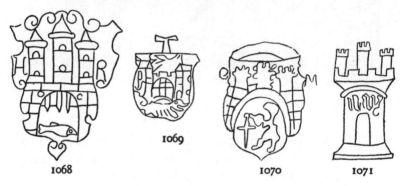

1068   1069   1070   1071

And o'er her breast floated *the sacred fish* ;
And in the space to left of her, and right,
Were Arthur's wars in weird devices done,
New things and old co-twisted, as if Time
Were nothing, so inveterately, that men
Were giddy gazing there : and over all
High on the top were those three Queens, the friends
Of Arthur, who should help him at his need."

In front of fig. 1068 floats the sacred Fish, and the waters
or flames at the base of fig. 1069 form the figure of a Fish.
The span of fig. 1070 is like a crescent moon, and underneath
this cornice is, "like the cross," a sword.

CHAPTER XVII

THE NIGHT OF FIRES

" The world has made such comet-like advance
Lately on science, we may almost hope,
Before we die of sheer decay, to learn
Something about our infancy ; when lived
That great, original, broad-eyed, sunken race,
Whose knowledge, like the sea-sustaining rocks,
Hath formed the base of this world's fluctuous lore."
P. BAILEY, *Festus.*

" There must have been a time when a simple instinct for poetry was possessed by all nations as it still is by uncivilised races and children. Among European nations this instinct appears to be dead for ever. We can name neither a mountain nor a flower."
ERNEST WEEKLEY, *The Romance of Words.*

FROM the evidence of fossil flora and fossil shells geologists conclude that there once existed a land connection between AMERICA and EUROPE. Tradition and documentary evidence alike attest the existence long ages ago of an Island once situated in the Atlantic Ocean and known as ATLANTIS.[1]

[1] " It is remarkable that recent paleontological researches should have established the fact of there having really existed an Atlantis in Tertiary times. The Tertiary shells of the United States are identical with a whole series of fossils in the same beds of France. Also the Tertiary vertebrate animals in France have their analogues either in fossil creatures or in living species in America. On this account geologists are justified in concluding that in the Tertiary epoch a land connection existed between the two continents. The fossil flora of the two continents give like results. Finally, COLLOMB and VERNEUIL have collected evidence to show that there actually did exist an enormous island to the West of Spain whose rivers formed the vast, marshy, and delta deposits of the Tertiary period in Spain."
—*Chambers's Encylopædia*, i. 546.

This great and highly civilised Continent is said to have been overwhelmed by the sea about nine thousand six hundred years before Christ.

Of the several accounts of this supposed catastrophe, one of the best known is that contained in the so-called TROANO Manuscript.[1]   This chronicle—one of the few Mayan documents that escaped destruction at the hands of Spanish missionaries—relates that " The year six KAN, on the eleventh MULAK, in the month ZAC, there occurred terrible earthquakes which continued without intermission until the thirteenth CHUEN.   The country of the hills of mud, the Land of MU, was sacrificed.   Being twice upheaved, it suddenly disappeared during the night, the basin being continually shaken by volcanic forces.   Being confined, these caused the land to sink and rise several times and in various places.   At last the surface gave way and the ten countries were torn asunder and scattered in fragments ; unable to withstand the force of the seismic convulsions, they sank, with their sixty-four millions of inhabitants, eight thousand and sixty years before the writing of this book."[2]

Another record of the same disaster is carved on a stone slab forming the lintel of a door in the ruined city of CHICHEN: "It is," says LE PLONGEON, "as intact to-day as when it came from the hand of the sculptor."   A third narrative exists in a Mayan Manuscript known as CODEX CORTESIANUS.   "Twice," says this figurative chronicle, " MU jumped from its foundations.   It was then sacrificed with fire.   It burst while being shaken up and down violently by the earthquake.   By kicking it, the wizard that makes all things move like a mass of worms sacrificed it that very night."[3]

SOLON was informed by an Egyptian priest that at the

[1] It is now at Madrid.   [2] Quoted in *Queen Moo*, p. 147.
[3] *Ibid.*, p. 148.

time of the destruction of Atlantis a great war was raging
between the Greeks and Atlanteans, and that the flower of
the Hellenic army perished in the cataclysm.   SOLON's
story, as recorded by PLATO, is to the effect that when in
Egypt he inquired of the priests whether they knew anything worth mentioning about the times of old.   "On one
occasion," says PLATO, "when he [SOLON] was drawing them
on to speak of antiquity, he began to tell about the most
ancient things in our part of the world."   Thereupon one
of the priests, who was of very great age, said : "O Solon,
Solon, you Hellenes are but children, and there is never an
old man who is a Hellene."   SOLON, hearing this, said :
"What do you mean ?"   "I mean," replied the priest,
"that in mind you are all young ; there is no old opinion
handed down among you by ancient tradition, nor any
science which is hoary with age."   After intimating that
Greek genealogies were no better than the tales of children,
the Egyptian priest then acquainted SOLON with what he
affirmed to be the true history of antiquity.   "There was,"
said he, "an island situated in front of the straits which
you call the Columns of Heracles ; the island was larger
than Libya and Asia put together, and was the way to other
islands, and from the islands you might pass through the
whole of the opposite continent which surrounded the true
ocean ; for this sea, which is within the Straits of Heracles,
is only a harbour, having a narrow entrance ; but that other
is a real sea, and the surrounding land may be most truly
called a continent.   Now, in the island of Atlantis there was
a great and wonderful empire which had rule over the
whole island and several others, as well as over parts of the
continent, and, besides these, they subjected the parts of
Libya within the Columns of Heracles as far as Egypt, and
of Europe as far as Tyrrhenia.   The vast power thus
gathered into one, endeavoured to subdue at one blow our

country and yours, and the whole of the land which was within the straits ; and then, Solon, your country shone forth in the excellence of her virtue and strength among all mankind, for she was the first in courage and military skill, and was the leader of the Hellenes. And when the rest fell off from her, being compelled to stand alone, after having undergone the very extremity of danger, she defeated and triumphed over the invaders, and preserved from slavery those who were not yet subjected, and freely liberated all the others who dwelt within the limits of Heracles. But afterward there occurred violent earthquakes and floods, and in a single day and night of rain all your warlike men in a body sank into the earth, and the island of Atlantis in like manner disappeared, and was sunk beneath the sea. And that is the reason why the sea in those parts is impassable and impenetrable, because there is such a quantity of shallow mud in the way ; and this was caused by the subsidence of the island." [1]

The theory has frequently been put forward—more particularly by the late IGNATIUS DONNELLY—that the submersion of ATLANTIS was the material basis from which originated the almost universal legend of a great Flood.

Various attempts have been made to identify the British with the Hebrews, a theory that no doubt has to some extent been fostered by the identity between British and Hebrew names and place-names, and in 1831 Lord Kingsborough published an enormous work in which he sought to prove not that the British but that the *Mexicans* were the Lost Tribes of Israel. [2] The greater probability would seem to be that some of the earliest tides of emigration set from

---

[1] *Plato's Dialogues*, Timæus, ii. 517.

[2] The Spanish historians, ACOSTA and TORQUEMADA, were so much struck by the similitude, and yet utterly unbelieving in the theory of a Hebrew origin, that they were obliged to look upon the Mexicans as a parody of the Devil's in the New World on the chosen race in the Old.

West to East, and that the lost cradle of civilisation was not
" somewhere in Asia " nor in Scandinavia, but at some point
midway between Europe and America. That the ancient
civilisations of Europe were due to a *maritime* people is, to
some extent, pointed by the fact that they all radiated from
the Mediterranean.   "The nations," said PLATO, "are
gathered around the shores of the Mediterranean like frogs
round a marsh."   Donnelly's theory, which he supported
with a weighty collection of evidence, was that the human
cradle was ATLANTIS, and that the civilisations of EUROPE,
MEXICO, PERU, EGYPT, and the MISSISSIPPI Valley were all
offshoots or colonies of the parent Atlantean Island.

LE PLONGEON, who spent many years exploring the
language and antiquities of MEXICO, affirms that " one-third
of this tongue (the Maya) is pure Greek."   "Who," he
asks, " brought the dialect of HOMER to AMERICA ? or who
took to Greece that of the Mayas ? " [1]

The primitive and radical character of British place-
names—particularly River names such as DEE, TAW, WYE,
and Lake names such as EWE and AWE—points to their profound and immeasurable antiquity. The giant mound or
barrow forming part of the prehistoric Temple at AVEBURY
is the largest structure of this character in the world ; it is
as unparalleled as STONEHENGE, and was believed by Donnelly
to be the primitive and parent form of all the American
tumuli and pyramids. Similarly the rock temple of CARNAC
in Brittany may justly be assumed to be an older and less
advanced form of art than the temple of KARNAC in Egypt.

The Breton peasants venerate the memory of MERIADEK,
who may probably be equated with the Babylonish MARDUK
or MERODACH, and they still cherish the tradition of a
wondrous *hundred*-gated Cathedral of Is.[2] This mystic
Church of Light must be related to the material Temple of

---

[1] Quoted in *Atlantis*, p. 349.   [2] Le Braz (A.), *Night of Fires*, p. 158.

BELUS, whose *hundred* brazen gates were one of the wonders of BABYLON, and also to the *hundred*-gated Holy City of THEBES. Similarly the Breton BOLBEC may be compared with the once mighty and world-famous BAALBEC.

In BRITTANY there exists to this day a worship of Fire, which in its elaborate ritual probably preserves the exact spirit and ceremony of prehistoric Fire-worship. To appreciate this cult one should consider it from the local standpoint, and for this purpose one cannot do better than contemplate it through the Celtic mind of M. ANATOLE LE BRAZ. Describing a modern Night of Fires, this Breton poet writes :

" I glance round at the crowd. Everyone is leaning forward, all necks being eagerly craned toward the pyre.

" For a moment the flame flickers, then, with a dry sound, the gorse begins to crackle, and fiery tongues leap forth as from the mouth of an oven. Up the sides of the *Tan-tad*[1] they climb, and are soon licking the foxgloves and iris, so that their stalks shiver and bend, while, at the same time, from the throats of the two hundred men, women, and children, a cry breaks forth, a frantic clamour, shouted in unison :

" ' *An tan !*[2] . . . *An tan !* . . . '

" Mothers lift up their sleeping babies, and with outstretched arms hold them in the air before the sacred flame, crying : ' May the blessing of Monseigneur Saint Peter rest upon our little ones ! '

" Quickly though it has been built, there has yet been time for the fog to find its way into the bonfire, so that it gives forth a thick smoke, which gradually envelops the whole summit ; and a strange, fantastic sight it is, this swarm of human beings, standing in the midst of the grey, eddying clouds, the whole scene lighted by the quick

[1] " Fire-Father."   [2] " The Fire."

flashing of the flames. . . . And on the bare summit
Fire reigns triumphant, Fire, the Father of Safety, Fire that
ever drives away evil terrors and brings consoling thoughts,
Fire, the Living Idol of earliest ages, which still in the
undying consciousness of Celto-Bretons wakes an echo of
the ancient Cult !

" With roars and heavy growlings like the strong breath-
ing of some mighty monster, the entire mass of the *Tan-tad*
bursts into flame, its huge, red crest bristling, so that in
the distance the circle of the surrounding mountains sinks
into deeper shadow, as the light of the fire grows ever more
and more intense. The sky, from which the mists have
now been torn, hangs like a high, motionless sea, with here
and there groups of cloud islands, dyed royal purple from
the reflection of the flames.

· · · · · · ·

" ' *An tan !* . . . *An tan !* . . . '

" Each time that the flame, roused by the night breeze,
bursts forth afresh, the shout is taken up, widening away
into space, dying, sinking into a faint echo, a vague,
melancholy vibration.

" During an interval of silence, a curious, sickly-looking,
little man approaches the fire, and snatching out a brand
flourishes it round his head, crying :

" ' Hearken, hearken to the Song of the Fire ! '

" His trim appearance, the fineness and whiteness of his
hands, his crooked legs, with knees bent outward, all mark
him as one of the country tailors who spend their days
sitting like Buddhas beneath the straw roofs of barns,
armed with needles thick as a cobbler's awl, patiently
sewing away at the heavy garments worn by the Breton
labourer. . . . Son of a race created but for the inner life,
which since birth has been endowed with the gift of poetry,
he spends the long, sedentary hours meditating over the

episodes of marvellous stories, or composing the verses of his songs.

"'Yes, indeed! Sing us your Song of the Fire!' cries the crowd to the tailor of Croaz-Houarn.

"Then, still swinging his brand, he breaks forth into song, and from the narrow chest of this deformed creature issues a splendid voice, so manly in tone, so full in volume, that its accents seem to shake the distant walls of the very shadows of night. And this is the song he sang:

"'Hola ye boys! Hola ye girls! . . . Leave your meal half eaten; Leave the spoon within the bowl; . . . For the holy night is here; For the Night of Fires is at hand: I behold the great light upon the mountains; I behold the fires of Saint John and of Saint Peter. . . . Hasten to your task, each of you! Leave there the spoon within the bowl, Take up the faggot on either shoulder; He who lingers last upon this holy night, Will be the last to enter Paradise.'

"The sweat is pouring from the brow of the singer; he wipes it off with the cuff of his sleeve, pausing a moment to regain his breath, while the assembly take up the chorus, in whose Biblical sounding verse gleams a reflection of the lofty night landscape, lit by the flames of bonfires—

"'Behold, the Night of Fires is here,
A great light shines upon the mountains!'

"'Bravo! Well done! *potr ar vesken*' (man of the thimble), cries Pierre Tanguy by way of encouragement, and the little tailor begins again more gallantly than ever.

"He shows the people of every degree, householders, farmers' wives, herdsmen, waggoners, servants, even babes at the breast, climbing in endless procession toward the sacred precinct. Then he enumerates all the heights around Motreff, crowned that night by fires 'like giant towers.' And especially does he glorify the fire of Croaz-Houarn which 'rises high above the others as the spire of the church over the roofs of the village.' He speaks of the splendour of the flame, of the sparks 'whirling like a dance of stars,' of the doors of heaven opening 'with a sound of music,' and Saint Peter without on the door-sill, his great white beard to windward, blessing the fields of the district, promising prosperity to those who cultivate them :

> " ' Scatter the ashes of the fire,
>   And you shall see the harvest grow !
>
> ' Hang the charred brand above the bed,
>   And you shall see the children grow ;
>
> ' He who composed and sang this song
>   Is but a humble man and poor ;
>
> ' Henri Rohan, by trade a tailor,
>   Has sung it for the Tan-tad.' " [1]

The instances of Bonfire customs collected by Dr FRAZER [2] clearly evince their original sanctity. In GREECE the women jumped over the all-purifying flames, crying : " I leave my sins behind me," and in most districts the *form* of the fire was symbolic. Thus, " in Swabia the 'fire of Heaven ' as it was called was made on St Vitus's Day (15th June) by igniting a *cart-wheel* which, smeared with pitch and plaited with straw, was fastened on *a pole* twelve feet high, the top of the pole being inserted in the nave of the wheel. This fire was made on the summit of the mountain, and, as the flame ascended, the people uttered a set form of words with eyes and arms directed heavenward." [3]

The British BELTAN fires were sometimes called BALTEIN, and in all probability *tan* or *tein*, fundamentally " shining

---

[1] *The Night of Fires*, pp. 36–42.
[2] *Golden Bough*, ii. [3] *Ibid.*, ii. 270.

one," is identical with the Chinese term *tien*, which means *day*, *sky*, and *God*. The Celtic word *tan*, meaning *fire*, is apparent in many directions. It occurs not infrequently in conjunction with *san*, meaning *holy*, and the combination of *san tan* appears to have been, probably unconsciously, Christianised into "St Anne." St Anne, the supposed Mother of the Virgin Mary, is the patron saint of Brittany. There is a St Anne's Hill at Avebury, and on 6th August an annual fair is held there known as Tan Hill Fair. In the Isle of Man there is a signal station at "St Anne's or Santon"; at St Anne's Head, Milford, there is a lighthouse, and the combination of a lighthouse and the name St Anne will be found in other directions.

In Borneo there is a Santan Point, and where the modern lighthouse at Damietta now stands—originally Zoan or San—is now known as Tanis. There is a Santander in Mexico, another in Peru, another in Colombia, and a Santander town and province in Spain.

The "St Anne's Beacon" in Cornwall is written "St Agnes," and at St Agnes in the Scillies stands a well-known lighthouse. Agni was the Aryan God of Fire; *ignis* is the Latin for *fire*; and the words *montagne* and *montagna*—radically *mount Fire*—probably developed into the generic term for an exceptionally large hill by reason of the fact that the highest, most conspicuous, and most commanding point in every district was always selected as the Beacon,[1] Galley, or Fire Hill.

The word *tan* or *tein* reappears in *mountain*[2] and, slightly varied, in place-names such as Pertinny or Bartiney, the sacred Fire Hill near Land's End, a district once known as Belerium or Bolerium.

Near Penzance there is an ancient, elliptical structure known as Kerris Roundago, and northwards of Land's

---

[1] *Be ac on.*   [2] Latin *montana*, Spanish *montanha*.

End is CARN CRIES—the Carn of *ak ur is,* the Great Fire Light—"whose summit," says BLIGHT, "was crowned with a beacon."[1]

The word BER or PER, used in CORNWALL as a generic term for *hill,* may be equated with *pur* or *pyr,* the Greek for *fire.* The word *pyre,* meaning with us a funeral fire, is the base of *pyramid* (Greek *pyramis*), and the pyramid or cone was apparently at one time a universal symbol of the Primal Fire. The Brahmins express SIVA, the God of Fire, by a pyramid ; and in the Buddhist Temples of JAPAN the Five Elements—Ether, Air, *Fire,* Water, and Earth—are denoted respectively by a Ball, Crescent, *Pyramid,* Sphere,

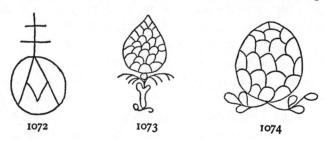

1072   1073   1074

and Cube.[2] "The element of Fire," says PLUTARCH, "is the Pyramid," and he observes further that "of the Pyramid everybody will recognise the *fiery* and movable character."[3] PLATO assumed the Pyramid to be *first* of all forms, and PLUTARCH maintains that "the only *first* form is the Pyramid."[4]

In fig. 1072 a cone, mountain, pyramid, or Great A appears within the Eye, Circle, or Roundago of CHEOP, KERRIS, or CERES. At CHIAPA in South America the Great Father was worshipped under the name ICONA[5] (the Great one A ?),

[1] *A Week at Land's End,* p. 184.
[2] Chamberlain (B. H.), *Japan,* p. 42.
[3] *On the Cessation of Oracles.*   [4] *Ibid.*
[5] Buckley (T. A.), *Great Cities of America,* p. 271.

and the word *cone* may possibly be due to this figure having been the symbol of *ic-one*, the Great One. The Fir cone was peculiarly the symbol of the Fire of Life because the Fir[1] tree was formed like a flame.[2] It was thus regarded as the Universal Root, the foundation of all things, and the boundless Power from which all flesh was nourished. The Anglo-Saxon for a mountain was *firgen*; the Gothic was *fariguni*.

The builder of the Great Pyramid of GHIZEH was King CHEOPS or CHUFU; and CHUFU, which may be compared with FUJI, the name of the cone-like, sacred fire-mount of JAPAN, in all probability meant *feu*, Fire, *ji*, Ever-Existent.

One must postulate a root *fu*, meaning *fire*, to account for such words as *feu*, *fuoco*, *fuego*, *fuse*, *fuzee*, *feuer*, *fever*, *fire*, etc. PAN was known in some localities as FAUNUS, *i.e.* *fa unus*, the "One Fire," and PHŒBUS may probably be equated with *feu obus*, i.e. *fire ball*. The word *fawn* in Old French was *faon* or *fan*, and the article known as a *fan*, which is a world-wide symbol of royalty, was seemingly thus named because it radiates like the sunbeams of the rising or setting Sun. The Hebrew for a palm-tree was *phenice*, whence probably PHŒNICIA and also VENICE. The fabulous PHŒNIX, said to have been born of fire, resolves into *fo en ix*, the Fire, the One Great Fire.

In the following emblem the Bird of Fire is represented in the *feu*. In JAPAN the Phœnix is known as the *Foo* and sometimes as the *Ho* or *O*. The Chinese call the yellow Phœnix a *To Fu* (resplendent fire?), and say that whenever the world is peaceful the note of the *To Fu* "will be heard like the tolling of a bell."[3]

---

[1] "At first sight," says Max Müller, "the English word *Fir* does not look very like the Latin *Quercus*, yet it is the same word."—*The Science of Language*, p. 247.

[2] King, *The Gnostics*, p. 133.

[3] Gould (C.), *Mythical Monsters*, pp. 369, 370, 372.

F<small>A</small> is the root of *fate*; of *fête*, i.e. *fair*; of *fare*, meaning *food*; and of *fair*, meaning *beautiful* and *just*. Archæologists have frequently commented upon the fact that fairs are often held upon dates corresponding with the ancient fire festivals. *Fa* is the root of *feyther*[1] or *father*, and of *faith* (French *foi*). The radical *fay* is an English word meaning *fairy*, and the Egyptian divinity T<small>YPHO</small> is probably related ideally to T<small>OFOA</small>, the name of a volcano in the Friendly Islands. F<small>UDO</small>, "Fire Resplendent" (?), is the name of the Japanese God of Wisdom who is represented as encircled

1074*a*

by Fire, and among the Chinese the supreme God of the World is worshipped under the name F<small>UHI</small>, F<small>OE</small>, or F<small>O</small>.

According to Northern mythology, one of the three sons of the All-Father B<small>ORR</small> was named V<small>E</small>. The German for *father* is *vater*, the enduring *fire* or enduring *vie*=*life*; the F<small>IJI</small> Islands are alternatively known as F<small>IJI</small> or as V<small>ITI</small>. S<small>IVA</small> was the God of *vehement* Fire; J<small>OVE</small> is a synonym for Z<small>EUS</small>; and one of the forms of J<small>EHOVAH</small> is J<small>AHVE</small>, the "Ever-Existent Fire or Life."

The pyramids are now deemed to be "really nothing more than tombs," but I suggest that in form and intention they originally symbolised the fourfold immovable A, the Universal *Maintainer*, the Primal Peak and Great First Cause, oriented due East, West, North, and South.

[1] The Egyptian for *father* was *atfe*.

In the Maya alphabet the letter A was expressed by the pyramidal form Λ; by the Egyptians A was expressed by *akhoom*, the "eagle," and by *aak*, the "reed." *Aak* probably meant primarily "Great A," and *akhoom*, "Great Sun." Temples and monuments in the pyramidal form are found accurately oriented in INDIA, CHINA, AMERICA, JAVA, and the POLYNESIAN Islands. That they symbolised the Sun and were something beyond tombs may be inferred from the fact that *within* Egyptian tombs small model pyramids have been found bearing inscribed adorations to the Sun.[1]

In MEXICO the pyramids were known as *teocallis*, from *teo calli*, meaning the "House of God"; and many pyramid names still seemingly preserve traces of the primitive and elementary A. Thus, among the most notable of the Egyptian pyramids are those at GHIZEH (*ag iz a*, "mighty light A"?); ILLAHUN ("Lord Everlasting Immutable One"?); ZUMA (*iz um a*, "Sunlight A"?); RIGAH (*ur ig ah*, "mighty Fire A"?); SAKKARAH (*is ak ur ah*, "light of the Great Fire A"?); and LISCHT (*licht=light*?).

At UXMAL in MEXICO there is a group of *seven* pyramids which in all probability will be found to be ranged in the form of the Seven Stars of the Great *Bear*. The miniature and primitive pyramid that we term a *barrow* or *berrow* in mediæval times was spelled *berw*.[2] This word is seemingly related to *pero*, a *bear*, and in all probability it once meant *bear* or *père* HU. In some parts of England a *barrow* is termed a *howe*[3] and sometimes a *low*—terms seemingly but a slight corruption of HEW or EL HU. My etymology thus strengthens the probability that the *barrow*[4] or *howe*[5] was

---

[1] *Chambers's Encyclopædia*, viii. 505.
[2] Skeat.
[3] At HOWERA in Egypt there is a pyramid.
[4] At BARROW in Lincolnshire are the remains of a prehistoric temple.
[5] Compare surname HOWE.

once regarded as a symbol of the immutable Father Hu. The word *pile* must be equal to *peel*, which, as has been seen, implied a *fortress, tower*, or *stronghold*; it also meant "a stockaded enclosure"; and the *palisade* around the Lion of fig. 1007 (*ante*, p. 122) is probably intended for a *peel*. Near PENZANCE are the ruins of some prehistoric, circular huts known as the *crellas*, and this word cannot differ from the Spanish-American *corale*, nor from the Zulu *kraal*, meaning a stockaded or defended circle.

Barrows or *peels* served the multifarious purposes of strongholds, beacons, shrines, judgment-seats, and burial-places. The verb *to bury* probably once meant to put into a *barrow* or a *bury*, and *to entomb*, to place within a *tump* or *tumulus*. To *inter* is now understood as consigning to *terre*,[1] the earth; but the Parsees still consign their dead to *towers*, and may be said to "entower" them. In Syria the word *tor* means a mountain;[2] in Britain *tor* means a conical hill.

In Wales the ancient churchyards are found in the form of a *circle*; the Norsemen consigned the dead to their Mother the *Sea*; and among most nations the idea of burial seems to have been to return the body to some symbol of its primal Parent—to TOMBA, the "Shining Sun Father."

The greatest barrow in the world is the English SILBURY at AVEBURY, and it is a remarkable coincidence that the daily gauge of the shadows of the Great Pyramid in Egypt and of SILBURY in England is almost exactly identical.[3] SIL, as in *ceiling*, meant primarily the Fire or Light of God, and may be compared with the surname SEELEY, with *silly* and *zeal*, and with the place-names SEAL near DERBY, and ZEAL in Cornwall.[4] The name AVEBURY is alternatively

---

[1] *Tur*=the enduring or strong.
[2] Lepsius, *Egypt, Ethiopia, and Sinai*, p. 552.
[3] Cox (R. H.), *A Guide to Avebury*, p. 32.
[4] Compare also SILCHESTER, SILSBY, SILSDEN, SILTON, etc.

spelled AUBURY or ABURY, and thus the curious fact results that the largest *tumulus* in the world is situate at a site evidently once known as the Burg, Barrow, or Bury of A or AWE. In Ireland barrows are called *lawes*, and in SCOTLAND *law* also means a mound. In Sclavonic *gora* means a *mountain*, and may be equated with *crau* or Great Fire AU, the Savoyade term for *mountain*.

In various parts of Britain barrows are known as *mottes*, *moots*, *moats*, or *mudes*. During a lawsuit the Judge used to sit on the summit of the Law or Moot-hill, and, as already suggested, the word *moot* is probably identical with MUT or MAAT, the Egyptian *Justice*. The moot-hills were also the general meeting and pow-wow places where the people arranged to *meet* and to discuss *moot*—*i.e.* debatable—points.

In some districts the moot-hills are termed *toot-hills*, and Wyclif uses this word as meaning a *watch-tower*. Among the variations and compounds of *toot*—a term evidently identical with *tat* or *tad*, meaning *father*—are TOUTHILL, TOTHILL, TUTTHILL, TUTBURY, TOOTING, and BELTOUT. The *toot-hills* being watch-towers, we may assume that a *toot* upon a horn was once a watchman's warning.

The author of *Byeways in British Archæology*[1] illustrates a very notable toot-hill existing to this day in the church-yard of PIRTON, and he adduces this with much other interesting evidence in support of the theory that many Christian churches were erected on the sites of pagan sanctuaries. The TOTHILL Street near Westminster Abbey is an inference that a toot-hill once stood in that neighbour-hood, and it is evident that Christian churches often owe their inconvenient but commanding position on the summits of remote hills to the fact that they superseded pagan Hill-shrines. In the Middle Ages the churches served all the varied purposes of the ancient *mottes*. Law was

[1] P. 60.

dispensed in the churchyards ; the village stocks or *coppes* [1] stood in the church porch, and the churches themselves were employed as secular meeting-places, theatres, law courts, markets, schools, forts, armouries, and beacon towers.

Basilica, the Greek word for *church*, is evidently a later form of *basil*. In Brɪks there is a place called BASILDON, and near BEER ALSTON in Devonshire is a spring under the churchyard bearing the curious title of " the Basil." [2] It is likely that this spring was once a very holy Well. *Basileus* in Greek means *king*, and it is exceedingly curious that the rector of BEER ALSTON till recently claimed and bore the title of " arch-priest." [3] The Old Irish for a *church* was *domnach*, probably meaning *dom on ak*, the House of the Great One. The word is evidently allied to DOMINIC, the proper name, and to *dominus*, a *lord*. [4]

The word *steeple*, originally spelled *stepel*, does not differ from *staple*—Anglo-Saxon *stapol*—meaning a post or pillar. *Staple* also means a chief market, a mart, and a public store-house. In German *stapel* means a *heap* ; in Dutch it means a *pile* or heap and also *the stocks*. The *pel* or *pol* occurring in all these terms is no doubt the rudimentary *pele* or *peel*, originally the divine POL. *Stable* is *stability*, and the *pel* of *steeple* reappears as *bel* in *belfry*. As archæo-logists are aware, the word *belfry* has only a fortuitous relation to bells ; the word originally meant a watch-tower, a protecting shelter, and is found varying into *berfray*, [5] *berfroi*, *berefrit*, etc. The second syllable *fry* or *fray* is

---

[1] In Edward III.'s time the stocks are mentioned as *coppes*. The round holes for " copping " the ankles were presumably regarded as great eyes.

[2] Baring-Gould, *Devon*, p. 96.   [3] *Ibid.*

[4] The Greek word *ecclesia* occurs in England in the more primitive form *eglos*, *i.e.* the Mighty Lord of Light, and may be recognised in the place-names EGLOSKERRY, EGLOSHAYLE, ECCLESTON, ECCLESHALL, ECCLES-FIELD, etc.

[5] Compare place-name BARFRESTON.

suggestive of fire; it is common knowledge that belfries were used as fire or beacon towers, and etymology suggests that belfries are the direct and unbroken sequence to BEL fires.

The piles and pyramids of the ancients seem usually to have had an altar or an ever-burning fire upon their summits: in the city of MEXICO six hundred of these pyramidal fires rendered other illumination at night superfluous.[1] An essential feature of the American pyramids was the chapel or *naos* at the supreme summit of the edifice.[2] The Temple of the Seven Spheres in ASSYRIA was built upon the summit of a gigantic pyramidal mound called BIRS, and the gods there worshipped are inscribed as " ASSARAC and BELTIS, the shining BAR, ANI, and DAGON."[3]

In addition to or in lieu of *fire* there appeared sometimes on the pyramid summits twin obelisks, and sometimes a cyclopean golden image of the Deity. The British judge perched on the top of a moot-hill was no doubt regarded as a humble image, deputy, shadow, and viceregent of the Supreme DOOM or el AW.

The Chaldeans built not only their temples but also their palaces in pyramidal form. " They ' lifted their eyes to the hills' on the north-east ('the Father of Countries') and imagined it the abode of the gods, the future home of every great and good man—'a land with a sky of silver, a soil producing crops without tilling'—'the mountain of BEL in the east, whose double head reaches unto the skies like a mighty buffalo at rest, whose double horn sparkles as a sunbeam, as a star.'"[4]

The name BABIL or BABYLON probably meant " Father BEL." The great mound BABIL among the ruins of BABYLON

---

[1] Spence (L.), *Mythology of Ancient Mexico and Peru*, p. 37.
[2] Anon., *Ruins of Sacred and Hist. Lands*, p. 261.   [3] *Ibid.*, p. 62.
[4] Anderson (R. E.), *Extinct Civ. of East*, p. 34.

represents the Temple of BEL, which was a pyramid of eight square stages. At the summit stood an image of gold forty feet high, two other statues of gold, a table, and two other colossal objects—all of the same precious metal.[1]

The Chaldean name for pyramid or *mountain-peak* was *ziggurat*, the Mighty Light, the Fiery Heat (?).

There is an injunction in Ezekiel, "Upon the top of the mountain the whole limit thereof round about shall be most holy. Behold, this is the law of the house."[2] At the summit of the pyramid herewith is a round Eye or Circle ; a *ronde*, *i.e.* One Shining Fire, or *is ur ac el*, the

1075

light of the Fire, the Great God ; and one of the most familiar symbols of Freemasonry is the All-seeing Eye posed upon the apex of a cone or pyramid. The Chinese have a "Heaven's Eye Mountain," and the Egyptians regarded the Pole Star as an *Eye* upon the summit of the Point or Pivot of the Universe.[3]

Cop was Saxon for a mountain ; and *kopje*, the Dutch for hill, may be resolved into *ak op je*, Great Eye Ever-existent. The word *heap* cannot differ from *hoop*, and *tip* and *top* yield "shining Eye." The word *apex* may be resolved into *ap ek se*, "great fiery Eye" ; and the Greek word *acme* is equivalent to *ack ome*, Great Sun, or *akhoom*, the Egyptian

[1] Anderson (R. E.), *Extinct Civ. of East*, p. 35.   [2] xliii. 12.
[3] Churchward (A. W.), *Signs and Symbols*, p. 326.

name for the letter A. The Arabic for *high mound* is *kom* ;
in English *comely* (Anglo-Saxon *kumli*) means *beautiful.*
The Anglo-Saxon *cymlic,* meaning *exquisite* and *fair,* may be
resolved into *com like* or " like the great Sun." The Mexican
temple with all its courts and purlieus was called the *teopan,*[1]
the Shining One Eye ; and *teocalli,* the term for the central
pyramid before it meant " House of God," probably implied
te oc al li, resplendent Great God Everlasting.

The Sclavonic for "an isolated hill" is *chlum,* ever-
existent Lord Sun ; the Irish for *hill* is *drum,* " enduring
Sun " ; and the Gypsy word for *hill* is *chumba,* ever-existent
Sun-Father.

In his travels in MASHONALAND BENT came across a
"curiously lofty mountain called CHIBURWE." This
mountain, which he describes as " almost round " and
as "a stronghold," is alternatively known as CHIBURGA.[2]
Bryn, the Welsh for *hill,* may be resolved into *bruin* or
bearun, the One Father.

Barrows had fires lighted upon their summits, and
sometimes in lieu of fires there was substituted some other
well-recognised symbol of fire, such as the fir-tree.
GRANT ALLEN has urged, with some reason, that the pine-
trees found so frequently on round barrows in the South of
ENGLAND are the descendants of those first planted there
by the original barrow builders, since the Scottish pine is
not now indigenous to that district.[3]

It is easy to conceive the emotions with which primitive
and poetic man viewed what we call a volcano or VULCAN.
The volcano was a natural gigantic cone or barrow, an
august symbol of the Primal Force, the Vital Fire ; and
everywhere volcanoes bear names appropriate to *vol ac an,*
the Strong and Great One. In ICELAND and in SCOTLAND

---

[1] Spence, p. 36.   [2] *Ruined Cit. of M.,* pp. 266, 267.
[3] *Evol. of Idea of God,* pp. 50, 51.

there is HECLA, the "Great Everlasting"; in South America
are JORULLA, "the aged Fire, the Lord Everlasting," and
COLIMA, "the Great God, the Sun A." The loftiest
volcano now active is COTOPAXI in ECUADOR; and the upper
part of COTOPAXI, the "Great Hot Eye, the Great Fire," is
said to be "a perfect cone." Among the ANDES is SANGAY,
"the Holy Mighty A"; in MEXICO are ORIZABA, the
"Golden Light Orb A," and CHIMBORAZO, the "Ever-existent
Sun, the Orb of Fire, the blazing O"; in the MOLUCCAS is
SION; in JAVA is PAPANDAYANG[1]; and in MEXICO, near
MAYAPAN, is the famous pyramid named PAPANTLA,[2] i.e.
"Father PAN, the Resplendent Everlasting." In JAPAN
is BANDAISAN, and the peak of BANDAISAN is named
KOBANDAI. The Druids applied the word ban to "coni-
cally-shaped mountains,"[3] such as BANNAU BRYCHEINIOG
or BRECON Mountain, and the syllable may evidently be
equated with ben and pen.[4] The peak of VESUVIUS is known
as Monte SOMMA, a word that is doubtless related to ASAMA,
the Japanese volcano; to ZUMA, the Egyptian pyramid, and
which, like IZUMA, resolves into the "light of the Sun A."
Summer is the season of Sunlight; SOMERSET is an English
place-name; and summit means the Utmost and the
Highest.

BENT mentions an African mountain which he describes
as like "a gigantic thimble." Its name JOMVGA, i.e.
JOMVIGA, resolves into "Ever-Existent Sun, the Fire of
the Mighty A"; in the name VESUVIUS we find vie twice

[1] In Mexico is the volcano POPOCATEPETL.

[2] For the sake of brevity I have everywhere decoded la as meaning
"everlasting," but according to Le Plongeon, "LA in the Mayan language
means 'that which has existed for ever—The Eternal Truth.'" (Sacred
Mysteries, p. 54.) The religious centre of Mexico and the largest pyramid
there was CHOLULA, i.e. "the ever-existent, everlasting Truth of Truths" (?).

[3] Morgan (O. M.), T.P.'s Weekly, 29th March 1912, p. 403.

[4] An Egyptian word for obelisk (ob el is ik) was ben-ben.

occurrent[1]; and the place-name JAVA is in all probability identical with JAHVE and JOVE.

The ruins of the Great Temple at ZIMBABWE exhibit the combination of sanctuary and fortress, a fact that prompted BENT to the inquiry : "Why did the inhabitants so carefully guard themselves against attack?" His supposition was that the gigantic ruins of that district were the work of some alien colonising race who were constantly on guard against native hostility.[2] It is a correlative fact that British hill-names, such as FUR TOR, BEL TOR, ALEX TOR, BRENTOR, BOW TOR, etc., not only enshrine the folk memory of primitive fire-worship, but that many of the great hills retain the idea of a light *stronghold*, *dun*, or *den*. The highest hill in HANTS is SIDON ; in WESTMORELAND are CONIS-BURGH and CONISTON, and in DEVONSHIRE is CONIESDOWN. The highest point of EXMOOR is DUNKERRY ; in DEVONSHIRE is COSDAN ; in CORNWALL is BLACKADON ; in LANCASHIRE is CRIBDEN ; and in LEICESTERSHIRE is BARDON. The view from the summit of BARDON commands, it is said, one quarter of England.

On certain occasions in many English localities the villagers still climb to the sacred earthworks that crown the eminences and maintain to some extent the rites of the prehistoric past. Notably is this the case at SILBURY[3] and St. MARTIN's HILL at AVEBURY, and at CLEY[4] HILL in WILTSHIRE.[5]

But to enumerate and unravel the names of Fire Hills is an apparently never-ending task. In his description of the dying down of the bonfires in BRITTANY M. LE BRAZ

---

[1] The French *vif* means lively, and may be equated with the English *five*. In SCOTLAND is FIFE.

[2] P. 176.

[3] Compare SILSDEN and DENZELL Down, near ST ISSEY, Cornwall.

[4] *Ac-el-a*, Great God A Hill.

[5] *Byeways in British Archaeology*, p. 194.

observes : "As the glow of the Tan-tad fades, the surrounding landscape, which until now has lain drowned in a sea of shadows, gradually clears, rising out of the abysmal depths of nothingness, retaking its form and familiar aspect. Sharper and sharper the ridges cut the vast horizon with their stern, rugged outline. It is like standing in the midst of a granite land but newly risen out of chaos. And around the circumference of the immense circle, on the backs of the hills massed one behind another, like flocks of sheep, are the flaming fires, sweeping the sky with their broad, bloody gleams. I try to count them, but minute by minute new ones are appearing, and I am continually obliged to begin over again. With outstretched finger the Vicar tells me their names.

"'This one opposite is Kervrec'h. That is Rosmeur . . . and that, Beg Aoun, the Peak of Fear. Then over there you have Saint Adrien, Balanek, Toul-laëron. . . .'

"But even he loses himself in the litany of barbarous names. The whole country resembles a mysterious camp, starred with bivouac fires. Such must it have appeared during those nights of long ago, when the hordes of nomads came rolling toward the west, lighting their evening fires in the unbroken calm of the then uninhabited region."[1]

[1] *The Night of Fires*, pp. 44–45.

CHAPTER XVIII

THE STONE HINGE

" When we look at huge cromlechs, at these vast circles, accurately planned
—though here and there unfortunately a stone missing, like a tooth from a
giant's jaw—at those colossal monoliths, the presence of every one of them
in such desolate spots is little short of a miracle. They suggest unheard-of
labour. How did they get there? . . . No driver's whip could have urged
on to completion such a gigantic task; no richest guerdon of jewels, gold,
or skins offered by affluent monarch or exalted priest of those days could
have repaid the toil. Yet there these stone circles, monoliths, menhirs,
cromlechs stand, the wonder of succeeding generations of all religious
opinions, belief, or unbelief—altars may be many of them 'To the Unknown God.' Monarchies, republics, systems have grown up, matured,
vanished. Slaughter and battles have raged round them. Cruelties, intoler-
ances, terrible superstitions, emotional outbursts of divers sorts have they
seen since first they stood up mute, impassive, sphinx-like, facing high
heaven.

.   .   .   .

" The dreams of barbarous sacrifice and writhing victims, yelling multitudes,
and strange rites will not stand the search-light of modern spade-work ; the
cold-water douche of our latest antiquarian knowledge. No place of religious
human sacrifice was here."   J. HARRIS STONE.

IN seemingly all ages and among all nations Stones and
Rocks have been worshipped as symbols of the Deity.

MITHRA is said to have been born from a Rock, to have
wedded a rock, and to have been the parent of a Rock.[1]
" Of the Rock that begat thee thou are unmindful," complained MOSES[2] to the Israelites ; " Unto thee will I cry

[1] Borlase, *Ant. of Cornwall*, p. 145.
[2] Deuteronomy xxxii. 18.

O Lord my Rock," wrote the Psalmist ;[1] and the modern Christian still sings, semi-comprehendingly, "*Rock* of Ages cleft for me, let me hide myself in Thee."

The Kafirs of INDIA say of the stones they worship, "This stands for God, but we know not his shape ";[2] the Maoris of NEW ZEALAND represent their tribal deities by stones set up in the ground ;[3] and a Holy of Holies to the ancient Persians was the peaked rock named BAGISTANE[4] or BEHISTOON.

According to Deuteronomy, the God of Israel "is a rock, his work is perfect," and the writer continues, "As an eagle stirreth up her nest, fluttereth over her young, spreadeth abroad her wings, taketh them, beareth them on her wings : so the Lord alone did lead him."[5]

Here, in one breath, the poet idealises God as a *Rock* and as an *Eagle*, and the two words are similarly correlated. *Roc* or *rukh* was Arabian and *rekh* was Egyptian for the giant *eagle* or *phœnix*.[6] The Cornish and Breton for *eagle* is *er*, and the word *rock*[7] is apparently composed of the syllables *er ock*, or " Great Fire." The Assyrians represented the God NISROCH as eagle-headed, and the Semitic word *nisroch*, which also meant *eagle* and *magnificent*, resolves into *oniseroch*, the " one Light, the Great Fire."

In English the word *rock* means also a *distaff*, and a *Blue Rock* is the common pigeon—symbol of *pi ge on*, the Father, the Ever-existent one.[8] The French for rock is *pierre*, Father Fire ; and PETER the Rock does not, of course, differ from *pater*, the Enduring Father. *Petra*, the Greek for rock,

---

[1] Psalm xxiii. 1.   [2] Gomme (G. L.), *Ethnology of Folk-lore*, p. 27.
[3] Cowan (J.), *The Maoris*, p. 110.
[4] Buckley (T. A.), *Great Cities*, p. 74.
[5] xxxii. 11, 12.   [6] Also called *bennu*.
[7] In Kent *rock* becomes *rag, e.g.* " Kentish rag."
[8] The Arabians term the Ruler of the fabulous Golden Age GIAN BEN GIAN.

and *patera*, the Latin for a disc or circle, apparently both owe their existence to *pater A*, the Rock, or JUPITER, whose way is Perfect.

The name PETER enters largely into place-names such as PETERBURGH, PETERHEAD, etc. The ancient city at the foot of Mount HOR named PETRA was originally known as SELAH, a word which in Hebrew means *rock*.

In Cornwall is a ST PETROCK and a PETHERICK, and I have already suggested that ST PATRICK of Ireland, who is fabled to have raised the dead, opened the eyes of the blind, and expelled serpents, was none other than the Rock of Ages. LE ROUZIC observes that in BRITTANY "everywhere the menhir was symbolic of an immortal God." [1] One of the largest of the BRETON menhirs is that known as PEDERNEC ; it stands twenty-five feet high and on one of its faces there are carved "three cup hollows." [2] The name PEDERNEC resolves into *peder on ek*, the "one Great Father," or the "Enduring one Great Parent." In *peuhen*, a Breton name for *menhir*, one may recognise the Celtic *hen*, meaning *ancient* ; the remaining syllable *peu* may no doubt be equated with *pa*.

According to the ancient ecclesiastical records of WALES known as the Iolo MSS., the native name of ST PATRICK was MAENWYN or Sacred Stone, and he was the Son of a certain MAWON. [3] In Celtic *mayon*, *myin*, and *maen* mean a *stone*, and these local modifications vary again into the monosyllabic *man* or *men*. *Men*, the Celtic for *stone*, may be equated with the Egyptian *men*, meaning "*to abide*," "*to be stable*," and with *mon*, meaning *alone* or *solitary*. [4] The "oldest idol"

---

[1] *Megalithic Monuments*, p. 28.

[2] Baring-Gould, *Brittany*, p. 104. Some of the BRETON menhirs are carved with the same curious spirals that are used by the Maoris of New Zealand.

[3] Morgan (O. M.), *T.P.'s Weekly*, p. 403, March 29, 1912

[4] The Cornish for *pigeon* was *kylobman=ak-il-ob-man*.

of the Arabs was an unhewn stone, worshipped under the name MANAH [1]—*lone* A (?)—and this idea of *oneness* is also retained in our English word st*one*. The *st* of *stone* may possibly be the divinity SET or SUT. We still apply the word *sett* to the square stones used for paving purposes. SUT, the Powerful, was the Egyptian God of the *South*—whence seemingly the French *sud* = *south*. Near Harrow is SUD-BURY, the Hill or Barrow of SUD, and the numerous English SUTTONS are thus indirectly "SUT Towns." At STANTON DREW in Devonshire are megalithic monuments ; and the root *stan*—as in *stanch* or *staunch*, *standard*, *staniel* (a kind of hawk), *stang* (a pole or stake), STANLEY, STANHOPE, STAINFORTH, STAINES, and innumerable name-places—evidently does not invariably mean *stone*. SUT was the God of darkness, and it is curious that country people pronounce *soot* "sut." SET, the powerful, is perhaps the root of *stag*. Among the Hittites SET, the "one universal divine being," was known also as SUTEKH, "the omnipotent." [2] SUTEKH seems to have been alternatively spelled ZTAK and was sometimes referred to as JA-ZTAK. He was hailed as "the Great Messenger, the supreme Ensnarer amongst the Gods," and was also entitled the "God of the Heights."

" Who can escape from thy message ?

" Thy word is the Supreme Snare which is stretched towards Heaven and Earth." [3]

SUTEKH or ZTAK is probably the origin of the words *stake* and *stick*, and of *stock*,[4] meaning a *log*—the symbol of *el og*, the Mighty God. In BRITTANY "during the night of the twenty-third of June, it is no exaggeration to say, that from the highlands in the centre to the low-lying coast, or,

---

[1] Borlase, *Ant. of Cornwall*, p. 169.

[2] Anderson (R. E.), *Extinct Civ. of East*, p. 100.

[3] See "The Book of Souls," *The Quest*, iii. p. 723.

[4] Compare STOKE PERO, STOKE POGIS, etc., and numerous STOCKTONS—stockaded towns (?).

in Breton words, from Argoat to Armor, there is not a village, a hamlet, a farm lying solitary in the midst of its fields, no, nor even a sabotier's hut, buried beneath the woodland covert, where the inhabitants do not consecrate the symbolical log, invoking the sacred flame or prostrating themselves around the ashes, according to the particular cult they follow. Through the course of ages the meaning of the various rites has been lost, but forms and gestures remain exactly as they were thousands of years ago."[1]

It would seem that in many languages *stone* or *rock* was entitled by some word denoting the strong, abiding, and immutable Fire of Life. The Semitic words *luz* and *sela*, both meaning *rock*, resolve respectively into "Lord Light" and "Fire Everlasting." In Old Scandinavian *stone* was *hellu*, the "established God everlasting"; in Sclavonic it was *kamen*, the great AMON; and in Arabic it was *hagar*, the "established mighty Fire." The Latin for stone is *saxum*; the Teutonic is *hamarr*.

The great rocks of which AVEBURY Temple was constructed are found scattered in great profusion at sites called PIGGLEDENE and LOCKERIDGE DENE. The Wiltshire Archæological Society have recently acquired and protected from further depredation twenty-two acres at these *denes*, strongholds, or dens. The words LOCKERIDGE and PIGGLE suggest *el ok ur ij*, great God, the aged Fire; and *op ig el*, OP, the Mighty God.

It is on record that Patrick, Bishop of the Hebrides, desired to build a Christian church wherever he found a pagan stone or monolith, and many of the holiest shrines of Christendom now stand on the sites of prehistoric rock sanctuaries. "Perhaps nothing could be more impressive," says Mr Stanley Cook, "than the Sakhra (compare Pyramid SAKKARAH) of the Holy Temple at Jerusalem, where, amid

[1] Le Braz (A.), *The Land of Pardons*, p. 131.

the associations of three thousand years of history, the bare rock, with hollows, cavities, channels, and subterranean caves, preserve the primitive features without any essential change."[1]

In Exodus there is an injunction, " If thou wilt make me an altar of stone, thou shalt not build it of hewn stone : for if thou lift up thy tool upon it, thou hast polluted it," and it is probable that many of the Celtic crosses of Christianity were tooled upon the unhewn rocks of paganism.

White pebbles known as " Godstones " were commonly placed, even within recent times, in Irish graves, and the place-name GODSTONE implies the supreme antiquity of the word *God*.

On one of the peaks of the moors near STUDLAND in DORSETSHIRE is a huge inverted cone of indurated rock known as the AGGLESTONE or HAGGLESTONE. This might no doubt be equally well termed the *Eagle* or *Mighty God Stone*. One of the names of MERODACH or MARDUK was NERIGAL, *i.e. on ur ig al*, " the one Fire, the Mighty God."

One of the largest monoliths in England is that at DRIZZLECOMBE in DEVONSHIRE. The first part of this name resolves into *dur iz el*, the Enduring Light God ; the second part *combe* may have meant a hollow in the hillside, but primarily *comb*—presumably from its rays—meant *ac om be*, " Great Sun Father." This symbolism appears to be the only reasonable explanation for the frequent appearance of combs in prehistoric tombs—particularly in those of the Bronze Age. In the Saxon period an ordinary comb was a well-recognised grave gift, and in later history combs were reserved for burials of ecclesiastical shining lights. A comb was the emblem of ST BLASE[2] : a comb (Icelandic *kambr*) is

---

[1] *Rel. of Ancient Palestine*, p. 20.
[2] Dawson (L. H.), *A Book of the Saints*, p. 24.

equivalent to a crest, and the word *crest* does not differ from
CHRIST. The crest on the Helmet of Salvation—illustrated
ante, p. 19, vol. i.—is the blazing *iris* of CHRIST, the Light
of the World. When the body of St Cuthbert was dis-
interred at Durham Cathedral, there was found upon his
breast a plain, simple, Saxon comb of ivory.[1] It was no doubt
a sign of the cross or of *ak amber*, the Great Sun Father.[2]

Monoliths were sometimes known as *amberics*, and one
of the Cornish monoliths is known as MENAMBER *i.e.* the
Stone AMBER or *Sole* AMBER. AMBRES—whence, no doubt,
the name AMBROSE—was one of the titles of the Celtic
JUPITER; and at Stonehenge is the village of AMBRESBURY.
On the River RAY near BICESTER is AMBROSDEN; in the
Midlands there are several AMBERLEYS; in Sussex is a
River EMBER; and in Devonshire is UMBERLEIGH. The
Wiltshire AMBRESBURY or Mount AMBRE was sometimes
known as AMBLESBURY; it is now called AMESBURY.[3] Referring to the Temple at AVEBURY, STUKELEY observes,
ungrammatically : "all the stones our whole Temple were
called *ambres*, even by our Phœnician founders, but this
[the centre stone] particularly. The Egyptians by that
name still called their obelisks."[4]

At BELSTONE near OKEHAMPTON there is a curious old
cross and a remarkably fine logan rock known as "the bell-
stone." STUKELEY describes many of the barrows at STONE-
HENGE as campaniform or bell-shaped; and the name BEL
enters largely into West of England names such as BEL TOR,
BLACKISTONE, and BLACKATON—the last near PADERBURY
TOP.

The GREEKS symbolised MERCURY, APOLLO, NEPTUNE,

[1] Johnson (W.), *Byeways*, p. 311.
[2] The Saviour God of SIAM—the Land of Sun Fire—is SOMMONACODUM,
i.e. is om mon acodum, the Light of the Sun, the Sole Great Hot Sun (?).
[3] AMES=sunlight—is an English surname.   [4] *Avebury*, p. 24.

and HERCULES under the form of a square stone ; VENUS was worshipped by the Paphians as a white *pyramid*; BACCHUS by the Thebans as a *pillar*; WOTAN by the Scandinavians as a *cube*; and SOMMONACODUM by the SIAMESE as a black pyramid.[1]

A *conical* stone was the emblem of BEL ; and at EMESA the Romans worshipped the Sun under the name of ELEGABALUS in the form of a black, conical stone, which it was believed had fallen from Heaven. The word ELEGABALUS may be resolved into *eleg abalus*, the Mighty God, the obulus or Ball. The *cube*, wherein there is again occurrent the idea *ac ube*, Great Orb, was regarded as an " index or emblem of Truth, always true to itself ";[2] and the cube, as PLUTARCH points out, " is palpably the proper emblem of rest, on account of the security and firmness of the superficies." [3] The sacred stone at MECCA is termed the *kaabeh* ; at KABAH in South America are the ruins of a prehistoric city ;[4] in the WEST INDIES is the Island of CUBA ;[5] and in Cornwall are ST CUBY's or ST KEBY's WELL, and CUBERT TOWN.

The Infinite and Perfect ONE was often represented by a stone globe, and seemingly these orbs were sometimes gilded. There is a place-name GOLDEN BALL on one of the SCILLIES, and at AVEBURY a " GOLDEN BALL HILL." The Celtic *Clachabrath* or rocking-stones were spheres of enormous size, balanced with such nicety that the slightest touch caused them to vibrate. In IONA, the latest asylum of the Caledonian Druids, one of these *Clachabraths* was to be found at the beginning of the nineteenth century, but it was defaced and rolled over into the sea by the ignorant and superstitious natives.

[1] Reade (W.), *Veil of Isis*, p. 97.
[2] Borlase, *Ant. of Cornwall*, p. 108.
[3] *On the Cessation of Oracles.*
[4] *Ruins of Sacred and Historic Lands*, p. 277.
[5] The natives termed the centre of CUBA, CUBAKAN.

In CORNWALL a rocking-stone is called a *logan*. There is a town near CAMBOURNE called ILLOGAN, and the word *logan* seems to imply that the tilting-rock was regarded as *il og an*, "our Lord the Mighty One." This idea is supported by the statement of OSSIAN that the bards used to walk chanting round the rocking-stones, making them move as oracles of the fate of battle.[1]

Allied to *logan* is *kloguin*, the Welsh for *a great stone or rock*.[2] We may resolve *kloguin* into *ak el og Hu in*, the Great God, the mighty, unique Mind.

The most celebrated of all logan rocks is the Cornish one situated on the fortified headland near TREEN, *i.e.* the "one Tower" or "Enduring One."

At the conclusion of the Night of Fires the Breton peasants wind in procession thrice round the dying embers, and exclaim three times : "God pardon the souls of the dead." At the end of the third circuit each man takes a round stone, upon which, with his thumb, he marks the sign of the cross ; these round stones are then laid reverently in concentric circles at the foot of the dying Tan-Tad.[3] In IRELAND, as in SCOTLAND, white pebbles are ceremoniously placed upon or within graves, and in the Apocalypse a white stone is mentioned as the symbol of justification.[4]

Round stones are still known as *cobbles* or *cobylstones*, and the word *cobble* may have arisen from either their circular ("Great-eye") form or from their symbolic meaning. The word *pebble* was in Anglo-Saxon *papol stane*, Father POL or BEL Stone ;[5] and in India the sacred white, round stones are known as *pindas*.[6] Among the objects found in prehistoric tombs are ammonites and the fossils called "heart-urchins."

---

[1] *Chambers's Encyclopædia*, viii. p. 756. [2] Borlase, p. 180.
[3] *Night of Fires*, p. 51. [4] ii. 17.
[5] Compare place-name PEEBLES.
[6] Oldham (C. F.), *The Sun and the Serpent*, p. 176.

At DUNSTABLE a tumulus when uncovered revealed the skeletons of a mother and child entirely surrounded by a circle of fossil sea-urchins, the symbolism of which has already been considered (*ante*, vol. i. p. 318).

On a little island near SKYE is a chapel dedicated to St Columba;[1] and on the altar of this chapel is a round, *blue* stone, said to be invariably moist. This ambrosial, holy stone is bathed occasionally by fishermen desiring favourable winds; solemn oaths are vowed[2] upon it, and it is sometimes applied to the sides of people afflicted with the stitch.[3] The stones of STONEHENGE are traditionally "mystical and of a medicinal virtue." The inner circle are known as *Bluestones*, and the altar itself consists of what JOHN SMITH describes as a "bluish marble interspersed with white, glittering sand."[4] The painstaking STUKELEY says : " I examined it with a microscope. It is a composition of crystals of red, green, and white colours cemented together by Nature's art, with opaque granules of flint or stony matter."[5] This trinitarian composition of the *blue* altar-stone is suggestive of the passage in Exodus, " And they saw the God of Israel : and there was under his feet as it were a paved work of a *sapphire* stone, and as it were the body of heaven in his clearness."[6]

According to Rabbinical tradition, the two stone tables of the Mosaic Law were of sapphire or "heaven blue."[7] These two tables and the two obelisks that are so frequent a feature in ancient sanctuaries were obviously forms of the Twins. One may see not infrequently the single sphere or the two stone balls of perfection surmounting the twin pillars of modern doorways; designs that have doubtless

---

[1] *Columba* or *colombe*, a *dove=ak ol um ba*.
[2] The words *vow* and *foi* are probably identical.
[3] *Chambers's Encyclopædia*, viii. p. 228.
[4] Smith (J.), *Choir Gawr*, p. 60.   [5] Stukeley (W.), *Stonehenge*, p. 5.
[6] xxiv. 10.   [7] *Bible Folk-Lore*, p. 69.

survived by reason of their architectural simplicity and excellence.

In EUROPE, SYRIA, NORTH AFRICA, INDIA, and JAPAN are found monuments consisting of unhewn stones piled into the form known somewhat indiscriminately as a *dolmen* or *cromlech*. Fig. 1076 seemingly represents one of these objects, and the designer of fig. 1077 by the addition of a fourth stroke has constructed a *hieralpha* or sacred A. Attached to fig. 1077 is the crosier or pastoral staff which was used by the Druids and which is still the symbol of a bishop or *episcopus*. I have already suggested that the letter P is in form related to the Shepherd's crook, and it is curious that the shape of the Greek letter *pi* (π) is very similar to that of a cromlech.[1]

1076   1077

From the emblems herewith it would appear that the cromlech was identified with PA, the All-Father. The designer has formed the summit of fig. 1079 like a *bow*, and the general form of all these emblems and the A emblems on p. 72, vol. i., is that of A and T, the first and the last letters of the Hebrew alphabet.

The syllables *a* and *tau* occur significantly in various directions. The words *auteur* and *author* may be compared with *athir*, the Celtic for *father*, and with *ether*, the All-Per-

---

[1] The word *cromlech*, which in France is applied to stone circles, is said to be composed of the Celtic *crom* (crooked) and *lech* (a stone); but, fundamentally, *crom*, as in CROMWELL and in the hill-name TREN CROM, is *ak ur om*, the Great Sun-Fire. Like *cam* and *zigzag*, *crom* probably came to denote *crooked* because of the crooked jags of the lightning flash. Whether this supposition be sound or otherwise it is obvious that "crooked stone" is as senseless an appellation for a stone circle as it is a flat-topped geometrical monument.

vading and All-Embracing. LAYARD alludes to the Assyrian ASHUR as ATHUR; and in EGYPT the cult of HATHOR was so widely spread that her name was used as a generic term for goddess.[1] HATHOR or ISIS was conceived usually as One, but sometimes there were said to be Seven HATHORS—an allusion evidently to the Seven Stars of the Great Bear or ARTHUR. In fig. 316, p. 116, vol. i. the A-*tau* was attached to the Bear, and this symbol of the First and Last is presumably the root of the words *eternitas, eternal,* and *eternity.* The Latin for *author* is *auctor,* i.e. *actor,* the Great Tor, the Eternal Author of the

1078   1079   1080

Universe. *Actor* is the Greek for a chief and is cognate with HECTOR, the "great bulwark" at the Siege of Troy. The bowl of a volcano is named its *crater* or *ak ur ator,* and the *cra-* may here be equated with *akra,* the Greek for *hill-top.* In Sanscrit *kr* means "to make," and this syllable is no doubt the root of our *creator,* i.e. a *maker.*

One of the most famous of the EXMOOR Tors is named HAY TOR, *i.e.* HATHOR (?).

In JAPAN one meets with sacred monuments known as *torii,* which in form are similar to A and T conjoined, and the word *torii* may perhaps be restored to *atorii.* "Every traveller in Japan," says a modern writer, "is acquainted

[1] Tiele (C. P.), *Religious Systems of the World,* p. 6.

with the *torii*, or sacred gateway, which so frequently attracts the eye. It is always constructed (whatever the materials used) in the same way. It has two upstanding columns, or posts, slightly inclined inwards towards each other, and across them a horizontal beam with widely-projecting ends, and below this another beam, which has its ends mitred into the columns. This sacred entrance is found across the path in Japan wherever it approaches a spot of hallowed ground. It is, however, unlike the sacred portals of other lands, from the circumstance that it does not necessarily indicate the close proximity of a temple. It is to be found over hill and

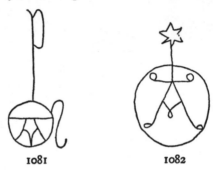

1081　　　　　　　1082

dale, at the entrance to a valley, placed high up along a mountain path, even in the deep recesses of the immemorial woods ; sometimes even on the edge of the rice-fields, at others on the shore of a lake. If one passes beneath it and follows the path of which it is the portal, one is almost sure sooner or later to come to a temple, or more often a simple shrine. In the latter one will find nothing ; that is the strangeness and mystery which strikes all who have come across these simple shrines. But, all the same, there is a reason for its being placed there. Close by there will be some example of Nature's wildness or loveliness—a grove of magnificent and stately trees, some exquisite view, a twisted and ancient pine-tree (to the Japanese an emblem of length of days), or perhaps an exquisite pool. The shrines are not there for idols, but to consecrate the beauty surrounding them.

" Sometimes, indeed, one may look in vain for anything suggestive of a reason for the presence of the shrine. It may have been placed where it is merely because of the exquisite and impressive solicitude of its environment. Often the path beneath the *torii* leads merely to some beauty spot, and ends in something which to the Japanese heart is more sacred than either shrine or temple." [1]

Some such similar spirit to this seems to have animated the cromlech builders of prehistoric Britain. That these were a maritime and colonising people may be inferred from the fact that with rare exceptions cromlechs are found *only along the coasts*.[2] In ENGLAND they are confined almost entirely to CORNWALL and DEVON ; in WEST WALES they are numerous ; in SCOTLAND they are rare ; in IRELAND they are abundant. In the county of SLIGO [3]—SIL, the mighty O ?—there are no less than one hundred and sixty-three.

That *cromlechs* or *cromlehs* were symbols of the fiery A or AU is sometimes suggested by their site names. On the Cornish hill called CARN LEHAU there is a well-known cromlech, and LEHAU may be resolved into " everlasting HAU or AU." Similarly the cromlech in MONKTON FIELD near AVEBURY enables us to resolve MONKTON into MON-ACTON. One of the greatest of the rocks at CARNAC is termed MENEC ; there is a monument on the Cornish hill named CARN MENELEZ [4]—either Sole Lord Light or Stone of the Lord of Light.

---

[1] Clive Holland, *Things seen in Japan*, pp. 197–199.

[2] Wm. Wright, *The Prehistoric and Early Historic Inhabitants of England*, p. 4.

[3] In Sligo are the GAMPH or OX Mountains. GAMPH=*ag am fe*, the Mighty Sun-Fire (?).

[4] In Abyssinia MENELIK is a royal name.

One of the most famous of the Cornish cromlechs is that at ZENNOR—a name understood to have meant "sacred land," but which, according to my roots, originally meant Sacred Fire. In Devonshire cromlechs are often termed *Shilstones*,[1] and one of the DEVONSHIRE hills is named SHELL TOP. Shells were frequently placed within primitive graves; yellow-robed VISHNU is generally represented holding a shell and a circular disc; in POLYNESIA the Chiefs wear upon their breasts as the peculiar badge of royalty a piece of *clam*-shell cut into a circular disc,[2] and the word *shell* points to the conclusion that the fan-like flutings of the shell were responsible for its symbols of *ish el*, the "Light God." The extending rays of the *scallop* or *escallop* no doubt identified it with ST JAMES, the "ever-existent Sunlight," and the word *escallop* may be resolved into *es ak ol op*, the light of great lord the Eye. In the British Museum there are several exquisite Greek statuettes of APHRODITE, the Goddess of Love, winged with, protected by, or emerging from, twin scallop-shells, and in the emblem herewith a shell is associated with the rod, pole, staff or spike of the Holy ONE. It may thus perhaps be assumed that the English SHELL TOP and "Shilstone" bore originally the sense of *ish el*, the Light of God. The Shell emblems here illustrated evidently had that holy significance.

One of the most famous of the Israelitish stone-shrines was the so-called "House of God"[3] at SHILOH, and in Genesis the word *Shiloh* is used in the sense of an expected Messiah. "The sceptre shall not depart from Judah, nor a lawgiver from between his feet, until SHILOH come; and unto him shall the gathering of the people be."[4] In ISAIAH a variant of the same word occurs in the passage, "Forasmuch

---

[1] Baring-Gould, *Devon*, p. 53.
[2] D. Rannie, *My Adventures among South Sea Cannibals*, frontispiece.
[3] Judges xviii. 31.   [4] xlix. 10.

as this people refuseth the waters of Shiloah that go softly
. . . he shall pass through Judah . . . and the stretching
out of his wings shall fill the breadth of thy land, O
Immanuel." [1] A variant of the same word is Siloah, where
at one time there was a famous *tower*.

The Breton words for *altar* are *dolmen* and *aoter*, and the
Breton for *author* (French *auteur*) is *penn abek*. In our
word *altar* is seemingly retained the original symbolism of
el tur, the Enduring God.

In the Old Testament there are numerous allusions to
altars of twelve stones, and one of the wonders of Wales is

1083   1084   1085

a colossal rock table, supported originally by eleven upright
pillars. The twelve precious stones set in the breastplate of
the Jewish High Priest are termed *logeion* by Philo. They
were arranged in four rows to distinguish the four seasons of
the year, and were said to be a symbol " of that *Reason*
which holds together and regulates the Universe." Josephus
calls these twelve *logeion* Essene [2]—a word which resolves into
the " One Essence " or " One Light."

On reference to the Logos emblem on p. 66 it will be
noted that surmounting the Serpent there are *thirty* circles.
The Grand circle of Stonehenge consisted of *thirty* upright
pillars, and the two circles within the egg enfolded by the
Avebury Serpent consisted each of an inner ring of twelve

<hr />

[1] viii. 6, 8.   [2] *The Canon*, p. 169.

stones and an outer circle of *thirty*. Of an Eastern Sanctuary
Pausanias records: "There stood next the Statue square
stones *thirty* in number; the Pharians worship them, calling
each by the name of some divinity; but more anciently, and
afterwards among the Greeks, white stones received honours
as symbols of the Gods."[1]

There are *thirty* days in a month; the *thirty* joints in the
body of the scarabæus were believed to correspond with the
transit of the Sun through one sign of the Zodiac;[2] and
according to Zoroastrian theosophy, there were *thirty*
presiding *Izeds*.

By the Druids *thirty* years were regarded as an age or
generation.[3] *Thirty* was the number of the Grand nobles of
Mexico,[4] and *thirty* was the number of the Gnostic Æons.
These Æons or great Powers were arranged in fifteen pairs,
"or the sacred number Five three times repeated,"[5] and
this is precisely the form of the thirty circles at the summit
of fig. 908 (p. 66). The pillars of the Parthenon at Athens
(the "Maiden's Chamber"), built in honour of Athenæ,
number eight in one direction and *thirty*, *i.e.* fifteen pairs, in
the other.[6]

---

[1] *Achaica*, xxii. 3.   [2] *Ruins of Sacred and Histor. Lands*, p. 200.
[3] Borlase, *Ant. of Cornwall*, p. 93.   [4] *Atlantis*, p. 350.
[5] *The Gnostics*, p. 263. King translates their names as "Depth, Silence,
Mind, Truth, Reason, Life, Man, Church, Comforter, Faith, Fatherly, Hope,
Motherly, Charity, Eternal, Intelligence, Light, Beatitude, Eucharistic,
Wisdom, Profundity, Mixture, Unfading, Union, Self-born, Temperance,
Only-Begotten, Unity, Immovable, Pleasure."
[6] The following lines sum up some curious coincidences at Salisbury
Cathedral:

"As many days as in one year there be,
So many windows in this church you see.
As many marble pillars here appear
As there are hours through the fleeting year.
As many gates as moons one here does view;
Strange tale to tell, yet not more strange than true."
(Quoted in *Wiltshire*, F. R. Heath, p. 250.)

At CLASSERNISS in the Island of LEWIS there is a circular stone temple consisting of twelve equidistant obelisks. The four cardinal points of the compass are marked by lines of obelisks running out from the circle, and in the pole or centre of this Zodiac is a stone thirteen feet high " of the perfect shape of a ship's rudder."[1] This Rudder-stone doubtless symbolised the Guide, Steersman, or Pilot of the Universe— the Point within the circle of Perfection or Infinity. " The beginning of Wisdom," says an Egyptian papyrus, " is the cry of AMON, the rudder of (Truth)."[2]

The name CLASSERNISS seemingly contains the memory of " ac el ASSUR, the one Light." Among the Israelites the greatest national celebrations were held at the stone sanctuary of GILGAL. In Hebrew *gilgal* means also a circle, and the word was seemingly *ag il ag al*, the Mighty God, the Mighty God. In BRITTANY the term *galgal* is applied to a certain variety of stone monument.[3]

The most celebrated of all circular stone temples is STONEHENGE, which is said to be somewhat similar to one in ARABIA, at a place called KASEEM (the Great Sunlight ?).

In HOMER's time—

" On rough hewn stones, within the sacred cirque
Convok'd, the Hoary Sages sat,"[4]

and that British " cirques " were similarly once Law Courts is evident from their traditional name in certain districts of " Doom stones." As late as the fourteenth century, stone circles were also used in Europe for coronation functions.[5] According to BORLASE, the King stood at the centre stone

---

[1] W. Reade, *Veil of Isis*.
[2] Renouf, *Hibbert Lectures*, p. 228.
[3] LE ROUZIC, p. 23.
[4] *Iliad*, xviii. ver. 504.
[5] Borlase, *Ant. of Cornwall*.

known as the *ambre*, and his nobles, *peers*, or *barons*, ranged themselves around him, each standing at his representative stone or pillar. It is still customary for British monarchs to be crowned over the piece of sacred rock now under the Coronation Chair at Westminster Abbey. This ancient stone, brought from the Hill of SCONE in SCOTLAND, was probably a symbol of *se kone*, the Fiery *Cone* or *Great One*.

The British Bards refer to a mystical structure—believed to have been STONEHENGE—as " The Great Stone Fence," the " Circle of the World," and the " Stone Cell of the Sacred Fire." [1]   STONEHENGE was also known as CAER SIDI, *i.e.* the Seat or Fort of SIDI. The author of *The Canon* says that SIDI was SATURN, from whom we derive *Saturday*, the ancient Sabbath or Day of Rest. The Saxons called it *Seaterdag*, or the day of the *Seater* or *Sitter*, *i.e.* the day upon which the Great Workman sat Himself down, as represented in figs. 800 and 925 (*ante*, pp. 4 and 78).

The reign of SATURN was proverbially the Golden Age, whence the celebration of the *Saturnalia* ; and SATURN [2] is identical with CRONUS=*Time*, whence *chronometer*. The supposed reference to STONEHENGE by DIODORUS SICULUS mentions it as a Temple of APOLLO, a *temenos* or enclosed circle. This word *temenos* must be allied to *tommen*, the Welsh for *barrow*, and, as has already been suggested, *tem* or *tom* is the root of *temps* and *time*. *Tommen* may thus be resolved into Sole TIME or Stone TIME, and *temenos* into the light of sole, stable, and abiding TIME. The name KRONOS yields *ak ur on os*, the Great Fire, the One Light ; and STONE- HENGE, whence were probably issued the edicts for sowing and all other seasonal functions, served thus as a gigantic Timekeeper, Chronometer, or Clock. The word *clock*

---

[1] Anon., *The Canon*, p. 230.

[2] The name SATURN was perhaps SET or SUT *ur en*, the Fiery One. The syllable SET may be resolved into IS-ET, *Light* and *Heat*.

(French *cloche*) means a Bell, and in the days before clocks were invented the time was tolled by a Bell.[1]

In Egypt KRONOS was named KEB,[2] the "Great Orb," and this everlasting KEB is evidently the root of *kebla*,[3] meaning a stone circle. In *septum*, the Latin term for a circle of stones, is again occurrent the idea *is ep tum*, the light of the Eye or Orb, *Tum* or TIME, the resplendent Sun. All *tempes* or *Tem*ples may indeed be described as originally Time Fathers, Time Tellers, Time Keepers, or Time Bells. TIME, the Father of *Truth*, has already been identified with Father THAMES, and the source of the River THAMES is at a spot named TREWSBURY. KRONOS, according to the author of *The Great Dionysiac Myth*, is equivalent to "KARNOS, KARNAIOS, KARNAIVIS, the horned God ; Assyrian KARNU ; Hebrew KEREN, horn ; Hellenic KRONOS or KARNOS."[4] The Temple of KARNAK in Egypt and the prehistoric Stone rows at CARNAC in Brittany were probably alike erected to the honour of KARN Ac, the Great Karn. *Cairn* or *carn* is a generic term for a barrow or heap of stones, and in Cornwall CARN—as in CARN BREA,[5] CARN GALVA,[6] etc.—means a hill. The word may be resolved primarily into *ak ar en*, the Great one Fire, and *caer*, meaning *fortress*, *seat*, into *ak ar*, the Great Fire.

CAER SIDI, which resolves into CAER *Si di*, the "Seat of Resplendent Fire," figures in legend not only as STONE-HENGE but also as the magic Land of Everlasting Summer. Thus, in the Poems of the Welsh Taliessin[7] :—

---

[1] Close to the Temple at AVEBURY is CLACK HILL, and in Scotland is CLACKMANNAN.

[2] Budge (W.), *Legends of the Gods*, p. 215.

[3] Stukeley (W.), *Abury*, p. 5.

[4] ii. 127, 129.

[5] Pronounced BRAY, *Father A* (?).

[6] AG AL VA= *Mighty Lord of Life* (?).

[7] Poem XIV.

" Perfect is my chair in Caer Sidi,
Plague and age hurt him not who's in it.

. . . . . .

About its points are oceans' streams,
And the abundant well above it,
Sweeter than white wine the drink in it."

In some localities stone circles are known as King
Arthur's Tables, and the Round Table of Slav Fairy-Tale
may similarly be equated with the Perfect Chair in CAER
SIDI. CAER SIDI seems also to have carried many correlative meanings, among others "Revolving Castle,"
"Four-cornered Castle," "Castle of Revelry," "Kingly
Castle," "Glass Castle," and "Castle of Riches."[1] This
whirling Mystery — sometimes described as the Sacred
Chalice or the Holy Grail—is described as turning with
greater speed than the swiftest wind, and its walls are said
to have been lined by archers who shot so vigorously that
no armour could withstand their winning and irresistible
shafts. Sir JOHN RHYS compares the word *sidi* with *sidyll*,
" a spinning-wheel." Fable relates that HERCULES laboured
at a spinning-wheel or *omphalos*, and the word *om phallus*
suggests that the resistless shafts of CAER SIDI were the
arrows of enkindling light, the spokes or spikes of the
ZODIAC, AXIS, or ELIXIR,[2] the spires, spears or spores of
the Mighty HUEEL.[3]

In CORNWALL Stone circles used to be known as *dawns
men*—a term explained by BORLASE to mean "dance stones."
It is known that on certain festival days the ancient Britons
dyed themselves blue, and that, together with their wives
and children, they danced *in circles*, bowing to the altar.

Sacred circular-dancing called *Orchesis* is frequently

[1] Squire, *Celtic Mythology and Legend*, pp. 366, 367.
[2] The word ELIXIR is from *el iksir*, Arabian for "Stone of Philosophy."
[3] Compare surnames WEALE, WHEELER.

mentioned by the early Fathers of Christianity, and there was also a ceremony of dance and song called *Chorostasia*. In the church at Antioch CHRYSOSTOM (*c.* 347–407) relates that there was a sacred all-night festival, a *Chorostasia* in imitation of the Angelic Dance and ceaseless hymnody of the Creator.[1] "Above, the angelic hosts sing hymns of praise ; below, in the churches, men in-choired faithfully mimic them with the very same praise service. Above, the Seraphim chant forth the hymn Trisagion ; below, the mortal crowd re-echo it above. Of those in Heaven and those upon the earth a unison is made — one general assembly, one single service of thanksgiving, one single transport of rejoicing, one joyous *dance*."

The name *carole*[2] was given by the Troubadours to a *dance* or *ballet* in which the performers moved slowly in a circle, singing as they went,[3] and there is no doubt that the Christian *Choir*, *Carol*, and *Chorale*, are all adapted survivals of pre-Christian rites. Among the Mexicans and Peruvians the sacred song-dance was brought to an extraordinary state of perfection. At Great Festivals two choral dances and hymns were rendered to the Sun, each strophe of which ended with the cry of *Hailly !* Referring to the all-night festival of the *Therapeutæ*, Philo says : "This is how they keep it. They all stand up in a body, and in the middle of the banqueting-place they first form two *Choroi*, one of men and the other of women, and a leader and conductor is chosen for each, the one whose reputation is greatest for a knowledge of music. They then chant hymns composed in God's honour in many metres and melodies, sometimes singing together, sometimes one *Choros*, beating the measure with their hands for the antiphonal chanting of

---

[1] See "The Sacred Dance of Jesus," G. R. S. Mead, *The Quest*, ii. p. 56.
[2] Cornish people pronounce it KUR-R-RL.
[3] *Dancing*, Lilly Grove, p. 131.

the other, now dancing to the measure and now inspiring it, at times dancing in procession, at times set-dances, and then circle-dances, right and left."[1]

Close to the great amphitheatre of STONEHENGE are the villages of ORCHESTON ST GEORGE and ORCHESTON ST MARY —possibly at one time the *tons* or *towns* of the performers of the pious *orgies*, the headquarters of the two *Choirs* or *Choroi* that officiated at STONEHENGE Circle. The name ORCHESTON, or town of *Orchesis*, might be rendered ORCHESTRA's TOWN ; the word *orchestra* being allied to *orchesmai*, "I dance." The suffixes ST MARY and ST GEORGE suggest that the women-singers represented MARY, the Queen of the May, and the men GEORGE, the solar Husbandman, the vital Urge.[2]

Dancing formed part of the initiation ceremonies of the ancient Mysteries, and to such a degree of refinement was it carried that the theologies of certain sects were said to be more clearly expressed by gesticulations than by the words of a professed rhetorician. The Hindoos paid their devotions to the Sun by a dance imitative of his motions, and this, their only act of worship, was performed every morning and evening.

In one of the choral odes of SOPHOCLES, PAN is addressed by the title of *Author and Director of the Dances of the Gods* ; by the Gnostics PAN was represented seated, playing upon his pipes, in the centre of the Zodiac, and in the Orphic Hymns PAN is described as *Zeus, the mover of all things*, the *Pervader of Sky and Sea*.[3] In one of the Hymns to APOLLO the Sun-God's parents are said to be " delighted to perceive the mighty *Mind*, their dear Son, thus sporting among the Gods."[4]

---

[1] Cf. *The Sacred Dance of Jesus*.
[2] The word *orchis* in Greek means *testicle*. The "slang" *bollux* is evidently the twin POLLUX. *Castrate* is possibly cognate with CASTOR.
[3] Payne-Knight, pp. 138, 139.
[4] *Ibid.*

The dances known as *heys, reels,* and *jigs* were originally, without doubt, exercises in honour of HEY, the Immutable A ; *ureel,* the Fire Lord ; or *jig,* the Ever-Existent Mighty One. All these, and doubtless many others such as the *chopine,* were *hops* or *hoppings* in honour of CHEOP PAN.

Near CHIPPING NORTON in Gloucestershire, at a site named ROWLDRICH, are the remains of a famous stone circle.[1] *Rhol,* the Celtic for a wheel or circle, may be equated with *reel,* and the name ROWLDRICH will thus resolve into the wheel of *dur ich,* the Enduring *aitch,* the Steadfast, immutable, aged One. Near DURHAM is a CHOPWELL ; at the summit of CHIPPING HILL in ESSEX are the remains of a double-ditched camp ; and on SHAP FELL[2] in WESTMORE-LAND is a Druidic circle, or *chapel* as the Scotch term it.[3]

It is probable that *sing, song,* and *sung* have an intimate relation with *Sun,* and that the words *hymn, chant,* and *pæan* are similarly connected. The word *chorus,* allied to *choros,* meaning in Greek a band of dancers and singers, appears to be resolvable into *ac horus,* the Great HORUS. The French for *chorus* is *chœur,* pronounced like *cœur,* a heart ; the Greek for the " feathered frenzy with an angel's throat," which we English people call a *lark* or *laverock,* is *koros* ; and the French for *lark* is *alouette,* a word seemingly allied to *louer = praise.* The personal application of the symbolic praising Birds herewith is probably expressed in Quarles's lines :—

> " Rouse thee, my soul, and drain thee from the dregs
> Of vulgar thoughts ; screw up the heightened pegs
> Of thy sublime Theorbo *four* notes higher
> And high'r yet, that so the shrill-mouthed choir
> Of swift-winged seraphims may come and join
> And make the concert more than half divine."

---

[1] See Stukeley, *Abury.*
[2] The *Fell* of Shap Fell is seemingly the same word as *ophel,* the Hebrew for *hill.*   [3] Borlase, *Cornwall,* p. 193.

The words *chorus*, *choros*, and *koros* must be allied to *Kuros* or CYRUS, meaning the Sun.[1] In Greek *choiros* means a *pig*; *choiras* means *rock*; and *guros*—whence *gyre*, a circular course —means *ring* or *circle*. The root *gor* appears in this latter sense in the Welsh word GORSEDD, meaning a mound of earth and a circle of standing stones. In Cornish *gawr* meant *gigantic*, and *gorsedd* may alternatively be understood as either *Great Seat* or a *Circular Sitting*. Even to-day the proceedings of the Welsh Eisteddfod are partly conducted in *gorsedd* form, of which the rule is that it be held in a conspicuous place " face to face with the Sun and eye of Light."[2]

1086   1087   1088

There is no power to hold a *gorsedd* under cover or at night, but only where and as long as the Sun is visible in the Heavens. Sir JOHN RHYS observes : " In the absence of documentary evidence bearing on the history of the *gorsedd*, we have to judge of it as we find it, and it is remarkable that everything connected with it seems to suggest that it is but a continuation of a court of which the Celtic Zeus was originally regarded as the spiritual president : witness the circle of stones, the importance attached to the sun and the eye of light, and also the nature of the prayer pronounced by the officiating ' Druid.' "[3]

STONEHENGE was known as the " Gorsedd of Salisbury,"

[1] " The Persians say that CYRUS (Kuros) means the Sun," *Hesychius.* *Cf.* Payne-Knight, p. 154.
[2] Rhys (J.), *Hibbert Lectures*, p. 209.   [3] *Ibid.*

and *gor*, meaning a *circle*, is manifest in many directions. It is recognisable in GORHAMBURY, where the ruins of a pre-historic amphitheatre yet remain upon the hill by St Michael's Church. *Gaur* is again recognisable in *marguerite*, the gold-eyed, white-spoked *day's eye*; and the Sun-wheel flowers of the *artichoke* [1] are similarly responsible for its Italian name *girasol*—from the Latin *sol*, the Sun, and *gyrus*, a circle. The Cornish for *daisy* was *egr*, the "great Fire or Light," and the English of MARGUERITE is MARGARET or PEGGY. *Peggy*, *i.e.* Mighty Eye, is the Persian for "a pearl" or "child of light"; [2] in ENGLAND pearls used to be known as *margarets*,

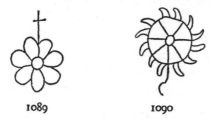

1089   1090

and the word *pearl* or *perle* resolves into *per le*, the Father Everlasting.

There is a PORGUARNON in Cornwall "which is enclosed by hills, giving the place somewhat the appearance of an amphitheatre; hence its name." [3] In CORNWALL are also several so-called *plan an guares*, *i.e.* "places of play" or "amphitheatre plains." On one of these near PERRAN-ZABULOE is the locally-known Perran [4] Round, a remarkable amphitheatre one hundred and thirty feet in diameter, with the traces of *seven* tiers of seats. Around this centre have been discovered "countless human remains," and the spot

[1] "The Light, the resplendent, Existent Great One."
[2] Swan (H.), *Christian Names*, p. 76.
[3] Blight (J. T.), *A Week at Land's End*, p. 62.
[4] PERUN. Compare Cornish MENPERHEN, where is "a large pyramidal stone twenty feet high, probably an ancient idol."—Borlase, p. 162.

"was clearly resorted to as a burial-ground of special sanctity."[1]

The word *gore*—primarily the Mighty Fire—was also applied to things triangular, and tailors now use this word to signify a three-cornered piece of material. By felicitous coincidence the giant *gore* of the Albert Hall stands upon Kensington Gore, a site believed to have been so named because it was once a triangular patch of Kensington Parish.

STONEHENGE was known traditionally as CHOIR GAUR, a term which may have meant *gigantic choir* or—deriving *choir* from Greek *choiras*, rock—the "Rock Circle."

At STONEHENGE there is an OGBURY, *i.e.* the Barrow of OG, and near AVEBURY there is an OG Valley, an OGBOURNE, and a River OG. The Israelites were seriously embarrassed by a memorable King OG, whose name is interpreted to mean "long necked," "gigantic," and "he who goes in a circle."[2] The GOG and MAGOG of London and Cornish tradition were once probably the "Mighty of Mighties," and MA or Mother "Mighty of Mighties": in Cambridgeshire are the GOGMAGOG Hills. The Egyptians worshipped an OGDOAD or Company of Eight original Gods who were called the Fathers and Mothers of the world, and the root OG is obviously at the base of *okto*, the Greek for *eight*. The Sanscrit word for *eight* is *ashtau*,[3] and the King OG of the Old Testament "dwelt at ASHTAROTH" (Joshua xii. 4). At Avebury is ASHBURY, and at Stonehenge ASHLEY.

The Mayas conceived Heaven to be in the form of an *Eight*-spoked wheel, and this Excellent Wheel of Good LAW is a revered symbol in INDIA, in CHINA, and in JAPAN. Among the Japanese it is known as *rimbo*, a word which may be resolved into *urim bo*, the "Father of Lights," or into *ur im bo*, "Fire Sun Father."

---

[1] Salmon (A.), *Cornwall*, p. 215.   [2] *Bible Folk-Lore*, p. 73.
[3] In Hebrew *eshta* means *fire*.

The Chinese divided their year into *Eight* seasons, the cardinal points being SING, FANG, HEU, and MAOU, and the original idea of the OGDOAD or Eight forms of the Lord of Time would appear to have been the seven planets circling around the Polar Axis. According to Dr Churchward, the division of the Zodiac into twelve points was a comparatively late conception.[1]

The sacrosanctity of Mount FUJI is probably due partly to the fact that it has a flattened top (a "truncated cone"), which causes it not only to resemble A, the primal peak,

1091

but also the Aleph-Tau or Ataw of the Eternal. The crater of FUJI is, moreover, *eight*-sided, and its alternative name "HORAISAN" may in all probability be equated with HORIZON, defined by SKEAT as meaning "the bounding or limiting circle." The Greek *Orizon* may be resolved into *or is zone*, the "Wheel of Golden Light," and the English, French, and Latin "HORIZON" suggests the Wheel of HORUS, a God who was frequently addressed as "HORUS of the Horizon."[2] "HU," says Dr Churchward, "was also a name of HORUS, as we find from the eightieth chapter of the *Ritual*. "I have seized upon HU from the place in which

---

[1] *Signs and Symbols of Primordial Man*, pp. 208, 327.
[2] Renouf, *Hibbert Lectures*, p. 229.

I found Him " ; also " I am the Craftsman who lighteneth the darkness, and I come to dissipate the darkness that light should be." [1]

In Sanscrit the word *ghar* means *diffusion or shedding of light*, also *bright and to make bright* ; and *ghrina* means *heat of the Sun*.[2] In *gorsedd* and CHOIR *Gaur*, as also in *gorgeous*, we have no doubt this same root ; and there is little doubt that *Caer Sidi* or STONEHENGE was, as the name implies, a seat or stronghold of the Resplendent Fire.

The name STONEHENGE is assumed to mean " the hanging stones," but the word *henge* is more probably equivalent to our modern *hinge*.

Among the ancients it would seem to have been a favourite idea to found a hinge or culture centre. Peruvian legends tell how the offspring of the Sun and Moon, two divine beings named MANCO CAPAC and MAMA OGLLO, descended from Heaven near Lake TITICACA. They had received commands from their Parent to traverse the country till they came to a spot where a golden *wedge* they possessed should sink into the ground, and at this place to form a culture centre. The *wedge* disappeared at CUZCO, which Garcilasso et Inca de la Vega (the most important of the ancient chroniclers of Peru) interprets as meaning " navel," or, in twentieth-century idiom, " Hub of the Universe." [3]

CAERLEON, the seat of King Arthur, where are the ruins of a vast amphitheatre, was alternatively known as CARDUEL or CARDOIL, and as *cardo* is the Latin for *hinge* and *kardia* the Greek for *heart*, the name CARDUEL may be resolved into the " Heart, Core, or Hinge of God."

At DORDOGNE in FRANCE—a district that has provided a rich harvest of prehistoric human remains—is PETROCORII,

---

[1] *Signs and Symbols of Primordial Man,* p. 381.
[2] Müller (M.), *Science of Language,* ii. 387, 388, 400.
[3] *Mythologies of Ancient Mexico and Peru,* Lewis Spence, p. 47.

again, seemingly, the " Rock *Core*, or Heart." The modern name PERIGORD is supposed to be a " corruption" of the more ancient PETROCORII, but it appears to be quite a distinct word—PERI, as in *peri*scope, meaning here, there, and everywhere, and GORD being phonetically GAUR.

The first two syllables of CUZCO, the City of the Golden Wedge, resolve into *ac uz*, the Mighty Light. The German word for wedge is *gehre*, and in Anglo-Saxon *gar* meant dart or spear-point. The Greek for *thorn* is *akis*, and for a sunbeam *aktis*, " the great resplendent light." In the eight-spoked wheel herewith the spikes, spokes, spears, spores, or spars are designed like flames or thorns. Among

1092

the Breton peasantry the sacred wheel is even yet venerated, and, like their crosses, is decorated with tinkling bells.[1]

The MAMA OGLLO of Peru, the " Mighty Mother Everlasting," may be considered in connection with OGMIUS, a British name for HERCULES,[2] the Spinner. Among the Druids OGMIUS, whom RHYS equates with the Greek LOGOS,[3] was represented as an old man followed by a multitude, whom he led by slender and almost invisible golden chains fastened from his lips to their ears. He was regarded as the " Power of Eloquence," and might be termed the *coax*.

The Egyptians represented the Creator under the name

[1] Johnson (W.), *Byeways in British Archæology*, p. 202.
[2] HUR-AC-UL-ES, the " Immutable Fire, the Great Lord of Light."
[3] *Hibbert Lectures*, p. 16.

KHNUMU—*ak en um Hu*, the "Great One, the Sun Hu"—
as a Potter making man upon a wheel.[1] The French for
a potter's wheel is *tour*, a word which we use to mean
circular journey; and all stone circles probably materialised
the idea of the Spinning, Potter's, or *Pater's* Wheel, the
Tour de Force.

In PERU, where the worship of the Sun lingered until
the Spaniards reached those hapless shores, the consecrated
virgins of the Temples wore crowns of sunflowers made of
pure gold, and during worship they carried the same precious
blossoms in their hands. In EUROPE JESHU was regarded

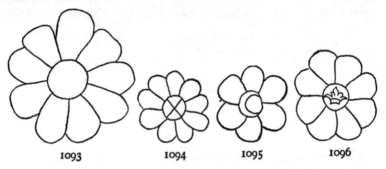

1093   1094   1095   1096

as the Marguerite, the Marigold or Goldflower of the
World, and he is thus referred to by early Christian writers,
e.g. "The queen of all the maidens gave birth to the
Creator and Consoler of mankind when *the Goldflower* came
into this world and received a human body from St Mary,
the spotless virgin."[2]

The *girasole* herewith is figured like the chrysanthemum
of JAPAN, the Land of the Rising Sun. In the centre of
fig. 1094 is the cross of *Lux*, in fig. 1095 is the Crescent
Moon, and in fig. 1096 there appears a Crown of Flame.

From its habit of turning sunwards the Sunflower was

---

[1] Petrie, *Religion of Ancient Egypt*, p. 32.

[2] *Blickling Homilies*, A.D. 979, quoted in *The Romance of Symbolism*,
S. Heath, p. 158.

regarded as the Symbol of Constancy, and sufficient evidence has perhaps already been adduced to confirm the suggestion that Stone circles or *Gorsedds* were symbolic of the Immutable Sun. The King or " Son of the Sun" standing at the *ambre* or central pillar typified the Sun-God, and the surrounding Nobles represented the variously conceived supporters of the Lord of Time. The definite number of stones which constituted a *gorsedd* may be equated, if twelve, with the twelve months; if nineteen—and this peculiar number constituting " Nineteen Maidens" is very usual— with the twelve months *plus* the seven days; if thirty, with the thirty days of the month. The mystic number thirty-three—noted *ante*, p. 142, vol. i.—in all probability stood for Thirty *plus* the Supreme Trinity.

The number of stones in the outer circle of STONE-HENGE is sixty—twelve times five; in the inner circle the number is thirty; and in the inmost circle of " Blue Stones" it is nineteen. DIODORUS relates: " They say, moreover, that APOLLO once in nineteen years comes into the Island, in which space of time the stars perform their courses and return to the same points, and therefore the Greeks call the revolutions of nineteen years the Great Year." [1] Three different qualities of stone were used in the building of STONEHENGE, some of which are foreign to the neighbour-hood and must have been dragged at incalculable labour from afar.[2] The general form of the Temple, which is orientated to the midsummer sunrise, is that of a horseshoe or oval enclosed within a circle, and in all probability the quality, as well as the form and number of the various stones, was symbolic. The only unhewn rock within the purlieu is that known as the " Hele" or " Sun Stone," and

[1] Quoted in *England's Riviera*, J. H. Stone, p. 125.
[2] Variously assumed to have been Brittany, Avebury, Pembroke, Ireland, and " the remotest parts of Africa."

it has been pointed out by BARCLAY that the five main trilithons are like the five fingers on an extended hand—graduated in height. They thus resemble a gigantic glove, comb, saw, or *broccus*, "facing the midsummer sunrise as if waiting to greet the Sun." [1]

Dr Frazer, who has noted the frequency in ancient times of octennial tenures of the kingship, observes that in EGYPT "the King who embodied the Sun-god seems to have solemnly walked round the walls of a temple for the sake of helping the Sun on his way." [2] This function, as also the carolling and dancing, was doubtless an imitation of the Sun in its course, and is additional evidence that much of the ceremonial of kingship was based upon its analogy with the Solar System.

It has frequently been pointed out that the Three Feathers of the Prince of Wales and the head-dress of Three Feathers, which are *de rigueur* at Royal Drawing-rooms, are the direct descendants of the Three Rays, and there is little doubt that they once typified the Three Sun-beams, Good Thought, Good Deed, Good Word. In EGYPT an ostrich feather symbolised MAAT, the Goddess of Truth, [3] who is represented with a single feather upon the forehead. Most of the Egyptian gods are decorated with a head-dress of two feathers, probably symbolic of the twin powers, Goodness and Knowledge. The Sanscrit for *feather* is *patra*, and the European *feather* or *veder* may be equated with *father* or *vater*. In figs. 1097 and 1098 the solitary plume or *penna* of the Universal Father is associated with the Heart of Charity.

Commenting upon the extraordinary collection of pre-historic mounds in OHIO, which includes circles, octagons, crosses and pyramids, insects and animals, DONNELLY ob-

---

[1] Barclay (E.), *Stonehenge*, p. 50. [2] *Golden Bough*, iii. 77.
[3] Petrie, *Religion of Ancient Egypt*, p. 14.

serves : " One of them is a threefold symbol like a bird's foot ;
the central mound is 155 feet long, and the other two 110
feet in length." [1] This gigantic CLAW or Broad Arrow, of
which fig. 1099 seems to be an example, was evidently
another form of the Three Lights, and the word *claw*
apparently originated from the similarity of a bird's *claw*
to the sign of *ac el aw*, the Great God A or Aw. In this
country the national mark of the broad arrow is branded
upon the clothing of those who fall into the clutches of EL
Aw. Another form of the same *claw* [2] is the barbed spear or
arrow-head known as a *pheon* or *feon, i.e.* the One Fire. A

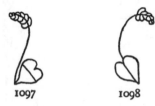

1097   1098

pheon surmounts fig. 1100, and the idea may be equated
with *paon* or *pavo*, the many-eyed *peacock*.

The Temple of the Azure Heaven at PEKIN (*op ak in*,
the " Eye of the Great One " ?) consists of a triple circular
terrace, and the marble stones forming the pavement of the
highest terrace are laid in nine concentric circles. On the
Cornish coast between SENNEN and ST JUST, oriented due
west, are the remains of a stone Temple consisting of three
interlaced circles. There is a circle of vast stones on Salakee
(*is al ak eye*) Downs, SCILLY ; another at TRESCAW (*tur es ak aw*),
Scilly ; another at BOSCAWEN (*bos ac aw en*), near PENZANCE.

In the centre of the eight-lobed *marguerite* or *girasole*
herewith is what may be read as the wavy M of MARY, or

---

[1] *Atlantis*, p. 376.
[2] The mediæval English *cliver*, a claw, is evidently the same word as
clover, cleaver, and *clever*.

as a hieroglyph of the Great Serpent. Prehistoric mounds in serpentine form are found in various parts of the world, always, apparently, on mountain-tops. In the Egyptian *Book of the Dead* there is an allusion to a certain " Hill of Bat." " There is the Hill of Bat ; the heaven rests on it. Sabak,

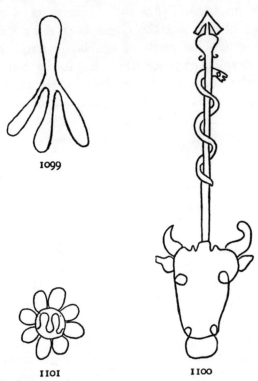

1099

1101   1100

Lord of the Bat in the east, is *on the hill,* in his temple upon its edge. There is a snake upon the brow of that hill about 30 cubits long, 10 cubits broad ; 3 cubits in front of him are stone. I know the name of this snake on his hill— Eater of Fire is his name." The Chaldean for Serpent was *acan,* and at Glen FEECHAN (*feu akan,* "Fire Serpent") in ARGYLLSHIRE there is a Serpent-mound 300 feet in extent. The back or spine of this Serpent was found beneath the peat-moss to have been formed by a scrupulous adjustment of stones, and the sinuous winding and articulations of the vertebral spinal arrangement are anatomically perfect.[1]

But the most majestic, the most colossal, and probably the most ancient,[2] of all serpent shrines is that which once stood at AVEBURY in ENGLAND. The sanctuary at AVEBURY, which embraced avenues of unhewn rock extending in the form of a snake over nearly three miles of country, is believed to have been the "greatest megalithic monument in the world," and Aubrey rightly considered that "Avebury doth as much exceed Stonehenge in grandeur as a cathedral doth a Parish Church."

From the partly-conjectural plan herewith, as drawn by STUKELEY in 1740, it will be seen that the Sanctuary consisted of the Circle of the Universe or World coiled within the folds of the Serpent of Eternity. Within the main circle or Egg of Time are the two smaller circles of Night and Day, and each of these twin circles—300 feet in diameter —was almost three times larger than the entire circuit of STONEHENGE.[3]

In the Old Testament there are frequent allusions to Sanctuaries and Holy places constructed upon hill-tops, and AVEBURY was undoubtedly one of the many such. In the neighbourhood it was regarded until comparatively recently as so holy that no reptiles could live there, and if any were

---

[1] See *Atlantis*, p. 205.

[2] The date of Stonehenge is unknown, but judged from the orientation and the wear and tear of the stones, it is believed to be only one half the age of Avebury. "The men who built Avebury and are buried in the chambered burrows on the surrounding hills, belong to the later or polished stone age, and must have settled in the country sometime between the last glacial period, 10,000 B.C., and the introduction of bronze between 2000 and 4000 B.C." —Lord Avebury, Introduction to *A Guide to Avebury*.

[3] The diameter of Stonehenge is 110 feet.

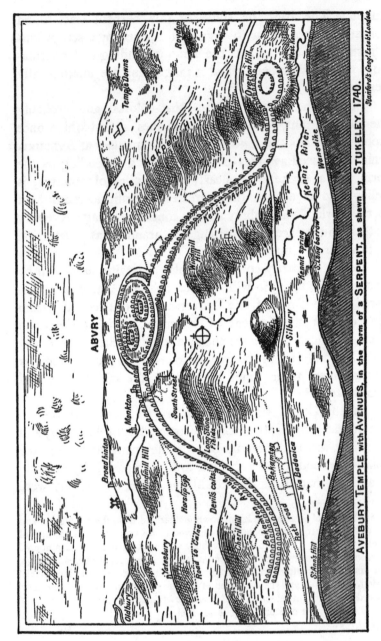

AVEBURY TEMPLE with AVENUES, in the form of a SERPENT, as shewn by STUKELEY. 1740.

Stanford's Geogᶜ Estabᵗ London.

1102

taken into the sacred precincts it was supposed that they immediately died.[1]

The Downs around AVEBURY are the meeting-place of the three main watersheds of the country, and they form the centre from which radiate the great lines of hills, north, east, and west. The Temple itself is placed at the junction of these radiating hills, and may possibly owe its situation to the felicitous symbolism of the surrounding landscape. Mr HIPPESLEY COX, who writes without any mystic or symbolic bias, observes : " The *triangle* of Downs surrounding Avebury may be considered the hub of England ; *from it radiate the great lines of hills like the spokes of a wheel*, the Cotswolds to the north, the Mendips to the west, the Dorsetshire hills to the south-west, Salisbury Plain to the south, the continuation of the North and South Downs to the east, and the high chalk ridge of the Berkshire Downs north-east to the Chilterns." [2]

From this centre spring also the sources of *five* rivers, and the whole district scattered over with tumuli and dew-ponds was once evidently a most Holy Land.

AVE, the root of AVEBURY, is likewise the root of AVALON or AVILLION, the mysterious Isle of Rest to which King ARTHUR was withdrawn to be healed of his wounds.

> " Where falls not hail, or rain, or any snow,
>   Nor ever wind blows loudly ; but it lies
>   Deep-meadow'd, happy, fair with orchard lawns
>   And bowery hollows crown'd with summer sea."

One of the quarters of the Garden of EDEN was the "land of ·HAVILAH, where there is gold ; and the gold of that land is good." [3] *Hav* is Welsh for *summer*, and our words *haven* and *heaven* originally implied *summer*, *rest*, and

[1] Preface by Lord Avebury to *A Guide to Avebury*, R. H. Cox.
[2] *A Guide to Avebury*, p. 55.
[3] Genesis ii. 11.

safety. The Elysian Fields might without inaccuracy be described as the Land of EVAN or BACCHUS, the Great Father Spirit.

The root *av* is again apparent in the name HAVAI or HAVAIKI, the Maori Isle of Souls, now spelled generally HAWAII. The spot in Japan where the original Twin Deities first descended upon Earth is still shown in the Island of AWAJI,[1] a name apparently identical with the Polynesian HAWAII or HAVAI. In all probability AV or AF, the root of APHRODITE, Goddess of *love*, may be equated with EVE, a name which in Hebrew means *life*. The *ivy* plant is notoriously long-*lived*; by the Christian DURANDUS it was regarded as the type of eternal *life*,[2] and probably for this same reason the *ivy* adorned the brows of BACCHUS. *Enef* in Cornish meant *soul*, and the words *life, alive*, and *love* may be understood either as " everlasting Life " or else " our Lord the Life."

An alternative form of the name EVE is CHAVAH or CHAVVA, signifying " the mother of all that lives." CHAVAH, the Ever-Existent Living AH, is closely akin to JEHOVAH, the Ever-Existent HOVAH, EVA, or living A. At the Greek Mysteries the worshippers used to raise loud shouts of *Hevah !* or *Evoe !* The natives of a tribe of NORTH AMERICA, discovered by Sir JOHN ROSS in his voyage towards the North Pole, used to assemble at midday in a circle, and then the oldest man called out three times " Ye-ho-wah ! " or " Yo-he-wah ! "[3] In Australia certain native tribes cry out "Ewah-ewah ! "[4] and in all probability the exultant shout of *Heva !* with which the Cornish fishermen of to-day greet the advent of a pilchard shoal, is the same

---

[1] Longford (J. H.), *Story of Old Japan*, p. 12.
[2] *Rationale Divinorum Officiorum*, i. 8 ; *c.* 37.
[3] Lord Arundell of Wardour, *The Secret of Plato's Atlantis*, p. 47.
[4] *Ibid.*, p. 73.

exclamation[1] JEHOVAH ! or YAHWE ! In Latin the word *ave* now means *hail !* but like *bravo !* it was probably once a beatific shout to the great God. The Breton equivalent for *bravo !* is *brav !* or *kenavo !* i.e. " The Great One, the living O ! "

The egg or *œuf*[2] (Latin *ovum*) was probably so named as being the germ of *life*, and the *bœuf*—Father Life—or *calf*, " Great Lord Life," is ideally identical with *aleph*, the Hebrew for *ox*. The Greek *alpha* is fundamentally *al ef a* ; and the *Caleph*, *Khalif*, or *Calipha* of the East, is a great chief. *Alif*, the Arabic for *alpha*, is the same word as the

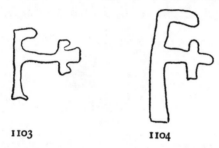

1103   1104

English *alive* and as *aloof*, i.e. *on high* or *aloft*, and an *elf* is the same as a *fay* or *fairy*. *Afar* may be equated with *heifer*, *ever*, and *over*.[3] The Latin for *ever* is *semper, i.e.* the " essence of the Sun Father " ; the *empyrean* is that which " pertains to elemental fire " ; the *empyrean* also means the sky, and that which is *above* or *abœuf*. *Af-ab*, the " living orb," is the root of *affability*, and *affec*—the " Great Life," the base of *affection*—is the same as *hafuc*, the Anglo-Saxon for *hawk*.

The letter *eff*,[4] which in the emblems herewith has been sanctified by a cross, is said to have been derived from the

---

[1] The expression *Heave-Ho !* may possibly once have been an invocation for fresh life and strength. [2] *Ophel* in Hebrew means *hill*.

[3] Compare surnames EVERARD, EVREMOND, etc.

[4] F is the root of HEPHÆSTUS, the Greek name for the Celestial Smith.

Egyptian hieroglyphic of the horned Serpent. "The two bars of our F are the survivals of the two horns, while the vertical stroke represents the body. In the letter Y, which comes from the same hieroglyphic picture, the two horns and the body of the asp are retained; but in the derivatives V and U the body has entirely disappeared, while the reduplicated character W is constructed of four strokes, which stand simply for four horns."[1]

This identity between *eff* and the Asp or sacred serpent is perhaps responsible for *ophis*, the Greek for *serpent*. The so-called *snake* Indians of ARIZONA (HORIZONA?) term themselves the *Hopii* or *Opii*—words not now in their

1105

language of everyday use,[2] but evidently cognate to the Greek *opis* or *ophis*. The primeval OP or AP is again traceable in APAP or APEP, the Egyptian name for the Great Serpent slain by HORUS. APAP, like SET, fell into disrepute, exactly like the *Pope* or PAPA of one generation often becomes the execrated "Antichrist" of a later.

The body of the snake herewith is marked with the sinuous curves of the celestial water, or it may be that these markings represent the intestines. The monstrous APEP is said to have "resembled the intestines."[3]

In PAPUA — the "Land of PAPA A" — there is a mountain popularly supposed to be the retreat of an immortal snake : some few claim to know the language

---

[1] Taylor (Dr Isaac), *The Alphabet*, i. 12.
[2] Lord Arundell of Wardour, p. 74.
[3] Budge, (W.), *Legends of the Gods*, p. lxxii.

of this snake, and they hold converse with the monster, whose reputation as an oracle is of the highest order. " I have," says a modern traveller, " made many endeavours to find the snake talkers, but they are never at hand when I am in the district. There may, or may not be, a big snake amongst the hills, but its record vies with that of the sea serpent." [1]

Ophis, the Greek *serpent*, may be equated with APIS,[2] the Sacred Bull of MEMPHIS, and with the Bull MNEVIS or *om on ephis*, " the Sun, the one living light " of HELIOPOLIS. *Ephis* or *ophis* is the same word as *hippos*, a *horse* ; *apis*, a *bee* ; and *apse*, a *bow*. The Teutonic for *bowman* is YVON, a proper name equivalent to the Welsh EVAN.[3] In Cornish *ephan* means *summer* and *even* means *patient*. The English *even* means *equal*, i.e. *ek Hu el*—French *egal* ; and AVON was so frequent a river name that it developed into one of the generic terms for *river*. All rivers and streams were regarded as manifestations and symbols of AV ON, the regenerative " One Life." Under the name HAPI the Egyptians hailed the River NILE as the inscrutable " Father of all the Gods," " the ONE," the Self-Begotten. HAP or HAPI, the NILE, cannot differ from HAPI—an alternative name for APIS, the Bull.[4] The word NILE, " One God," is

---

[1] J. H. P. Murray, *The Papuans*. " The Papuans, as a whole, are people of simple faith, and in their primitive state may be regarded as having a high sense of integrity. Whatever you do, never break your word with them. As aborigines, their word is their bond, and they have many other characteristics which are admirable. Strangely enough, they degenerate as soon as they come within the sphere of civilisation, and at times it is difficult to escape the reflection that the race pays a very high price for being deprived of its primitive morality, and picturesque, if savage, mode of life."

[2] The constant interchangeability of *p*, *ph*, *f*, and *v* is evident in such words as April=*avril*, apple=*aval*, etc.

[3] EVAN=EWAN. The Russian IVAN is considered the equivalent of JOHN.

[4] APIU was the Egyptian name for the City of THEBES, and the Sacred name for THEBES was AMON or NU AMON, the one HU, the lone A?

supposed to have been derived from *nakhal*, a Semitic word
for *river*. *Nakhal* resolves into "one Great God," and the
same idea underlies the British terms *brook*, *burn*, and *beck*.
In the West of England AVON is pronounced *awne*; AVE-
BURY is alternatively AUBURY, and it is evident that Av is a
synonym for A. Most of the preceding A or Aleph-Tau
emblems incorporate by means of their V-shaped cross-
strokes the idea A V. The Sunflower herewith is surmounted by A V; figs. 1107 and 1108 read I V; and in
the other designs following there appears the V I or V of
La Vie. The V on the breast of the Phœnix identifies

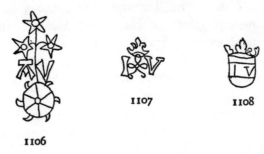

1106   1107   1108

that Bird of Fire with OHNIVAK, the "only Living Great
One."

A great *focus* of APOLLO-worship was at DELPHI, a small
town in PHOCIS. The Temple was shut in on the north
by a mountain barrier which was cleft in the centre into
two great cliffs with peaked summits, between which issued
the waters of the Castalian spring.[1] It was regarded as the
central point of the entire earth, and was hence called "the
navel of the earth." But originally it was called PYTHO, a
word obviously related to *Python*, the giant serpent, and to
the Egyptian sanctuary-city PITHOM. The name PITHOM
resolves into "Father TIME," and may be connoted with
ADAM = "Warm Sun." There is thus some scientific basis for

[1] Smith (Dr W.), *Classical Dictionary*.

the Allegory that mankind are the children of ADAM, the Warm Sun, and EVE, the Everlasting LIFE or BREATH.[1]

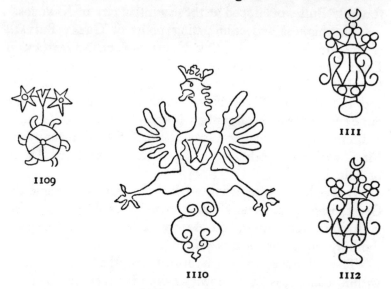

1109

1110

1111

1112

The Egyptians conceived the Supreme as AMON—meaning in Greek *hidden* or *inscrutable*—who created the pair ATHOR and KNEPH. The name KNEPH may be resolved

1113

1114

1115

into *ak on eff*, the One Great Life, and to this Deity are probably related the words *nave* and *navel*. KNEPH is sometimes referred to as KNEPHIS or CNUPHIS—he was typified by a serpent; and the name KNEPHIS is evidently

---

[1] A *cough* is *ak of*, *i.e.* a great breath (?). Compare proper names CUFF, GOFF, GOUGH, CAFFYN, and COFFIN.

ak on ophis, the "One Great Serpent." The word is no doubt similarly related to *canopy* and to *kanobus*, the title of the holy Bull worshipped at the Egyptian city of KANOBOS.

The highest and culminating point of GREAT BRITAIN is the mountain named BEN NEVIS, and at NAVESTOCK in ESSEX are the remains of an "alate" or winged stone temple.[1] The Coptic name for the River NILE was NEV, and the Russian River NEVA is blessed to this day in the same spirit as was the Egyptian NEV. The Lake of GENEVA is alternatively known as GENFER, the "Ever-Existent One Fire," and it is also known as Lake LEMAN, *i.e.* Lord AMON, or Sole A.

It would be interesting to learn under what name the Great Serpent at ABURY was known by its Builders. *Haie* is Arabian for *serpent*, and ABURY or AUBURY was perhaps the burg or barrow of this *haie*.

The Ridge upon which once stood the head, a point within a circle, is still known as the HACKPEN or HACKPEN Hill. *Hack* is an old English word for *serpent*,[2] and STUKELEY is of the opinion that *hack pen* meant "Serpent's head."[3] *Acan* was Chaldean for *serpent*, and the Mayan for *serpent* was *can*,[4] i.e. *ac an*, the "Great One." The Sacred Serpent of INDIA is termed *nag*, i.e. *on ag*, the "Mighty One," and as snake-worship was always associated with sun-worship, it is probable that our word *snake* may be resolved into *sun ake*, the "Great Sun."[5] Allied to *nag* and *snake* is *nachash*, the Hebrew for *snake*; and *nachash* resolves into

[1] Illustrated in Stukeley's *Stonehenge*.

[2] The same word is found in Cornish place-names such as BOTALLACK, translated as meaning "Abode of Serpent."

[3] "It is remarkable the remains of a similar circle of stones in Bœotia had a similar name in the time of Pausanias."—See Payne-Knight, p. 15.

[4] KHAN is the Afghan title for King or Ruler, and as late as the thirteenth century the Afghan rulers claimed to be *of serpent race*.—See Oldham (C. F.), *The Sun and the Serpent*, p. 117.

[5] Compare place-name SEATON SNOOK and proper name SNOOKS.

on ach ash, the "One Great Light" or Mighty Ash. One of the meanings of Hebrew *nachash* is "to become *wise*"; and similarly *sophos*, the Greek for *Wisdom*, and SOPHIA, the Virgin of Light, may be traced to *is ophis*, the "light of *ophis*," the Serpent, or the "light of the living light." The name OPHELIA is defined as meaning a Serpent, and the same signification underlies the surname ORME and place-names such as GREAT ORMES Head, ORMSKIRK, ORMISTON, and ORMSBY. *Orm*, the Teutonic for *serpent*, is the root of *worm* (German *wurm*); and in Hebrew *orm* means "wise, prudent, ready-witted." The Afghan for Serpent is *kirm*, i.e. *ak irm*, the "Great Worm"; in ENGLAND we have a River ERME which rises on EXMOOR.

The Greeks used the word *echis* to mean Serpent; *saraph*, a Hebrew term for *serpent*, cannot differ from *seraph*, nor from *cerf*, a *stag*; and all three expressions resolve into the essence of light of the Vital Fire. Our English *eel* is simply EL, and *conger* resolves into *aconagur*, the great one, the Mighty Fire. AVEBURY, in addition to "ABURY" and "AUBURY," was known as AVESBURY and ALBURY.[1] The AVES- may be equated with *ophis*, and the AL- with *eel* or EL. A Semitic word for *serpent* is *naas*, and one of the Gnostic sects worshipping SOPHIA, whom they identified with JESUS of NAZARETH under the form of a Good Serpent, was for this reason entitled the NAASENI. There is a place named NAASE, "the One Light," in KILDARE, Ireland, and it is a very curious coincidence that legend assigns the origin of the STONEHENGE stones to this very spot. It was supposed that Merlin by supernatural means transported the giant rocks from NAASE to Salisbury Plain, but that originally they were brought to Ireland "from the remotest parts of Africa."[2]

Perhaps the Builders of the AVEBURY Serpent knew it

---

[1] *Abury*, p. 19.   [2] Smith (J.), *Choir Gaur*, p. 5.

as an *anaconda* or a *boa*. The name Bo-A would be not inappropriate at Abury, and in the immediate neighbourhood there is still a Bowood, a *Bay* Bridge, and a Bytham =(Pythom) Farm. In China the *anaconda* or *boa* is known as the *pa* snake.[1] In Africa it was known as the *jaculus*, and in Jamaica[2] the natives term it *jacumama*, which they understand to mean *the mother of the waters*,[3] *i.e.* Labismina (?).

The Cornish term for Serpent was *bref*, i.e. *bereff*, the Father Life. That Eff was once a familiar root in the Avebury precincts is evident from the still existing Uffcot, Foxham, and Gopher[4] Wood. On the spurs of Overton Hill overlooking the Temple are *eight* large round tumuli,[5] and on Overton itself, the Stronghold of the Ever and the Over, stood until recently the stones of the Serpent's head. Stukeley observes that "this Overton Hill, from time immemorial the country people have a high notion of. It was (alas, it was!) a very few years ago crowned with a most beautiful temple of the Druids. They still call it the Sanctuary."[6]

The word *viper* (Latin *vipera*) may be considered as the French spell it, *vipère*, and understood as "Fire or Life Father." Near Avebury are Fifield and Clyffe[7] Pypard; and *Père* or *Bear* is again recognisable in the close-neighbouring Purton, Barton, Bourton, Barbury, and Berwick. The initial syllables of Bremhill and Bromham may be connoted with the neighbouring Boreham Downs and equated with Brahm.

Mr Cox observes of Avebury that "these national

---

[1] Gould (C.), *Mythological Monsters*, p. 235.
[2] This Jam- may be compared with *Jam* the Indian title.
[3] *Mythological Monsters*, p. 180.
[4] Gopher in Hebrew means a *wood*.
[5] Cox (H.), *Guide to Avebury*, p. 50.   [6] *Abury*, p. 31.
[7] Compare surnames Clyff and Ilyffe.

monuments are placed in the centre of a well-fortified triangle of land measuring about ten miles on either side, leaving BARBURY at the north apex."[1] At the south-east corner is MARTINSELL HILL, probably once MARTIN'S HILL, containing the remains of "a practically complete settlement of primitive man." On the neighbouring CLACK Mount is a well-preserved camp "of rather curious triangular construction, with a tumulus in its centre." On the side of WADEN HILL, nominally cognate with WODAN or WOTEN, there is a white horse. On EASTON HILL, the Stronghold of *ees*, are two round tumuli ; on HUISH HILL is "an almost perfect *rectangular* camp " ; and on KNAPP HILL is a group of five tumuli. BURDEROP Down brings us again into touch with *dur op*, the Enduring Eye ; and the same root is recurrent in SNAP,[2] in UPHAM, and in UPAVON—the site of the source of the River AVON. To the west lies CHIPPENHAM ; and it may be that the *Bup* of BUPTON is cognate with the Egyptian APAP or APEP, and with the applause *Hip! Hip! Hip! Hurray!* In TASMANIA the mythical giant snake is termed the *bunyip*,[3] *i.e.* the "Good Hoop" on the "universal Eye" (?).

Close to AVEBURY lies MORGAN'S HILL, suggestive of the Anglo-Saxon *morgen* or *morning*. MORGAN LE FAY was the half-sister of King ARTHUR, and, according to Sicilian tradition, she is still preserving him in a fairy palace, occasionally to be seen from REGGIO, in the opposite Sea of MESSINA. Mirages and cloud cities are known as *Fata Morgana*, and, according to RHYS, *morgen* means "sea-born, or offspring of the sea."

Near the Kentish MAIDSTONE at a place named AYLESFORD[4] is a cromlech called KITS COTY, the word *coty* being

---

[1] Cox (H.), *Guide to Avebury*, p. 34.
[2] SUN AP=Sun Eye. Compare surname SNAPE.
[3] *Mythological Monsters*, p. 180.   [4] Compare AYLESBURY.

evidently related to *quoit*, the Cornish term for cromlech. At Stonehenge is a Syrencot, and at Abury a Draycot Hill. The name Draycot suggesting *draco*, the Greek for *serpent*, implies that upon the summit of Draycot there may once have stood a quoit or cot of Dray, *i.e. dur ay*, the enduring Ay.

The Egyptians personified the Soul of all the Gods under the name Heka or Hekau, the "Great A or Au" (?), and this term served among them as a mighty talisman or "word of power." The English Temple of Stonehenge

1116

was a representation and a symbol of Time; the English Temple at Abury typified not only Time but also the greater Absolute, the all-embracing and more *awe*-full Soul or core of Time, the axis of Existence.[1] In the following Egyptian hymn Ra,[2] the "Fire of A," the Sun, the Mighty Eye, the Egg within the Serpent's coil, thus addresses Nu,

---

[1] Compare the Chinese Ode:
    "Like a whirling water-wheel,
    Like rolling pearls,—
    Yet how are these worthy to be named?
    They are but illustrations for fools.
    There is the mighty axis of Earth,
    The never-resting pole of Heaven;
    Let us grasp their clue,
    And with them be blended in One."

[2] *Ura* was Egyptian for *great*.

the one Hu, the celestial ocean, the unfathomable Mind or Oversoul :—

"Ascribe ye praise to the god, the Aged One, from whom I have come into being. I am he who made the heavens, and I set in order (the earth, and created the gods, and) I was with them for an exceedingly long period ; then was born the year and . . . but my soul is older than it (*i.e.* time). It is the Soul of Shu ; it is the Soul of Khnemu (?) ; it is the Soul of Heh ; it is the Soul of Kek and Kerh (*i.e.* Night and Darkness) ; it is the Soul of Nu and of Ra ; it is the Soul of Osiris, the lord of Tettu ; it is the Soul of the *Sebak* Crocodile-gods and of the Crocodiles ; it is the Soul of every god (who dwelleth) in the divine Snakes ; it is the Soul of Apep in Mount Bakhau (*i.e.* the Mount of Sunrise) ; and it is the Soul of Ra which pervadeth the whole world." [1]

[1] Budge (W.), *Legends of the Gods*, pp. 37, 38.

1117

CHAPTER XIX

THE GARDEN OF ALLAH

" Eternally the Mystic Rose,
Petal on petal doth disclose ;
Engraved with knowledge of all time,
Of every age and thought and clime."
W. T. HORTON.

" Spikenard and saffron ; calamus and cinnamon, with all trees and frankin-
cense ; myrrh and aloes, with all the chief spices : A fountain of gardens, a
well of living waters, and streams from Lebanon. Awake, O north wind ; and
come, thou south ; blow upon my garden, that the spices thereof may flow
out."—THE SONG OF SOLOMON.

THE MIZTECS of MEXICO have a tradition that the gods once
built a sumptuous palace, a masterpiece of skill, in which
they made their abode upon a mountain. This rock was
called "The Palace of Heaven," and there the gods first
dwelt on earth, living many years in great rest and content,
as in a happy and delicious land, though the world still
lay in obscurity and darkness. The children of these gods
made to themselves a garden, in which they put many trees,
and fruit-trees, and flowers, and roses, and odorous herbs.
Subsequently there came a deluge, in which many of the
sons and daughters of the gods perished. Every race upon
Earth seemingly possesses a variant of this idyllic tradition,
and traces of holy habitations *upon hill-tops* are more or less
universal.

It was equally customary among the ancients to portray

the Garden of the Gods as being situate on *an island* from whose centre towered a mountain-peak. The Indians of NORTH AMERICA tell of a Blissful Isle appointed for the residence of the good. In this land of spirits " there is no want; there is neither sorrow nor hunger, pain nor death. Pleasant fields filled with game spread before the eye, with birds of beautiful form. Every stream has good fish in it, and every hill is crowned with groves of fruit-trees, sweet and pleasant to the taste. It is not here, brother, but there that men truly begin to live. It is not for those who rejoice in those pleasant groves, but for you that are left behind, that we weep." [1]

In the eyes of primitive man almost all islands appear to have been idealised into the Gathering-Place of Souls, and poetically regarded as either golden clouds floating in an azure ocean, or precious stones set in a silver sea. Ancient island-names afford many proofs of this mystic origin of their nomenclature, and even within historic times the same idealising tendency is traceable.[2]

Among the Greeks the SCILLY ISLES were known as the HESPERIDES, and the fondness of the ancients for imagining and naming isles as " Fortunate " or " Blessed " is well known. It is not unlikely that the name SCILLY[3] is identical with *silly*, meaning innocent or blessed, and that it is

---

[1] *Folk-Lore and Legends* (*North American Indian*), anon., London, 1890, p. 87.

[2] Of this an instance is at hand in AOTEA-ROA, the native name bestowed upon NEW ZEALAND by the first MAORI immigrants. *Aotea* signifies *the ether*, the *bright light of morning*, the *brilliantly clear light of day*; and AOTEA-ROA literally interpreted means *The Long Bright Land* or *The Long Daylight*. This same word AOTEA-ROA was an ancient name for the Island of TAHITI, the last MAORI HAWAIIKA or Gathering-Place of Souls.—*The Maoris of New Zealand*, J. Cowan, pp. 93, 95.

[3] The etymology of the name SCILLY is not known. By some it is thought to have been derived from SILYA, a Cornish word meaning " conger eel "; others trace it to SULLEH, a British word signifying " The rocks consecrated to the Sun."

allied to the CEYL of CEYLON, whence towers the super-sacred " Adam's Peak." The special object of adoration upon ADAM's PEAK is an alleged footprint of BUDDHA. According to Major Oldham, " the foot emblem seems to be very ancient. It is, in fact, a form of memorial of the dead ; hence probably it was adopted by the followers of

1118

BUDDHA in remembrance of their great Leader."[1] Fig. 1118 may thus seemingly be read as an emblem of the idea :

> " Lives of great men all remind us,
> We may make our lives sublime ;
> And departing, leave behind us,
> Footprints on the sands of time."

The English AVEBURY, embracing within its precincts a veritable Holy Land of Hills, Springs, Rivers, and Dewponds, was without doubt modelled somewhat on the same lines as the Egyptian Temple Grounds, and as the GILGALS,[2] SHILOHS,[3] and High Places of the Old Testament : " I will open rivers in high places," says the writer of ISAIAH, " and fountains in the midst of the valleys : I will make the wilderness a pool of water, and the dry land springs of water. I will plant in the wilderness the cedar, the shittah tree, and the myrtle and the oil tree ; I will set in the desert the fir tree, and the pine, and the box tree together."[4]

[1] *The Sun and the Serpent*, p. 176.
[2] The word *gilgal* was Hebrew for circle.
[3] The word *shiloh* in Hebrew meant *place of rest*.
[4] xli. 18, 19.

It is probable that in ENGLAND there were many culture centres other than AVEBURY and STONEHENGE, and it may be that the Box-trees, which still grow so luxuriantly upon Box HILL in SURREY, are, like Mr Grant Allen's pines, the descendants of trees planted upon a prehistoric Hill-shrine.

At a time when the wooded lowlands and the river banks were alive with savage beasts, it is not unlikely that primitive man retired at nightfall to the security of the open downs ; whence the word *down*, a *stronghold*. Names such as EXMOOR, BRAZEMOOR, HAYES COMMON, HAWKESDOWN, ASHDOWN, etc., all containing the idea of *fire* or *great fire*, imply that downs were often the sites of fires which served the dual purpose of scaring away wild beasts and of symbolising the sacred and protective God of Fire. Words like *parish* and *arrondissement*, the "light of PAR," "the light of *ar rond*, the fire round," imply that originally *parish* meant the radius of such and such a tribal Fire. But it may also mean that most of the uplands were dedicated as sanctuaries, and that ENGLAND was once, like Egypt, dotted with Holy Places.

There is an invariable and inevitable tendency to idealise one's homeland, and thus to the Jews JERUSALEM was the Holy City, the idyllic Zion towards which were turned the yearning eyes of Semitic exiles. The NEW JERUSALEM of the Apocalypse—described as a twelve-gated solid cube[1] of pure gold, whose light was like a jasper stone—obviously differs only from the Garden of EDEN to the extent that primitive innocence differs from the purified innocence of Wisdom and Experience. The name JERUSALEM or URUSALEM[2] may

[1] "The length, and the breadth, and the height of it are equal."—Revelation xxi. 16.

[2] "Probably David only revived the ancient name, since a cuneiform tablet, written centuries before the Hebrew Period, seems to refer to that place under the form URUSALEM."—Anderson (R. E.), *Extinct Civilisation of the East*, p. 106.

be resolved into Eros *al em*, the City of Eros or Horus, our Lord the Sun.

The city of Eros does not differ symbolically from the Orchard of the mystic Rose. There is a silver rose figured in the Paradise of the Brahmins, and Dante similarly figures the innermost circle of the heavenly spheres as a rose perennial, "brighter than a million suns, immaculate, inaccessible, vast, fiery with magnificence, and surrounding God as if with a million veils."

> " How wide the leaves,
> Extended to their utmost of this Rose,
> Whose lowest step embosoms such a space
> Of ample radiance ! Yet, nor amplitude
> Nor height impeded, but my view with ease
> Took in the full dimensions of that joy.
> Near or remote, what there awaits where God
> Immediate rules and Nature awed, suspends
> Her sway ? "

It is said by the Brahmins that the Almighty has his permanent abode in the heart of the silver Rose ;[1] and the word *rhodon*, the Greek for *rose*, yields *don*, " the stronghold of *rho* = R = *ar* = the Fire."

The inmost centres of the flowers of Flame here illustrated are respectively the Pearl, the Cross of St George, and the Egg-encircling Serpent as at Avebury. The Persian word for *rose* is *gul*, i.e. " the Mighty God."

The Rose being regarded as the Heavenly Spirit of the Highest was by the mystics identified with Jesus Christ, of whom Vaughan writes :

> " 'Tis now clear day : I see a rose
> Bud in the bright East and disclose
> The pilgrim Sun."

---

[1] Waite (A. E.), *Real History of the Rosicrucians*, p. 11.

In the symbol here below (fig. 1125) the Rose has been ingeniously combined with the Solar Wheel of the HORIZON.

Prior to Christianity the Rose was identified with the Virgin SOPHIA. The Bride of *The Song of Solomon* is

described as the " Rose of Sharon " ; in Ecclesiasticus WISDOM is likened to a " rose plant in Jericho " ; and CINDERELLA [1] is similarly associated with a Rose.

[1] In ITALY she is called ROSINA, meaning Little Rose, and in Hungary is traced by a golden rose stuck into the gate-post of the house she enters.— *Cinderella*, pp. 297, 331.

A magic Rose is the heroine of the *Romance of the Rose*, and the symbolic character of this " bourgeois " poem is stated by the poet himself in the lines :

> " When I to you
> Of those things spake, 'twas with the view
> Of showing briefly what I meant
> In parable, thereto was bent
> My reasoning. Whoso'er should see
> The words of Scripture literally,
> Ere long would pierce the sense obscure
> That lies beneath their coverture.
> Uplift the veil that hideth truth,
> And bright it flashes forth forsooth.
> This shalt thou find if thou rehearse
> The noble stories writ in verse
> By ancient poets. Great delight
> Will flood thy soul if thou aright
> Dost read, for thou shalt see unrolled
> Secret philosophy of old,
> Profiting thou amused shalt be,
> And thine amusement profit thee,
> For oft their quip and crank and fable
> Is wondrous good and profitable,
> And much deep subtle thought they hide
> 'Neath veils torn easily asunder."

In *The Song of Solomon* the Bride—" my sister "—is described as " a garden inclosed." [1] The *Romance of the Rose* relates how a lover attains to a delicious garden surrounded by a wall, and the fair Rose dwelling within the centre of this paradise is eventually transformed into a maiden :

> " Through the magic power
> Of Venus, in that selfsame hour
> A wondrous miracle befel.
> The Rose became a damozel
> Of form and beauty past compare,
> Clothed in her own rich golden hair."

---

[1] *Song of Solomon* iv. 12.

In comparison with the "garden enclosed" of the Song of
Solomon and the wall-enclosed Garden of the Rose, peopled
with rare and strange plants, one may consider the Persian
conception of EDEN known as YIMA's Garden—a square
enclosure with a wall.   "There shall be no humpbacked,
none bulged forward, there ; no impotent, no lunatic, no
poverty, no lying, no meanness, no jealousy, no decayed

1126

tooth, no leprous to be confined, nor any of the brands
wherewith ANGRO MAINYUS (the Evil Spirit) stamps the
bodies of mortals." [1]

Fig. 1126 may be taken to represent either the Garden
of YIMA, "the Good Shepherd," the garden enclosed of *The
Song of Solomon,* or the Walled Orchard of the *Romance
of the Rose.*   In fig. 1127 the Rose Maiden, the AWAKENER,
the *rouse,* appears with three flowers springing from her
forehead.

[1] *The Teachings of Zoroaster,* S. A. Kapadia, p. 75.

SPENSER in *The Faerie Queene* regards the "daintie rose" as a symbol or ensample of God's "heavenly grace." The word *grace* may be equated with *groes*, the old British word for *cross*, and resolved into *ag eros*, the "mighty Rose or Eros."

> "Eternal God in His almighty powre,
> To make ensample of his heavenly *grace*,
> In Paradise whylome did plant this flowre." [1]

1127

The Orchard of the Rose—that Garden of Grace—is represented as being "peopled with strange plants," and it is difficult to say whether the flowers depicted herewith represent roses, flowers of flame, or stars. The cross-surmounted Hills of figs. 1136 to 1138 are perhaps what Vaughan terms the

> "Fair shining mountains of my pilgrimage,
> And flowery vales *whose flow'rs were stars*."

---

[1] Book iii., canto v.

The Solar Wheel depicted in fig. 1139 is surmounted by three *asters* or Star Flowers ; the heart of fig. 1140 is palpably

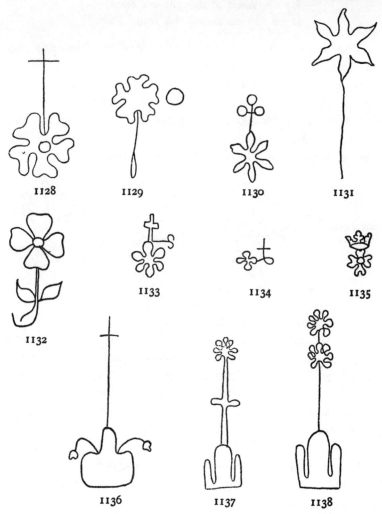

1128   1129   1130   1131

1133   1134   1135

1132

1136   1137   1138

a star ; and figs. 1141 and 1142 are romantic blossoms, akin to what must have been in the mind of the poet who wrote :

> "Man is the seed
> Of the unimaginable flower,
> By singleness of thought and deed
> It may bloom now—this actual hour." [1]

The word *aster* is cognate with As- or AZGARD, the Scandinavian Heaven, the "garden of light." In Norse *as* or *ais* was understood as "belonging to the Gods," whence place-names such as AISTHORPE, AISMUNDERBY, etc.[2] The most living-fire-like of all flowers is perhaps the *azalea* ; the great blossoms of the *pæony* or *pione* no doubt identified it as a symbol of *pa ony*, the "only Father" ; and the

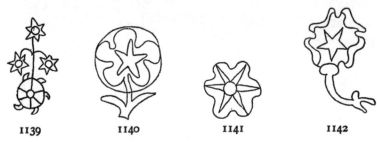

1139   1140   1141   1142

gorgeous spike of the *hollyhock* or "holy great one" is possibly intended in fig. 1138. Fig. 1143 consists of *five* hearts surmounted by the Z of Light, and its centre forms the M of Mary. CINDERELLA, who pined for seven years imprisoned in a cave, exclaims : "Here *Mary* was I named the *Rose* and *Star*"[3]—and CINDERELLA may be equated with the Eastern Queen of the *Five* Flowers. "The Hindu child," says Cox, "is still roused and soothed by the stories of the sweet Star Lady and the lovely Queen of the Five Flowers,[4] just as the young German and Norseman used to listen to the tale of the beautiful Briar Rose sleeping in

---

[1] Crowley (A.).   [2] Edmunds, p. 162.

[3] *Cinderella*, p. 409.

[4] LAYARD discovered in NINEVEH several figures of a divinity bearing a branch with *five flowers*.

death-like stillness until the kiss of the pure Knight rouses
her from her slumber." [1]

The Star Flowers surmounting these Solar emblems
ure usually three, but in fig. 1145 the number is *Five*, and
the spines of the Thorn or of the Briar Rose are con-
spicuously indicated. The Queen of the Five Flowers
" dwelt in a little house round which were *seven* wide

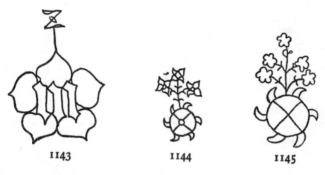

1143   1144   1145

ditches and seven great hedges made of spears." [2]   With
this we may compare the passage :

> " Wisdom hath built for herself a
> House and underpropped it with
> Seven Pillars." [3]

The star-flowered *jasmine* or *jessamine* was presumably
named after the Bright and Morning Star, said to have
sprung from the Root of JESSE.   The Jessamine was sacred
in CEYLON, and on one historic occasion a Cingalese Pyramid
or *Dagaba* was festooned from pedestal to pinnacle with
jessamine blossom.   On other occasions these Dagabas
were actually buried underneath a mountain of flowers, and
in one instance a dagaba was crowned with a hoop of
diamonds. [4]

[1] *Aryan Mythology*, p. 66. [2] *Ibid.*, p. 90. [3] Proverbs ix. 1.
[4] See Cave (H. W.), *Ruined Cities of Ceylon*, p. 86.

The Bride of King SOLOMON is entitled the Rose of SHARON and a Lily of the Valley, and this combination of the Lily and the Rose is perpetuated in the Christian name ROSALIE.[1] In fig. 1146 the *Fleur-de-lys, flowre de luce,* or *iris* is combined with a fiery rose ; and in fig. 1147 the *iris* is

surmounted by a rose-and-star flower. In fig. 1148 an *iris* forms the inmost centre of the mystic fourfold *rose* ; and in fig. 1149 the heart of EROS or *Love* or *Grace* is associated with an *iris*. The lily-flower appearing herewith within the circle of CHEOP, the Existing Eye or *iris*, has no doubt some relation to the passage in HOSEA, " In thee the fatherless findeth mercy. I will heal their backsliding, I will love

[1] ROSALINE=*Rose Alone.*

them freely : for mine anger is turned away from him.
I will be as the *dew* unto Israel : he shall grow as the lily,
and cast forth his roots as Lebanon." [1]

In Celtic the word *ros* means *dew*, and the Orchard of
the *Rose* is verbally and ideally identical with the New
JERUSALEM ; with the Garden of EROS or CUPID, the " Great
warm Hoop or Hub " ; with *iris*, an eye ; with *iris*, a lily ; with
IRIS, the rainbow-messenger of the Gods ; with *ros*, a hill ;
with *rhoss*, the white horse ; with *urus*, the great *bull* ; and with

1152   1153   1154

the Christ-child HORUS of the Horizon. In Greek the
word *eros* means a demigod or *hero*.[2]

A golden Iris constitutes the arms of FLORENCE or
FIRENZE, a city which sprang from and lies at the foot of
the rock-perched and inaccessible FIESOLE. The words
fleur and *flower* mean " living Lord of Fire " ; *flos* is *ef el os*,
the " living Lord of Light " ; and the name FLORINE means
" Sole Living Lord of Fire," or *feu sole*. The English *florin*,
a coin first struck at FLORENCE, now bears as its centre the
Cross and Star of ST GEORGE ; during the previous reign
it bore the image of BRITANNIA or MINERVA.

In fig. 1152 the *double* HU or *les yeux* surmount what is

---

[1] Hosea xiv. 3–5.
[2] Compare surnames ROSS, REES, ROWSE, ROSE, and RICE.

seemingly a FIESOLE, *i.e.* "Sole Fire and Life." In fig. 1155
a carnation or *dianthus* is a supporter to the fourfold meander
of the Supreme Spirit, and in fig. 1153 the same "resplendent
blossom " is sanctified by the cross.

The holy plants represented herewith are either *dianthuses*
or thistles. The Greek for *thistle* was *akantha*, the "great

1155

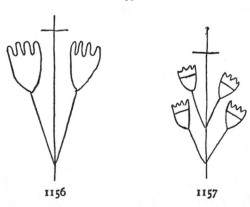

1156   1157

flower," and in Anglo-Saxon times *thisl* was a term for the
constellation of the Great Bear.[1] Porcelain reproductions
of the thistle have been found in Egyptian tombs, and in
those specimens at the Victoria and Albert Museum the
thistle flower is represented, not as mauve or purple, but
as a celestial *blue*. In some English counties the thistle is
termed a *daashl*[2] (German *dissel*), and this word—"the

[1] Müller (M.), *Science of Language*, ii., 402.   [2] Skeat.

resplendent light of God"—points to the probability that the *teazel's* plumes were deemed to be founts or spirits of the immortal sapphire, the "light of the living Fire." *Carduus*, the Latin for thistle, resolves into the light of *cardo*, the Heart, Core, Gore, or Hinge.

There is a variety of Thistle known as "Our Lady's"; there is also a "Lady Fern," "Lady's Finger," "Lady's Smock," "Lady's Mantle," and a golden "Lady's Slipper." These flowers, together with innumerable others, are all, so it is supposed, named in honour of the Virgin MARY, but it is more probable that their names antedate the Christian era. The blue flower known as "Love in a Mist" may be associated with the Wisdom who praises herself in the words, "I came out of the mouth of the Most High and covered the earth as in a mist"; indeed, so numerous are the wild flowers named in some relation to the Virgin that one may identify our manifold and elusive "Lady" with Mary of the nursery rhyme:

> "Mary, Mary, quite contrary,
>   How does your garden grow?
> Silver bells and cockle-shells,
>   And pretty maids all in a row."

The "pretty maids all in a row" are the mermaids or marymaids of the Water-Mother, whose singing made the music of the seven spheres. The harmony of the Orchard of the Rose is described by Chaucer as

> ". . . . wonder lyk to be
> Song of mermaidens of the sea.
>
> .   .   .   .   .   .
>
> It semede a place espirituel,
> For never yitt such melodye
> Was herd of man."

In fig. 1158 WISDOM is crowned with a cockle- or scallop-shell, and with the twin heads of a *uræus* or sacred serpent.

The Silver Bells in Mary's Garden are illustrated in the *campanulas*, or hare-bells herewith. There is a small flower

1158

which, from its resemblance to a circular mirror, has been named *campanula speculum*, or *Venus' Looking-Glass*. One may infer that the Blue-bell was also the Virgin's flower, and that its mystic value has been expressed in the lines, "O Thou mighty God, make me as a fair virgin that is clad

1159   1160

in the blue-bells of the fragrant hillside ; I beseech Thee, O thou Great God ! that I may ring out the melody of Thy voice and be clothed in the pure light of Thy loveliness : O Thou God my God ! "[1]

It is related that CINDERELLA, in addition to her robe of musical bells, was garbed sometimes "like the flowers of the field."[2] In an Armenian version CINDERELLA is described

---

[1] *The Equinox*, vol. i., No. 3, p. 25.   [2] *Cinderella*, p. 232.

as covered entirely in exquisite flowers, "so that no part of her clothes is seen," and elsewhere one of CINDERELLA's dresses is recorded as "made of all the flowers in the world." CINDERELLA, robed like the flowers of the field, may again be compared with WISDOM, of whom in *The Wedding Song* it is said :

> "Like unto Spring flowers are her garments,
> From them streameth scent of sweet odour."

"At our gates," says the Bride of King Solomon, "are all manner of pleasant fruits, new and old, which I have laid up for thee, O my beloved."[1] Dishes and festoons of

1161

flowers and fruits, the symbols of spiritual Plenty, are a commonplace feature of symbolic ornament, and in the typical example herewith the fruits are radiant with light. Figs. 1162 and 1163 depict the invitation of WISDOM, "Come unto me all ye that are desirous of me, and fill yourselves with my fruits."[2] The Birds (*aves*) and Butterflies (*psyches*) introduced among the foliage represent the Souls of the blessed feeding upon the pleasures of PARADISE.[3]

Fig. 1164, representing Peace, Wisdom, or Truth upholding the Vine and Honeysuckle, is expressive of the passage : "As the vine brought I forth pleasant savour, and my flowers are the fruit of honour and riches. I am the

---

[1] *Song of Solomon* vii. 13.
[2] Ecclesiasticus xxiv.
[3] Jenner (Mrs H.), *Christian Symbolism*, p. 81.

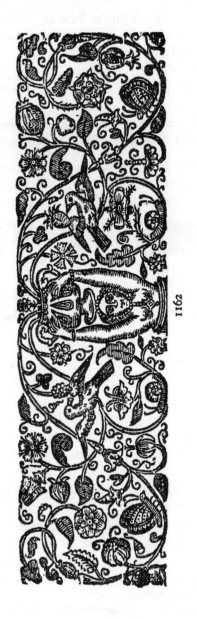

1162

mother of fair love, and fear, and knowledge, and holy hope :
I, therefore, being eternal, am given to all my children which
are named of him. Come unto me all ye that are desirous
of me, and fill yourselves with my fruits. For my memorial

1163

1164

is sweeter than honey, and mine inheritance than the honeycomb. They that eat me shall yet be hungry, and they
that drink me shall yet be thirsty. He that obeyeth me
shall never be confounded, and they that work by me shall
not do amiss."[1] The Greek for honey is *meli* or *melissa*,

[1] Ecclesiasticus xxiv.

and MELISSA was one of the names of Isis. The beautiful half-mermaid MELUSINE who appears in European legend must be another form of the celestial MELISSA who brings clusters of blossoms to the honey-drinkers. One of the legendary names of BRITAIN was "The Honey Isle of Beli," [1] and at AVEBURY there is a MELSOME Wood and a MILK Hill. Offerings of the first milk from their cows are still made in India to the Serpent NAGA [2] or DEVA.

CANAAN, the Promised Land of giant grapes, is described as flowing with milk and honey, and in the Song of Solomon is the passage, "Thy lips, O my spouse, drop as the honeycomb : honey and milk are under thy tongue." [3]

1165

The Holy Bear represented herewith as about to feed upon what is seemingly a cluster of honeycomb or a bunch of grapes illustrates the idea : "I am come into my garden, my sister, my spouse : I have gathered my myrrh with my spice ; *I have eaten my honeycomb* with my honey ; *I have drunk my wine* with my milk : eat, O friends ; drink, yea, drink abundantly, O beloved." [4]

The heroine of *The Song of Solomon* was "the keeper of the vineyards," and the Gospels attribute to JESUS CHRIST the claim, "I am the Vine." The word *vine* does not differ from *wine*, the "one Hu," the divine Mind or Reason ; and the word *reason* does not differ from *raisin*, a grape. The Greek for *grape* is *rax*, which is equal to REX, and both *raisin* and *reason* resolve into the HORIZON or "only ROSE."

---

[1] "The Honey Isle of Beli"="The Land of Balow."
[2] Oldham (C. F.), *The Sun and the Serpent*, p. 30.
[3] iv. 11.   [4] v. 1.

The Latin for a cluster of grapes is *uva*, and the word *grape*, "the mighty Fire, the Eye," is allied to *hip*, the little red berry of the hedgerow ; to *drupe*, the botanical term for any oval or round stone fruit ; and to *drop*. The *dewdrop* has already been illustrated as a symbol of the Enduring Eye.

The 80th Psalm is an extended elegy over the long-suffering and persecuted Vine of the Holy Spirit : "Return, we beseech thee, O God of hosts : look down from heaven, and behold, and visit this vine." ISAIAH bewails that "the Daughter of Zion is left as a cottage in a vineyard,

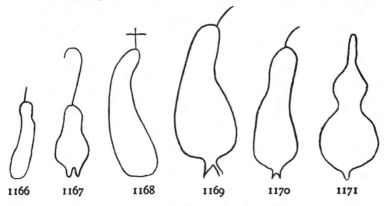

1166   1167   1168   1169   1170   1171

as a lodge in *a garden of cucumbers*, as a besieged city. Except the Lord of hosts had left unto us a very small remnant, we should have been as Sodom, and we should have been like unto Gomorrah."

We are familiar with the story of the Princess SUDOLISU besieged in her city, and we have met with WISDOM symbolised by a cottage or a lodge. Figs. 1166 to 1171 are classed by Mons. BRIQUET as "fruits," and from the cross surmounting fig. 1168 it is evident they represent *sacred* gourds, or the cucumbers of the Daughter of Zion.

In an Italian version of CINDERELLA a woman, according to augury, gives birth to a gourd, but, ignorant of the fact that there is a lovely girl inside, she exposes it in the forest. The gourd is found by the son of a king, who takes it home, and eventually marries the CINDERELLA within. This story is known as ZUCCHETTINA, which means "Little Gourd,"[1] and I surmise that the gourd was esteemed symbolically as being the distiller, the collector, and the treasurer of dew in a parched country. This may account for the introduction into certain versions of CINDERELLA of

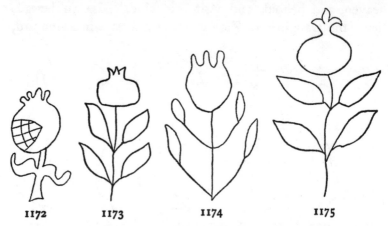

1172   1173   1174   1175

a great Gourd or pumpkin and its transformation into the crystal coach that eventually takes her to the ball.

The Garden of King Solomon's Bride is described as "an orchard of pomegranates, with pleasant fruits."[2] The pomegranate was regarded as the emblem of fertility, and its bursting seeds were held to typify the Resurrection. Fig. 1175 budding with an *iris* has evident relation to the passage, "I went down into the garden of nuts to see the fruits of the valley, and to see whether the vine flourished, and the pomegranates budded."[3]

The pomegranate is a symbol of the Virgin MARY,[4] and

[1] *Cinderella*, p. 133.   [2] *Song of Solomon* iv. 13.
[3] *Ibid.*, vi. 11.   [4] *Christian Symbolism*, Jenner, p. 99.

a magic pomegranate tree planted by Isabelluccia, and whose fruit she alone can pluck, enters into the Italian version of Cinderella.[1] There is an Indian story of a princess whose garden was hedged around with *seven* hedges made of bayonets. None should marry her but he who could enter the garden and gather the *three pomegranates* on which she and her maids slept.[2]

1176

In the early form of the " Foolscap " water-mark herewith Britannia, seated upon a triple-budded pomegranate, appears as Nucleolus within the Egg of the Universe.

Pomegranates formed part of the symbolic robe of the Israelitish High Priest. This garment was to be "all of blue." "And beneath upon the hem of it thou shalt make pomegranates of blue, and of purple, and of scarlet, round about the hem thereof; and bells of gold between them round about: a golden bell and a pomegranate, a

[1] *Cinderella*, p. 219.
[2] *Aryan Mythology*, Cox, p. 90.

golden bell and a pomegranate, upon the hem of the robe round about."[1]

Fig. 1177 is a flame-tipped, nondescript kind of fruit, and figs. 1178 to 1180 may be either figs, pomegranates, or pears.

The teeming seeds and the form of the *Fig* will account for its symbolism of the Womb of Life and for its title of *ef ig*, the "mighty life." The same root is also responsible for *vigour* and for *vegetation*, both cognate with the Latin *uegere*,

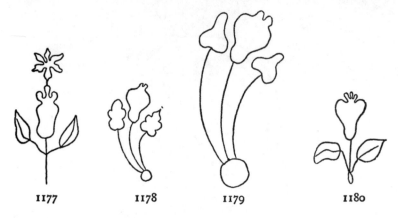

1177   1178   1179   1180

to quicken or *arouse*. FIGGIS is a British surname; and near SALISBURY is a circular earthwork known as FIGBURY[2] RING or CHLORUS' CAMP. The name CHLORUS may be resolved into *ac el* HORUS or the Great God EROS, the young-eyed, rousing, and *aguressive* Love or Life. CHLORIS was the Greek name for the Goddess FLORA.

In a French version of CINDERELLA entitled "Golden Bells" a magic pear-tree takes the place of the magic pomegranate. Its branches rise higher and higher beyond reach, except to FLORINE, the heroine, who says : "little pear-tree,

---

[1] Exodus xxviii. 33, 34.
[2] Compare proper name FAGGE.

bend for me to pick your bells." The branches then bow themselves and FLORINE gathers their golden fruit.[1]

The *pear* or *poire* may have been so named because it is formed like a pyre or pyramid. The Anglo-Saxon for *pear* was *peru*, *i.e.* père Hu, and the word *peru* does not differ from *perro*, a dog ; *pero*, a bear ; and *berw*, a hill, mound, or *barrow*. We again get the idea of *père Hu* in the pear-like fruit called a *quince*, i.e. *ak Hu ince*, the " Great Hu, the one Fire." There is a peculiarly conical kind of pear known as a jargonelle, a word supposedly allied to *jargon*, meaning

1181   1182   1183   1184

" a yellow diamond." *Jargon* resolves into the " Existent Fire, the Mighty One," and *jargonel* into the " Existent Fire, the Mighty One God."

The *pear* or *père Hu* was evidently esteemed also as an image and symbol of the human heart, and in the emblem herewith the fruits are unmistakably hearts.

The fruits of the raspberry are miniature *hearts*, and were presumably for this reason christened the berries of *eraspe* or Father EROS.

In EGYPT a pear- or heart-fruited tree named the *persea* was dedicated to ISIS. " Its fruit," says LE PLONGEON, " in the sculptures resembles a human heart, which vividly recalls the ON of the Mayas, that bears the Alligator pear."[2]

[1] *Cinderella*, p. 200.   [2] *Queen Moo*, p. 47.

The round fruit on the top of fig. 1184 may be an *orange*—the "golden ever-existent One" or the *Pearl* of Price—a *gooseberry*, or an *onion*. The onion was an emblem of God among the Egyptians, and probably likewise among the Druids, for it was a custom in England for girls to divine by it. According to Webster's Dictionary, *onion* is a name also given to "a single, large pearl, apparently because of its oneness or unity." The reason for the symbolism once attached to *onion* (the vegetable) was no doubt its spherical shape, the golden sheen of its outer skin, the pearly white of its inner texture, and the sheath within sheath, the ring within ring, of its growth.

> "Shall any gazer see with mortal eyes,
> Or any searcher know by mortal mind ;
> Veil after veil will lift—but there must be
> Veil upon veil behind."[1]

There is a golden, yellow fruit that grows in AMERICA known as the *persimmon* or "Jove's apple." Its scientific name is *diospyrus*, and the splendour of its colouring is some justification for the idea that it was the golden apple that grew in the Garden of the Hesperides.

The French word *pomme* and the English *apple* yield respectively "eye of the Sun" and "eye of POL": POL was one of the names of BALDUR, the Sun-God — the "enduring Ball." The Greek for *apple* is *melon*,[2] a word applied by us to a *gourd*[3] or *cucumber*,[4] and it is evident that many fruits and berries[5] were named from their similitude to the round Sun.

The Welsh for apple is *aval*, and thus AVALON, the Isle of Rest, is understood alternatively to mean "The Apple

---

[1] Arnold (E.), *Light of Asia.*   [2] =Om, the one God.
[3] *Ag our de*=mighty, shining fire.
[4] *Ac uc umber*=great, great Sun-Father.
[5] Compare *hips, haws,* goose—*i.e. ag uz*—berries.

Island." The heroine of *The Song of Solomon* is described as having been raised under an apple-tree.[1]

In mystic literature the apple-tree figures frequently as the Tree of Life,[2] and in fairy-tale the apple appears as the giver of immortal youth. CINDERELLA, according to an Armenian version of the story, knocks off the crown of a certain King AMBANOR by the dexterous throw of a diamond apple, and when the King, full of vexation, picks up the diamond apple, "the face of a most lovely girl looks forth at him as from a mirror." [3]

There is a SLAV story relating to an apple-tree "that bears the fruit of everlasting youth, and one of whose apples eaten by a man, even though he be dying, will cure him and make him young again." Something having gone awry with this apple-tree so that neither fruit nor flower will grow upon it, a messenger is despatched to the Palace of the Sun to ascertain the cause of the misfortune. When the weary APOLLO returns from his daily round and is resting sleepily upon his Mother's lap, the following dialogue takes place :

" Mother, what do you want ? "

" Nothing, my Son, nothing ; I was dreaming. In my dream I saw a large town, the name of which I have forgotten. And there grew an apple-tree, the fruit of which had the power to make the old young again. A single apple eaten by an old man would restore to him the vigour and freshness of youth. For twenty years this tree has not borne fruit. What can be done to make it fruitful ? "

" The means are not difficult. A snake hidden among

---

[1] *Song of Solomon* viii. 5.

[2] *The Quest*, vol. ii., No. 4, pp. 715, 716.

[3] This story, according to HANUSCH, is a most important reminiscence of ARMENIAN mythology, for in King AMBANOR is hidden the name of the ancient Armenian Spring-Goddess *Amanora*, to whom also points the flower-decked maiden.

the roots destroys the sap. Kill the snake, transplant the tree, and the fruit will grow as before."[1]

The Snake here introduced may imply, as also in the Garden of EDEN story and elsewhere, the creeping materialism that is so baneful to the fruits and flowers of AZGARD.

The Circles here illustrated are either some fabulous Fruit of Perfection or they represent cherries.

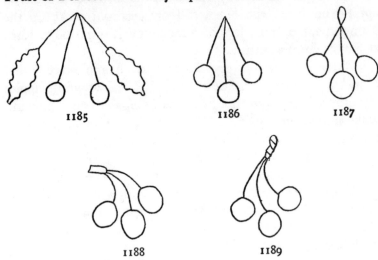

1185   1186   1187

1188   1189

Figs. 1188 and 1189 are unmistakably *cherries*,[2] a word that is identical with *cheres*,[3] meaning in Hebrew *orb of the Sun*, and with *charis*, the Greek for *grace*, cognate with our *charity* or *love*. *Cheery* means happy or light-hearted ; *ma chérie* is the French for *my darling* ; a *caress* is an *ac* EROS or *great love* ; and to *cherish* is to protect lovingly. According to Persian theology, the *Ized* entrusted with the care of the Sun disk was named CHUR ; there is a CHERHILL or Hill

---

[1] *Fairy-Tales of the Slav Peasants and Herdsmen*, p. 42.

[2] CHERRY is an English surname. According to Skeat, the word *cherry* (Mediæval *cheri*) was a corruption of *cheris*, the final *s* being mistaken for the plural inflection.

[3] MENCHERES was an Egyptian royal name.

of CHER at AVEBURY ; and CHER, the "Ever-Existent Fire," enters into innumerable place-names from CHERHILL, CHER-BURY, and CHERBOURG, to PONDICHERRY. The *naga* or sacred cobra[1] is in some parts of India known as the *chera*, and its worshippers term themselves in various localities the Cherus, Cheras, Seras, Kiras, or Keralas.[2]

The English *cherries* varies into the French *cerises*, German *kirsches*, Greek *kerasos*,[3] and the same root is responsible for *cherub* or *kerub*. The Hebrew Ark was surmounted by protective *kerubim* ; *ker* or *car* is Celtic for a fortress ; and *kirk* is Scotch for *church*.

Cherries, the ruddy little orbs of the Sun, are one of the myriad fruits of CERES, the Goddess of growth and giver of all increase. The name CERES—whence, no doubt, *crescere*, to grow, and thence *increase*—is resolvable either into *ac* EROS, *ac* HORUS, or *across*, the "Great Firelight." The Greek name for CERES or ISIS was DEMETER, *i.e.* the Resplendent Mother, and she was represented as holding a wheat-ear or a poppy. The flaming poppy was presumably a symbol of the *papa* or, as the American girl terms her parent, *poppa*.

The *per* of *pear*, *père*, and *parent* reappears in *prunus*, the generic term for trees of the cherry family. The words *prune* and Latin *prunum* resolve into "Sole Father" and "Sole Father Sun," obviously because the *prune*, *prunella*, or *plum* is round like the Sun-Ball. The French for *eyeball* is *prunelle de l'œil*, or "*plum* of the Eye" ; and the words *bloom* and *blossom* may be understood as *ball oom* and *ball os om*, i.e. Sun-Ball or Sunlight-Ball.

The Scandinavian for *blossom* is *bloma*, i.e. "ball of the

---

[1] *Ac ob ur A.*

[2] Oldham (C. F.), *The Sun and the Serpent*, pp. 152–160.

[3] It has been surmised that cherries first came from the Black Sea town named CERASUS, now called KHERESOUN.

Sun-Mother" or "beautiful Sun-Mother." The daughter of CERES, the Sun-Mother, was PERSEPHONE, a name resolving into *per is ef one*, the "parent of Light, the living one," and PERSEPHONE was worshipped under the alternative title of KORE. *Kore*, which is the Greek for *maiden*, is the same as CORA, the Irish Christian name, and it may also be equated with the Peruvian maize-goddess Mama CORA. At the Peruvian Harvest-homes an effigy of "Mama CORA" was put into a "certaine granary which they do call *Pirua*, with certaine ceremonies, watching three nightes; they

1190

put this Mays in the richest garments they have, and, being thus wrapped and dressed, they worship this *Pirua* and hold it in great veneration, saying it is the Mother of the Mays."[1]

This *Peru*vian word *pirua* is not very different from *peru*, the Old English for *pear*; and Mama CORA may be equated with *cœur*, the *heart*, the *cor* or *core* of the Universe, the "Presiding *Care*."

CORA still figures in British Harvest-homes under the name of "the Maiden" or *Kernababy*—a rude corn image made up from the last gleanings from the last field and treasured carefully from autumn to the ensuing spring. In all probability the *-baby* of this word is older than its

[1] See Lang (A.), *Custom and Myth*, p. 19.

modern sense, and means *baba*,[1] "parent of parents." In
KENT the Kernababy, Kernbaby, or Cornbaby is known as
the Ivy Girl,[2] and as the plant ivy does not enter into
harvest festivities, the Ivy Girl may no doubt be equated
with EVE, the Mother of all Living, or with the AVE- of
AVEBURY. In some parts of Scotland the *Ivy Girl* consists
of a "handful of Corn dressed out generally in the form of
a Cross,"[3] and the word *cross* will be recognised as merely
an inflection of CERES.

1191

In fig. 1192 CERES, the Ivy Girl, is flanked by cornucopias
or horns of increase ; in fig. 1191 she is crowned with the
crate or *corbeau* of the crops ; and in fig. 1190 the im-

---

[1] BABA was a royal name in Egypt, as was KHAMBABA in Persia. An old
title of PERSIA was ELAM ; and Oldham observes that King KHAMBABA ("the
Great Sun, the Father of Fathers") "seems to have been a personification
of the Sun-God."—*Sun and Serpent Worship*, p. 189.

[2] Knowlson (T. S.), *Orig. of Pop. Superstitions*, p. 70.

[3] *Ibid.*, p. 71.

plements and fruits of husbandry are associated with *ac er es*, the Great Firelight of DEMETER, the resplendent Mother. The word *crops* is an extended form of *ops*, riches, or *opus*, work.

Agriculture was by the ancients regarded as a religious art, and its processes were regulated by a belief in the agency of spiritual beings through whose kindly co-operation the infinite beauty and fertility of the earth was produced. In EGYPT, as also in PERU, the King put his hand to the plough as a sign of dignity and consecration, and in CHINA this custom still prevails. "There is," says a recent writer, "a

1192

ceremony called the Ceremony of Guiding Light, which takes place immediately after the Emperor has ploughed the first sod of the year. This ceremony falls under the department of the Worship of the Earth, which is permitted to the Emperor alone. It is the most solemn celebration of the year—it is as solemn as our Easter ceremonies, and, indeed, it is performed about the same time. And the extraordinary thing is, that this ceremony is exactly the same ceremonial dance as the Holy Sacrifice of the Mass. The Emperor, officiating, turns to the East and to the West at exactly the same time and with exactly the same genuflections as any Roman Catholic officiating priest. The music which is performed—the music of the Guiding Light—is just precisely a Gregorian chant. And at a given point little bells are rung, and censers swing before the altar. Three grains of rice are laid upon the Emperor's tongue, and he drinks a cup of rice wine." [1]

This drinking of *rice* wine is evidently a *Eucharist*, and the three grains of rice are seemingly another form of the triple ray of the *iris*, or of EROS, the *rising*, and *rousing*, and *increasing* sap.[2] Rice, a symbol of EROS (?), is still thrown as a benediction upon the newly-wedded, and the word *rice*— Latin *oryza*, Greek *oruza*, Arab *uruzz*, Afghan *wrijzah*, Spanish *arroz*—may be regarded as another of the arrows of EROS, another petal of the Golden ROSE.

1193

It is believed by some that the Scotch Island HARRIS was the Fortunate Island of the Ancients,[3] and by transposition of the syllables *ar is* they become ESAR, which is the Turkish name for GOD.

The Eastern term for *rice* is *paddi*,[4] and PADDY is a variant of PATRICK, whose symbol, the *shamrock* (Arabian *shamrak*), resolves into the "light of the Sun, the Great

---

[1] Hueffer (Ford Madox), in *The Bystander*, December 20, 1911, p. 638.

[2] Sap=*isap*, the essence of AP. The word is perhaps allied to the Egyptian *sa*, a mysterious and vivifying fluid imparted by RA. *Sap* is Gypsy for *snake*, and *sapience* means *wisdom*.

[3] See *Abury*, Stukeley.

[4] Compare place-name PADIHAM.

Fire." The honey-flowered *clover* or "Great Lover" may be dissected into *ac el ov er*, the Great God, the Living Fire, the *clever* One, the *Axe*, or "*Cleaver* of the Way."

In an Italian version of *Cinderella* the heroine is named LA GEORGIA,[1] the feminine of GEORGE, the husbandman, the Existent Fire, the Vital Urge.[2] The Emblem herewith surmounted by the motto, "Sow and be not doubtful," is elucidated by the passage, "Faith is the seed I sow ; good works are the rain which makes it fruitful ; wisdom and meekness are parts of the plough ; the mind is the rein ; and diligence is the patient ox."[3]

The objects below are described by Mons. Briquet as "yokes," and the meaning underlying them is probably CHRIST's statement, "My yoke is easy and my burden is light." The yoke[4] of CHRIST is identical with the pre-

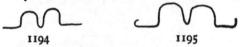

1194   1195

Christian yoke of WISDOM referred to in Ecclesiasticus, "Draw near unto me, ye unlearned, and dwell in the house of learning. Wherefore are ye slow, and what say ye of these things, seeing your souls are very thirsty ? I opened my mouth, and said, Buy her for yourselves without money. *Put your neck under the yoke*, and let your soul receive instruction : she is hard at hand to find. Behold with your eyes, how that I have had but little labour, and have gotten unto me much rest. Get learning with a great sum of money, and get much gold by her. Let your soul rejoice in his mercy, and be not ashamed of his praise. Work your work betimes, and in his time he will give you your reward."[5]

---

[1] *Cinderella*, p. 134.
[2] DEMETER was sometimes called GEMETER *i.e.*, the "Earth-Mother."
[3] From Buddha's Parable of the Sower, quoted in *Bible Folk-Lore*, p. 239.
[4] The word *yoke* means also the golden ball, the vital centre of an egg or *œuf*.   [5] Chap. li.

The essentiality of putting oneself under the yoke of discipline and toil is emphasised from the beginning to the end of the *Romance of the Rose*. The poet of this Gospel of Industry exhorts his readers, " To work, my masters, then to work "—

> " Unless in labour ye engage
> With right good-will, your lineage
> Must perish.   Seize ye then the plough
> With ready hands and cheerly bow
> Your backs in manner of the sail
> That bellies to the ruffling gale ;
> The plough-hales let your sturdy hands
> Grip, and across the fallow lands
> Drive the bright coulter, while the share
> Plays its due part, and then with care
> Scatter around the precious grain ;
> In faith 'twill render back again
> In autumn tide a manifold
> Rich harvesting of bearded gold."

The figure herewith surmounted by the motto, " His art in God," may be recognised as PIERS the Plowman, and read as an expression of the idea :

> " For such is His domain,
>   So closely near, so everywhere,
> All faithful hands can sow some grain,
>   And bring some seed to bear." [1]

PIERS PLOWMAN was a personification of the mediæval Poor Man's CHRIST.   " Conscience told me," says the author, " of CHRIST's resurrection, and how he gave his power to PIERS PLOWMAN, and anon departed into Heaven and sent the Holy Ghost to PIERS and to his fellows, and gave them many gifts. . . . And PIERS sowed them all—

[1] Duke of Argyll, *Poems*, 1894.

cardinal virtues, Prudence, and Temperance, and Justice, and Bravery." [1]

The name PIERS, a variant of PIERRE and PETER, resolves into *Pi ers*, "Father EROS," or the "Parent ROSE."

1196

The idea that the Orchard of the Rose or the Garden of EROS is *within* is far less theologic than poetic, and SHAKES-PEARE is the spokesman of all poets in the passage : "Our bodies are gardens ; to the which, our wills are gardeners : so that if we will plant nettles, or sow lettuce ; set hyssop and weed up thyme ; supply it with one gender of herbs, or

[1] *Piers Plowman*, Everyman's Library, p. 167.

distract it with many ; either to have it sterile with idleness, or manured with industry ; why, the power and corrigible authority of this *lies in our wills.*"[1]

The spade represented in fig. 1197 appears to depict the passage in Egyptian ritual, "I have grasped the spade on the day of digging the earth in Suten-henen," and the same idea is expressed by Marcus Aurelius when he says : "Look within. Within is the fountain of Good, and it will ever bubble up if thou wilt ever dig."

1197

A popular and childish version of this philosophic dictum is to be found in the invocation of Cinderella :

> "Little golden apple-tree,
> With my vase of gold have I watered thee,
> *With my spade of gold have I digged thy mould ;*
> Give me your lovely clothes I pray,
> And take my ugly rags away."[2]

In the designs herewith the "vase of gold" forms the fount whence spring the Rose and the flowers and fruits "both new and old."

[1] *Othello,* i. 3.   [2] *Cinderella,* p. 139.

Although the poets have systematically inculcated the idea that

> "*Here*, 'mid the bleak waves of our strife and care,
> Float the green Fortunate Isles,"[1]

no authentic mystic has ever maintained that Love's Gar-

1198

1199

den was nothing but a subjective and imaginary sphere. SWEDENBORG, a Seer, Scientist, and Philosopher, totally bereft of the poetic temperament, has described "from things heard and seen" an actual paradise of which, at the approach of children, "the clustering flowers above the entrance shot forth glad radiance."[2]   The writer of the *Romance of the Rose* affirms :

[1] J. R. Lowell.   [2] *Heaven and Hell*, 337.

> " For this fair dream I certify,
> To be no mockery or lie ;
> But all herein set down forsooth,
> Pure gold refined, and spotless truth."

The open-sesame to the Orchard of the Rose was no special shibboleth of any particular sect, but simply a ceasing to do evil, and a learning to do well.

> " 'Mid strife or slaughter be not seen,
> But hands and mouth alike keep clean ;
> Be loyal, kind, and piteous,
> And then shall you that marvellous
> And beauteous park at last attain."

It was said that the Queen of the Fortunate Islands, at whose look all the country round was rendered shining, first lulled her visitors to a preliminary sleep, and that afterwards they only who awoke to the appreciation of her supreme beauty were made welcome. " All this," says the poet, " is held a fable, but who first made and recited it, hath in this fable shadowed a truth." [1]

The Father of Queen Truth, who ruled in the Fortunate Isles, is said to be TIME, and in fig. 454 (*ante*, p. 182, vol. i.) PAN-footed TIME with his scythe or reaping-hook was represented as aiding his Daughter out of her cave-dungeon to the motto, " Time brings occult or hidden things to light." The mystic tenet, " Love to be unknown," and the silent hiddenness of WISDOM, or the humble hard-working CINDERELLA, are expressed in the lines :

> " Then bless thy secret growth ; nor catch
> At noise, but thrive, unseen and dumb ;
> Keep clean, bear fruit, earn life, and watch
> Till the white-winged reapers come." [2]

---

[1] *Cf.* Bayley (H.), *New Light on the Renaissance*, pp. 168, 169.
[2] Vaughan (H.).

The scythes or sickles herewith, symbols of the Reapers, probably express the passage, "Let us not be weary in well-doing : for in due season we shall reap, if we faint not."[1]   A hook was the attribute of SATURN or CRONUS, who was also known as "the ripener, the harvest-God."   The object surmounting fig. 1202 may be intended for "the new sharp

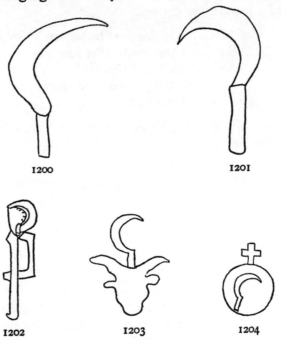

1200   1201

1202   1203   1204

threshing instrument having teeth" prophesied in Isaiah,[2] but I think it more likely an attempt to combine under one form the rake of the Sower with the sickle of the Reaper.

> "I am the Reaper.
> All things with heedful hook
> Silent I gather.
> Pale roses touched with the spring,

---

[1] Galatians vi. 9.　　　　　　　[2] xli. 15.

Tall corn in summer,
Fruits rich with autumn, and frail winter blossoms—
Reaping, still reaping—
All things with heedful hook
Timely I gather.

I am the Sower.
All the unbodied life
Runs through my seed-sheet.
Atom with atom wed,
Each quickening the other,
Fall through my hands, ever changing, still changeless.
Ceaselessly sowing,
Life, incorruptible life,
Flows from my seed-sheet.

Maker and breaker,
I am the ebb and the flood,
Here and Hereafter.
Speed through the tangle and coil
Of infinite nature,
Viewless and soundless I fashion all being.
Taker and giver,
I am the womb and the grave,
The Now and the Ever." [1]

1205

[1] Henley (W. E.), *Poems*.

CHAPTER XX

THE TREE OF LIFE

"In every well-conditioned stripling, as I conjecture, there already blooms a certain prospective Paradise, cheered by some fairest Eve; nor, in the stately vistas, and flowerage and foliage of that Garden, is a Tree of Knowledge, beautiful and awful in the midst thereof, wanting. Perhaps, too, the whole is but the lovelier, if Cherubim and a Flaming Sword divide it from all footsteps of men; and grant him, the imaginative stripling, only the view, not the entrance."—CARLYLE.

COLONEL KENNETH MACKAY who was President of the American Commission appointed to inquire into the conditions of government in PAPUA, relates: "As we rode back, George told me of the native conceptions of a future state, which struck me as very beautiful. Up on the Astrolabe Range there blooms invisible to mortal eye a great and gracious tree, in and around which dwell for ever, free from care and happy, all those who have lived good lives ere death claimed them. There lovers and loved relations will be reunited, while those who are already dwellers beneath its shade may and do come back to watch over the living, so that each soul yet on earth has an unseen but ever-present loving guide and helper. The wicked have to pass through sickness, pain, and trouble before they reach the tree, but eventually they, too, are gathered beneath its branches. The natives of the Astrolabe district say they know this sacred idyll is true, because those they loved and have lost have come back to them and told them so." The writer adds:

" I give this tale as it was told to me, and when one re-
members how old the Papuan is, how he has lived through
all the ages that have died, and the upheavals that have
made and unmade worlds since the continent of Lemuria
sank engulfed for ever beneath the waters of the Indian
Ocean, it is not hard to understand that he still possesses
dim memories of faiths learnt from lost peoples of higher
development when the world was younger and perhaps
nearer its Creator than it is to-day."[1]

There is a Mexican manuscript in the British Museum[2]
wherein two figures are represented plucking the fruits of
the so-called " Tree of Our Life." The Mayas and other
peoples of CENTRAL AMERICA always represented their sacred
trees with two branches shooting horizontally from the top
of the trunk, thus presenting the appearance of a cross or
TAU,[3] and the first Spanish missionaries in MEXICO found
to their great astonishment that the cross was already in use
there " as symbolising a Tree of Life."[4]

WODEN, the All-father, was said to have hung as a sacrifice
for nine days upon the tree IGGDRASIL, and the modern
Christian sings hymns to the CHRIST who suffered upon
" the accursed *tree*."[5] There seems at one time to have
been a widely-spread notion that the Cross of Christianity
was a *Tree*, and the belief in the saving and beneficial pro-
perties of that Holy Rood is still general. In figs. 1206 to
1210 there is an intentional blending of tree and cross, and
in fig. 1210 the Holy Rood or Rod surmounts a pyramid or
Calvary.

In the *Visions, Commands, and Similitudes, by Hermas*, an
Apocryphal work discarded by the Athanasian Council, the

---

[1] *Across Papua*, London, 1909.   [2] Add. MSS., British Museum, 9789.
[3] *Sacred Mysteries among the Mayas*, Le Plongeon, p. 134.
[4] *Bible Folk-Lore*, p. 243.
[5] It was not until A.D. 608 that CHRIST was represented as a man on a
cross.

Law of God is spoken of as *a tree* and as the Son of God. "This Great Tree which covers the plains and mountains and all the earth is the Law of God published throughout the whole world. Now this Law is the Son of God who is preached to all the ends of the earth. The people that

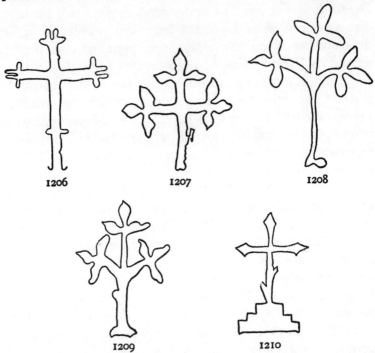

1206   1207   1208

1209   1210

stand under its shadow are those who have heard his preaching and believe."[1]

The Latin for *law* is *lex*, and the evergreen variety of oak-tree is called an *ilex*. When an oak-tree died the Druids stripped its bark, shaped its trunk reverently into the form of a pillar, a pyramid, or a cross, and still continued to worship it as an emblem of the great spirit.[2] Over and

[1] See *Aryan Sun Myths*, anon., p. 118.
[2] Reade (W.), *Veil of Isis*, p. 96.

beneath the sacred oaks used to be inscribed the word
THAU,[1] *i.e.* " resplendent Au." In fig. 1211 the holy tree is
shaped like *zeta*, the ancient Latin, Greek, and Phœnician
form of the modern letter Z. The word *zeta* may, as pre-
viously noted, be understood as *ze thau*, and resolved into
the " Fire or Life of Resplendent Au."

The twelve-leaved, three-rooted, eye-encircled tree here
illustrated is an heraldic *oak* or *aik*. Among the Hebrew
terms for *oak* are *el* and *allah* ; the Latin *robur* may be equated
with " Father RA " ; the Greek *drus* resolves into the " En-

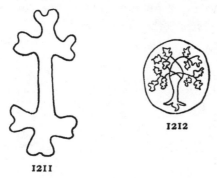

1211

1212

during Light " ; and the Latin *quercus* into *ak hu er ac us*.
The Welsh for *oak* is *deroo*, which may be equated with the
Sanscrit *dru*, meaning *wood* and *tree* in general.

Among the Chinese the Tree of Life was believed to be
a very wonderful *persica* or *peach-tree* situated in the Happy
Islands of the Eastern Ocean. It was said to coil up its

---

[1] The very learned Schedius, in his treatise *De Mor Germ*, xxiv., speaking
of the Druids, confirms exceedingly all that we have said on this head. He
writes : " that they seek studiously for an oak-tree, large and handsome, growing up with two principal arms in form of a cross, beside the main stem
upright. If the two horizontal arms are not sufficiently adapted to the figure,
they fasten a cross-beam to it. This tree they consecrate in this manner :
Upon the right branch they cut in the bark, in fair characters, the word HESUS ;
upon the middle or upright stem the word TARAMIS ; upon the left branch
BELENUS ; over this, above the going-off of the arms, they cut the name of
God, THAU ; under all the same repeated—THAU."—Stukeley, *Abury*.

leaves to a height of 3000 miles, and that "a golden cock is sitting upon it when the sunlight dawns."

The Egyptians supposed that "In the East of Heaven stands that high *Sycamore*-tree upon which the gods sit, the tree of life by which they live, whose fruits also feed the blessed." Thither at death went the souls of good men— "They go not as dead but as living." "They possess their heart, they possess their mind, they possess their feet, they possess their mouth, they possess their arms, they possess all their limbs."[1] The word *sycamore* may be resolved into *is ik amor*, the light of the great Love, or, more fundamentally, into *amor*, the Sun Fire.[2]

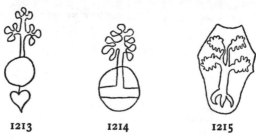

1213   1214   1215

In fig. 1213 the circle of the Sun is associated with a heart, and in this design, as also in figs. 1214 and 1215, the Tree is formed like fire.

The Fir-tree associated with the motto, "Without Thee Nothing," has doubtless relation to the God of Israel of whom it was said: "I am like a green Fir-tree. From me is thy fruit found."[3]

The Tree of Osiris was a conifer; a pine cone often appears on the monuments as an offering presented to Osiris; and the pine-tree was also sacred to Dionysos, to Atis, and to other gods of the awakening spring.[4] Fir

---

[1] Erman, p. 97.
[2] The Egyptian for *love* was *mer*. Compare name Murray, etc.
[3] Hosea xiv. 8.   [4] *Golden Bough*, J. G. Frazer, ii. 136, 144, 161.

cones have been assumed to possess a merely phallic significance, but the real reason for the sanctity of the conifers
was probably preserved by the Gnostics. According to
King, the fir-tree was "admitted into this system because its
spiry form imitates a flame, for which same reason its cone
was taken for the symbol of the element fire."[1]

The name *fir* may evidently be equated with *fire*, an idea
which is corroborated by the fact that the Welsh for *fir*-tree

1216

is *pyr*, *i.e.* the Greek for *fire*. The Greek for *fir* is *peuke*,
i.e. the Great Father or *Père*.

In some parts of Europe the *pear*-tree was regarded as
sacred,[2] and there is little doubt that the pyramidal form of
trees in general was partly responsible for their universal
worship. The conifers were peculiarly "coney" fires, but
the root *fer* or *ver* was applied in common to all *ver*dure
and all *for*ests or *for*êts. The golden *Furze*—at the first
sight of which LINNÆUS burst into tears—is a pre-eminently

---

[1] *The Gnostics*, p. 133.   [2] Faraday (W.), *The Edda*, p. 39.

fire-like bush. *Gorse* means the fire of the *gor* or " mighty Fire " ; it was sometimes called *gos*,[1] the " mighty light," and its botanic name *ulex* may be equated with *ilex*. The word *whin*, another name for gorse, may be equated with the *One*. The feathery fronds of the *bracken* or " Father Great One," especially when touched with the gorgeous colouring of autumn, equally suggest the blazing of a mighty fire. On Midsummer Eve the *fern* or " One Fire " was believed to burst into a bloom like burnished gold or wondrous fire, and whoever caught this bloom, which quickly faded and fell off, could understand the language of the birds and beasts, render himself invisible, and so forth.[2]

The Latin for a tree is *arbor*, " Fire Father " ; the French is *arbre*, *i.e.* arbor A ; the Italian is *albero*.

At the summit of the hill in DERBYSHIRE known as *Arborlow* is a Druidic circle of thirty stones. In LANARK-SHIRE there is an *Arbor Hill* described as a " conical eminence surmounted by the remains of an ancient fort." [3] *Broch*, the Scotch for a *fort* or *round tower*, is Cornish for the *yew* or *Hu*-tree. The sanctity of the yew-tree (Greek *taxus*, or " resplendent axis ") forms the subject of a special chapter of *Byeways in British Archæology*.[4]

In MEXICO the pre-eminently sacred tree was the pyramidal *Yaxche*. It is described as " a perfect cone from which the main branches shoot in a horizontal direction. Its leafy top seen from a distance presents the appearance of a half sphere of verdure." [5] The word *yaxche* resolves into *yak se che*, " great fire ever-existent."

The German for a *tree* is *baum*, or " Father Sun," and

---

[1] Compare surname GOSS, and place-names GOSPORT, GOSFIELD, GOS-BECK, etc. [2] Frazer (J. G.), *Golden Bough*, ii. p. 286.
[3] Bartholomew (J. G.), *Gazetteer*, p. 19.
[4] Johnson (W.). [5] Le Plongeon (A.), *Sacred Myst.*, p. 133.

in some parts of the world a similar tree to the pyramidal *yaxche* is termed a *baobab*, *i.e.* "Father HUBBUB" or "orb of orbs." In Hebrew *hobab* means *beloved*. The orb-like object illustrated in fig. 1217 is either a mystic Perfection or else a *cole* or *cabbage*. It was presumably its ball-like form that led to the symbolic estimation of *ak ol*, the "Great God," or *ac ab aj*, "the mighty aged orb."

Obab may be equated with APAP; and the *Poplar*-tree, once sacred to HERCULES, was obviously a symbol of the

1217   1218

Holy Rood, Rod, Pole, Spike, or Spire.[1] The sacred tree among the Buddhists is the *Bo*-tree, a name which may be equated with the European *Bay*, whose leaves were once a coveted crown of honour. In French *baie* means berry, or a *pip*. The laurel which was sacred to APOLLO resolves into *la ur el*, or "Everlasting Fire God," and *laurus*, the Latin for *laurel*, yields the Everlasting Eros, or the Fire Light.

The fruit-yielding tree labelled CHARITY is evidently a representation of the Apocalyptic promise, "To him that overcometh will I give to eat of the tree of life, which is in

---

[1] *Spire* = *Sepire* = "Fire Father"; compare also *cypress*, *spruce*, *juniper*, etc.

the midst of the paradise of God. . . . In the midst of
the street of it, and on either side of the river, was there the
tree of life, which bare twelve manner of fruits, and yielded
her fruit every month, and the leaves of the tree were for
the healing of the nations."

PLUTARCH states that of all the plants growing in EGYPT
the *persea* was the most sacred to the Gods, because its fruit
resembled a heart and its leaf a tongue.[1] Many leaves are
formed like hearts, and the word *leaf* is identical with *love*
and *life*. It is a scientific fact that a tree *lives* by its *leaves*,
and it is Swedenborg's leading dogma, " That Love is the
Life of Man." [2]

The Rose- or Eros-tree was, as already noted, regarded
as the home and abode of Deity. *Dendron*, the Greek for
tree, resolves into *den dur on*, the " den of the Enduring
One," and the flaming splendours of the *rhododendron* were
evidently once deemed to be a *den* or stronghold of the
Resplendent *Rho* or Fire. In Scotland the Mountain *Ash*
is named the *Rowan* or one RA. The British for an *ash*-
tree (Latin, *fraxinus*) was *onn*[3] or *one* ; the Anglo-Saxon was
wiggen, or the " one mighty Mind ; " and IGGDRASIL, the
Scandinavian Mighty Ash, resolves into *ig dur az il*, the
" mighty, Enduring, Light God." The last two syllables of
this name may be contrasted with the *hazel* and also with
the *azalea*, a variety of *rhododendron*.

---

[1] *Isis and Osiris.*

[2] " Some idea of love, as being the life of man, may be had from the heat
of the sun in the world, which, as is well known, is the common life, as it
were, of all vegetation ; from that heat, when it commences in the time of
spring, vegetables of all kinds shoot from the ground, are adorned with
leaves, afterwards with flowers, and lastly with fruit, and thus, as it were,
live ; but when the heat retires in the autumnal and winter seasons, they are
stripped of those signs of their life, and wither. Similar is the case of love
in man ; for love and heat mutually correspond to each other ; wherefore also
love is warm."—Swedenborg, *Divine Love and Wisdom*, i. p. 3.

[3] Edmunds, *Names of Places*, p. 247.

The *linden* was also seemingly once regarded as a stronghold of the *lin* or "the Lone," and its alternative name *lime* may be equated with "Lord Sun" or *elm*.

Lin does not differ from *oln* or *olan*, the Anglo-Saxon for *holly* or *holy*. The twisted, flame-like zigzags of the *holly* leaves were perhaps the special reason why this tree was named the *holy*. In olean*der*, ce*dar*,[1] el*der*, al*der*, german*der*, etc., there reoccurs the *dur* of "enduring"; the *laven* of *lavender* is "Lord Living One," and the same meaning underlies the fruitful *olive*,[2] and the mighty *agave* or *aloe*. "OLIVE LAND" was one of the names of EGYPT, and among the titles of HORUS, "the beautiful child of gold," was "child of the Olive-Tree."

In MEXICO the *agave*, which yielded drink from its juice, food from its root, paper from its leaves, pins and needles from its thorns, thread and cord from its fibre, and thatch from its leaves, was called "the miracle of Nature." The Greek for *agave* or *aloe* is *alon*, which may be Anglicised into "the Alone." *Alnus*, or the "only Light," is the scientific name for the *alder* or Enduring God. The *alder* in Anglo-Saxon was termed *aler*, and the powerful superstitions which still linger around the *elder*[3] are no doubt a survival of its one-time symbolism of "the Enduring God."

"I was exalted," says the protean Wisdom of herself, "like a cedar in Libanus, and as a cypress-tree upon the mountains of Hermon. I was exalted like a palm-tree in Engaddi, and as a rose plant in Jericho; as a fair olive-tree in a pleasant field, and grew up as a plane-tree by the water."[4]

We have already seen the Palm-Tree serving as a

---

[1] The *cedar* = incorruptibility, see *ante*, vol. i. p. 154.
[2] Compare names OLYFFE, JOLYFFE, OLAVE, OLAF, etc.
[3] See Appendix to *England's Riviera*, J. Harris Stone.
[4] Ecclesiasticus xxiv.

symbol of the Flaming Column, the Fire, or Tree of Life (*ante*, p. 39), and in fig. 1219 it is employed as a printer's mark. The Assyrian Tree of Life, as illustrated by LAYARD, consisted of an ornamented trunk or column surmounted by a seven-lobed palm leaf, and sometimes it has the appearance of a backbone.

In all probability the Palm was pre-eminently a symbol of the immutable and never-dying Fire, as being the only tree known to the ancients which never changed its leaves, all other evergreens shedding them, though not regularly

1219

nor all at once. The Phœnicians represented on their coinage a palm-tree encoiled by a serpent, and the Phœnician Deity was entitled BAAL TAMAR or "Lord of the Palm." *Tamar*[1] resolves into "resplendent Sun Fire"; *phenice*, the Hebrew for *palm*, may be Anglicised into "Fan light"—an obviously appropriate term; and *phœnix*, the Greek for *palm*, may be equated with the sole PHŒNIX, FEU, or VIE, the one Great Fire of Life. Among the Greek titles of BACCHUS was Lord of the Palm-tree or Ph-anax.[2] The word *palm* was probably once *paalom*, "Father Powerful Sun," or *op al om*, the "Eye of Lord Sun."

The word *almond* is affiliated by philologers with

[1] *Tamara Pua* is the name of the Indian mystic Rose of Paradise.
[2] Payne-Knight, *Symbol. Lang. of Ancient Art*, p. 15.

ÆGMOND, a proper name meaning "the protecting Eye."[1]
The fruit herewith is evidently a symbol of the almond-
tree of which one of the Gnostic Fathers wrote : "The
Father of the All is furthermore called by the Phrygians
Amygdalus, the *Almond-Tree*, not meaning the natural tree,
but the Pre-existing One, who, having within himself the
Perfect Fruit pulsating and moving about in his depths,
tore open his bosom and brought forth the Invisible,
Ineffable Son."[2]

The name *Almond* yields *al monde*, "Lord of the World,"
or "Sole Resplendent Lord." The Latins called the almond

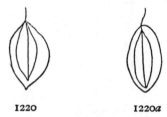

1220   1220*a*

amygdala, "the mighty Sun, the Resplendent Everlasting";
the Germans term it *nuss*, and its Egyptian name was *luz*.

The Egyptians depicted their sacred sycamore with the
head and shoulders of the Goddess NUT emerging from
among the branches. "O Sycamore of NUT," says the
Book of the Dead, "give me the air and water that is in
thee"; and there are representations of this Goddess in a
tree bearing bread or fruit and a vase of water.

It is proverbial that WISDOM is "a tree of life to them
that lay hold upon her"; and in the figures herewith, Mary,
the Water-mother or mermaiden, is formed like a tree.

In fig. 1223 the M of the Great Deep, or "*mem* the
waters," is formed suggestively like a Tree, a Root, a

---

[1] Edmunds, p. 164.

[2] King (C. W.), *The Gnostics*, p. 92. In Mediæval Breviaries the symbol
of the almond as the Womb of the World is often very naïvely exhibited.

Fountain of Living Waters, and the Source of the Spring of Knowledge.

The tree of MARY, the mother of the Mays, was essentially the *May* or Hawthorn, and in all probability the memory of " *Mem*, the waters," or Mama Cora, the Mother Fire, is preserved in the golden-bloomed *mimosa*. MAM TOR in Devonshire is said to mean the " Mother " Hill.[1]

The *maple* used to be spelled *mapul*, and the Anglo-Saxons termed it *mapulder*. Ideally and philologically it may be equated with the *Maypole*. The botanic term for maple-

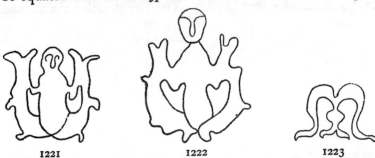

1221   1222   1223

tree is *acer*, *i.e.* the first two syllables of CERES and of CORA. The Peruvian name CORA or Mother of the Mays cannot differ from the British Mother CAREY whom KINGSLEY describes in *The Water Babies* as sitting " quite still with her chin upon her hand, looking down into the sea with two great, grand, blue eyes, as blue as the sea itself. Her hair was as white as the snow—for she was very very old—in fact, as old as anything you are likely to come across, except the difference between right and wrong."

The *Mimosa* has been adopted as the symbol of SOUTH AFRICA, and the *Maple* as the national emblem of CANADA—" Our Lady of the Snows." It is a felicitous coincidence that Mother Carey[2] of the stormy petrel, or " Mother Carey's chicken," and of the maple leaf, sat like " one peaked

---

[1] Compare CAREW and CAREY.   [2] Edmunds, p. 248.

iceberg." Situated in the centre of "Peacepool" this iceberg "took the form of the grandest old lady he had ever seen—a white marble lady sitting on a white marble throne. And from the foot of the throne there swum away, out and out into the sea, millions of new-born creatures of more shapes and colours than man ever dreamed. And they were Mother Carey's children, whom she makes out of the sea-water all day long."[1]

As well as the *may*, the *mimosa*, and the *maple*, one may judge that the *myrtle*-tree or *meurte* was a symbol of the resplendent *mer*, *mère*, or *mare*.

The conception of the Law, Wisdom, Love, or Spirit of God as a Tree may be compared with the allegory of the Parsees, that the Great Spirit planted the seed of a good fruit-bearing tree. He nourished it with the water of purity, cultivated it with honest industry and diligence, and watched its growth in divine contemplation of its blossoming forth good thoughts, good words, and good deeds. Suddenly from the North rushed forth the evil ARIMANES, and with one chill blast of snow and frost ("Falsehood" and "Wickedness," *vide Avesta*) smote and retarded the rising sap of the growing tree. Thus, from on high, war was declared between Good and Evil, between the Pious and the Wicked, between Light and Darkness— one preserving and the other smiting God's glorified works.[2] In the following emblem two sages are represented tending and watering the Trees of Wisdom.

It was a teaching of CHRIST that "The kingdom of heaven is like to a grain of mustard seed, which a man took, and sowed in his field : Which indeed is the least of all seeds : but when it is grown, it is the greatest among herbs, and becometh a tree, so that the birds of the air come

---

[1] *The Water Babies.*
[2] Kapadia (S. A.), *The Teachings of Zoroaster*, p. 31.

and lodge in the branches thereof." [1] Hence Mysticism has always taught that the Tree of Life grew primarily within the Garden of the Soul.

1224

" Plante, Lorde, in me the tree of godly lyfe,
  Hedge me about with Thy strong fence of faith ;
  If Thee it please, use else Thy pruning knife,
  Lest that, O Lorde, as a good gardiner saith,
  If suckers draw the sappe from bower on hie,
  Perhaps in tyme the top of tree may die.
  Let, Lorde, this tree be set within Thy garden-wall
  Of Paradise, where grows no one ill sprig at all."

[1] Matthew xiii. 31, 32.

The pruning-knives herewith possibly imply the Millennium, when swords shall be beaten into plowshares, and spears into pruning-hooks,[1] but more probably they illustrate the idea—"The vine that is not pruned grows to wood. So also man. The Word, the knife, clears away the waste shoots, compelling the impulses of the soul to fructify."[2]

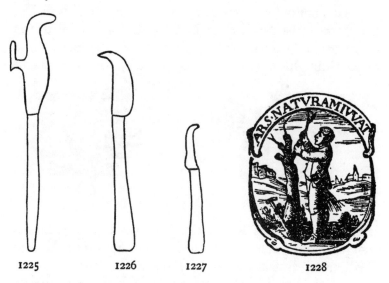

1225   1226   1227   1228

Fig. 1228 represents the operation of grafting, to the motto "Art vivifies Nature."

The Scandinavians conceived the Tree of Life as IGGDRASIL, the World-Ash,[3] the Oracle and Judgment-Place of the Gods, the Dwelling of the Fates, and the Source and Spring of Knowledge. Up and down the trunk of this

---

[1] Isaiah ii. 4.   [2] Clement of Alexandria.
[3] The symbolic sanctity once attaching to the Ash may account for the item of "natural" history: "Ash hath so great virtue that serpents come not in shadow thereof in the morning nor at even. And if a serpent be set within a fire and ash leaves, he will flee into the fire sooner than into the leaves."—Bartholomew Anglicus, 1260 (?).

mighty Ash a squirrel is said to have perpetually run, a squirrel which, according to RHINE legend, was "animated by the Voice of God," and whispered tidings into the ear of WOTAN of everything that transpired below.[1]

The French for squirrel is *écureuil*—phonetically *ek ûr œil*, "the Great Fire's Eye," and the emblems herewith are thus primarily symbolic of the All-seeing Eye. Their personal application rests probably on the mediæval idea that "when the Squirrel is hunted she cannot be driven to the ground, unless extremitie of faintnesse cause her to do so through an unwilling compulsion, for such is the

1229   1230

stately mind of this little beast that while her limbs and strength lasteth she tarrieth and saveth herself in the tops of tall trees, disdaining to come down for every harm or hurt which she feeleth ; knowing, indeed, her greatest danger to rest below amongst the dogs and busie hunters. From whence may be gathered a perfect pattern for us, to be secured from all the wiles and hungrie chasings of the treacherous devil ; namely, that we keep above in the loftie palaces of heavenlie meditations, for there is small securitie in things on earth ; the greatest ought to be our fear of danger, when we leave to look and think of heaven."[2]

It has very frequently been said that Mysticism bursts the shell of Dogma, and that it has preserved amid the

---

[1] B. Saintine, *La Mythologie du Rhin*, p. 127.
[2] Cf. Hulme (F. E.), *Natural History Lore and Legend*, p. 174.

jangle of conflicting creeds the sound kernel of Religion. BEHMEN observed that " the World is like some fruit, such as a plum or an apple, and has its rind-men, its pulp-men, and its core- or kernel-men ; all with the same faculties, only the first live merely on the surface of things, the last perceive how the outer form is determined by the central life within." [1]

The maxim that one must pierce below the husk of the external is represented by the squirrel cracking a nut, as in fig. 1229 and elsewhere. " We believe," said the mystics, " that the writings of Moses, the Prophets, and all earlier Teachers are not to be taken literally but figuratively, and as containing a secret sense hid under the mere letter. These writings are to be compared to a beautiful woman who hides her charms under a veil and expects her admirers to take the trouble of lifting it ; which is also the case with the Word of God being hidden under the veil of a figurative sense, which cannot be lifted even with the highest human ingenuity and greatest degree of wisdom without the assistance of divine grace. In other words, the things spoken of in the THORAH (Word of God) must not be taken literally according to the mere phraseology, but we must pray for the teaching of the Divine Spirit to be enabled to discern the kernel which lies under the mere shell or husk of the letter." [2]

The idea that the Scriptures—particularly the early chapters of Genesis—contained a hidden and mysterious sense was common among the early Fathers of Christianity. " What man," asked ORIGEN, " is so simple as to believe that God personifying a gardener planted a garden in the East ? that the Tree of Life was a real tree that could be

---

[1] *Dialogues on the Supersensual Life.*
[2] From the *Confession of Faith* of a Polish Cabalistic Sect known as Soharites. Cf. *New Baptist Magazine*, April 1827.

touched, and of which the fruit had the power of conferring immortality ?"

According to the Mosaic account of Creation, the Garden of Eden was protected by cherubims, and a flaming sword which turned every way to keep the way of the Tree of Life.[1] *Cherubims* as here mentioned is not another name for angels, but the *Cherub* of the writer of Genesis—like the *Cherub* of ASSYRIA, the *Cherub* of BABYLON, and the *Cherub* of the entire Orient—was a fabulous winged-animal[2] akin to a Griffin or Gryphon. The Mosaic idea of the protective Cherubim may be equated with the Persian conception of the innumerable attendants of the Holy One keeping watch against the attempts of AHRIMAN to destroy the tree HOM, situated in the region of bliss called HEDEN. According to Greek legend, the apple-bearing tree in the Garden of the HESPERIDES was guarded by a Serpent or a Dragon. The Hindoo sacred Mount MERU, whose summit towered into the golden light of Heaven, is said to have been guarded by a dreadful Dragon. The Chinese tell of a mysterious garden where grows a tree bearing apples of immortality guarded by a Dragon, and this winged Serpent —the national emblem of the Celestial Empire—is regarded as the symbol of Infinite Intelligence keeping ward over the Tree of Knowledge.

In the figure herewith a Dragon-guarded Tree is subscribed with the word BRASICA, fundamentally equivalent to *Persica*, a peach. The *Persica* was the Chinese Tree of Life, and among the Gnostics there was a sacred rite called *Persica*. The initiates into this Mystery were termed "Keepers of the Fruits," and, according to PORPHYRY, they "symbolically signified 'the power of Keeping or Preserving.'"[3] The word *Persica* is evidently allied to JASPER, a

---

[1] Genesis iii. 24. [2] Smith's *Bible Dictionary*, art. "Cherubim."

[3] Mead (G. R. S.), *The Mysteries of Mithra*, p. 62.

Persian proper name meaning "Treasure Master."[1] JASPER, the " Ever-existent Light Father," may be equated with the "first foundation," which was Jasper of the New JERU- SALEM : "And her light was like unto a stone most precious, even like a jasper stone, clear as crystal."[2] The name JASPER is the European KASPER, which also is interpreted to mean "Treasure Master." Fundamentally it resolves into *ak as per*, the "Great Light *Père*, *Pure*, or *Power*." In

1231[3]

1232

fig. 1232 a Dragon is seen guarding a garland of fruits surrounding the winged visage of EROS or JERUS, and the motto reads "By vigilance." Sometimes the Cock is found in emblem with the motto, "The vigilant custodian of things,"[4] and in fig. 1233 a cock-headed Dragon has its paw upon a horn or crozier ; in fig. 1234 the same Monster has under its protective claw the little House of Wisdom.[5]

---

[1] See Swan, *Christian Names*, p. 62.   [2] Revelation xxi. 11, 19.
[3] From *Printers' Marks*, W. Roberts.
[4] There are several examples in the BLADES' Library.
[5] "For this Mystery is the Gate of Heaven, and this is the House of God, where the Good God dwells alone ; into which House no impure man shall

Among the ancients there was a belief in two antagonistic Dragons, the one crooked, crawling, and slimy, the emblem of everything that was obstructive, loathsome, and disgusting; the other, winged, radiant, and beneficent, " The Reconciler, the Deliverer," the " Angel of the Dawn," the " Spirit of All Knowledge."

1233   1234

The opposition of those two Dragons was a leading tenet among the Gnostic *Naaseni*,[1] the followers of the

come, but it is kept under watch for the Spiritual alone; where, when they come, they must cast away their garments, and all become Bridegrooms, obtaining their true Manhood through the Virginal Spirit." Cf. *Wedding Song of Wisdom*, p. 74.

[1] The words NAAS and NAASENI are evidently affiliated with *nazar*, meaning *keep, guard, protect*, and with NAZARENES or NASAREES. Dr Wm. Benjamin Smith writes : " The epithet Nazoræus (variously spelled, the oldest spelling being most likely NAZARÆUS) is not derived from a 'city called Nazareth'; there was, in fact, no such city at the beginning of our era. The epithet is an appellation primarily of a Deity; it is formed after the analogy of Hebrew proper names ending in *iah*, as Zachariah, the *iah* representing *Jehovah* (pronounced Yahveh, Yahu, or Yah), and is derived from the familiar Old Semitic *nazar*, meaning *keep, guard, protect*, so that the Syriac ' Nazarya' is very nearly *Guardian-Yah*. The names Jesus and Nazaræus differ about as *Salvator* and *Servator*.

" The Nazarenes (or Nasarees) were in all likelihood the worshippers of Nazarya, and according to Epiphanius were 'before Christ and knew not Christ.' They are mentioned in Acts xxiv. 5, and Paul was one of them. They seem to have been hardly distinguishable from the *Jessees* also men-

Radiant and Perfect Serpent, whom they identified with JESUS CHRIST or SOPHIA ; and the antagonism of "the *Lord*" with "leviathan that crooked serpent" is one of the themes of ISAIAH : "In that day the Lord with his sore and great and strong sword shall punish leviathan the piercing serpent, even leviathan that crooked serpent ; and he shall slay the dragon that is in the sea. In that day sing ye unto her, a vineyard of red wine. I the Lord do keep it ; I will water it every moment : lest any hurt it, I will keep it night and day."[1] In the midst of this Celestial Vineyard there is said to have been a

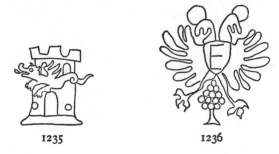

1235   1236

Tower, and in fig. 1235 the Dragon of the Absolute is flying guardingly before a Tower. In fig. 1236 the Eagle of Omnipotence is sheltering the symbol of His Vineyard or the Holy Grail.

Under fig. 1237—an emblem of the Holy Grail or Heavenly Hierarchy—there appears the motto " DUAU LE GARD," *i.e. Dieu* or the " Resplendent AU or AV " guards it. Under the Gate of Heaven symbolised in fig. 1239 there appears the same *le gard*, preceded by a monogram

tioned by Epiphanius, apparently an early name for the worshippers of the Jesus. Amid some uncertainty of detail the ground fact that Nazaree is derived from the Hebrew stem N-z-r, meaning *protect*, remains indubitable."
—Cf. *The Theory of the Pre-Christian Jesus*, The Open Court, 1910, p. 633.
[1] xxvii. 1–3.

which may be read AUM, or AA, or AVAN; and in fig. 1238 this same inscription appears beneath the symbol of the "Vineyard of Red Wine."

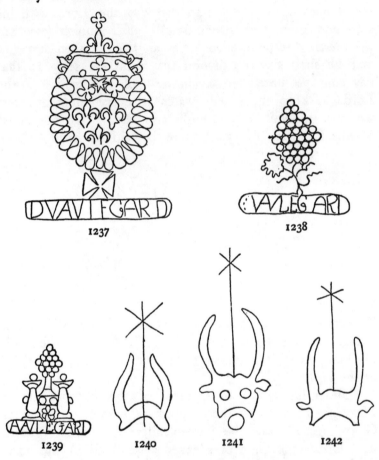

1237

1238

1239   1240   1241   1242

The act of guarding was typified by horns, and in the emblems herewith the cross of *lux* is shielded between the Horns of the Ox. "The image of the ox," says DIONYSIUS, "denotes the strong and the mature, turning up the intellectual furrows for the reception of the heavenly and productive showers, and the horns, the guarding and indomitable." [1]

The notion that *horns* exercised some potent, evil-averting, and *protective* influence has survived in the superstitious use of horse-shoes. Nailed upon farm buildings and elsewhere they are said to *guard against* ill-luck, and it is held to be essential that their position should be erect and hornlike, otherwise the luck runs out. The Dragon or *horned* serpent, as worshipped in Mexico and Egypt, although not a European reptile, is found represented on Gaulish coins and ensigns.[2]

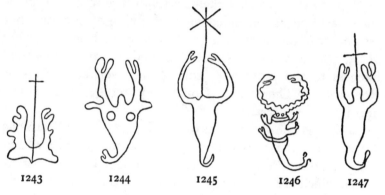

1243   1244   1245   1246   1247

The horns of fig. 1243 are those of an *Elk*, an *Axis*, or a *Roebuck*. Fig. 1244 is something like an *Elk's* head and something like a scorpion ; figs. 1245 and 1246 are pure and simple scorpions.

The Scorpion was the emblem of the Egyptian goddess Selk, whose title was "the great reptile, directress of the books." Selk — the "Light of the Elk," or *el ek*, the "Great God"—is portrayed with a Scorpion as her head-gear. Selk was also called the "Lady of Letters," from which she appears to have been the Goddess of Writing, and her

---

[1] *The Heavenly Hierarchy*, section viii.
[2] E. Anwyl, *Celtic Religion*, p. 30.

symbol was placed over the doors as the *keeper of books*.[1]
In BABYLONIA and ASSYRIA Scorpions were similarly regarded
as the *wardens* or *keepers*, and they are referred to particularly
in Babylonish literature as guardians of the Gateway of
the Sun.

> "Scorpion-men guard its gate,
> Of terror-inspiring aspect, whose appearance is deadly ;
> Of awful splendour, shattering mountains ;
> At sunrise and sunset they keep
> Guard over the Sun."[2]

Fig. 1247 has a remarkable resemblance to a "scorpion-
man" with arms extended prayerfully, and one can but
assume that the *scorpion* acquired its symbolism of *is ak or
pi on*, "the light of the Great Fire Father," from its formal
likeness to the protective arms of the everlasting Axis or
Roebuck. "The eternal God is thy refuge, and underneath are the everlasting arms."[3]

Scorpio is one of the signs of the Zodiac ; Seven Scorpions
are said to have accompanied ISIS as a bodyguard ; and in
fig. 1248 the little figure of Isis is equipped with tapering
horns, which are protecting the Circle of the Sun, or it may
be the Pearl of Price. Her head-dress is the Vulture-
symbol of the Great Mother,[4] or *val ture*, the "Strong
Tower." In PERU the *condor* or *vulture* was regarded as
the Messenger or Mercury of the Sun,[5] and it occupied the
same place in the sceptre of the Incas[6] as the two-headed
eagle now does upon the sceptres of the Emperors of

---

[1] Cf. Le Plongeon, *Queen Moo*, p. 67 ; and W. M. Flinders Petrie,
Religion of Ancient Egypt.

[2] Jastrow, *The Religion of Babylonia and Assyria*, p. 489.

[3] Deuteronomy xxxiii. 27.

[4] "The vulture was the Great Mother : we know not why."—Tirard, *Book
of the Dead*, p. 105.

[5] Spence, *Mythology of Mexico and Peru*, p. 55.

[6] INCA = *The Unique A*.

GERMANY and RUSSIA. In the emblem herewith the Bird of Fire is headed like a Serpent.

The Egyptians believed that "if he (the soul) comes to NUT or to *the Serpent which guards the Sun*, either of them greets him as her Son. She has pity on him and offers him her breast that he may suck, and thus he lives and is once more made a child." [1]

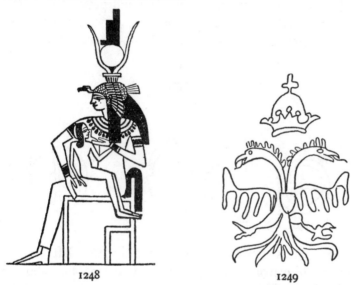

1248   1249

The word *guard*, i.e. *ag wara*, the "Mighty Ward," is traceable to the same root as that from which sprang AZGARD, the Scandinavian idea of the enclosured Light, the Park, or Paradise. Similarly the words *garner, garrison*, and *garden*, may be compared with the Phœnician *cartha*, the Norse *garth*, and the Russian *gorod*, all meaning a *guarded* and protected place. One of the Old English words for garden was *haigh* or *haw*, and the latter term survives in the name of the London church now known as "St Mary Woolchurch *Haw*."

[1] Erman, p. 97.

Branching from CHEAPSIDE is the street named BUCKLERS-
BURY, a name suggesting that at one time there stood here
a Bury or Barrow of "Buckler." A buckler is a protective
shield, and the word is radically the same as *buckle*. In
ancient Egypt the *Buckle* was regarded as a protective
amulet, and TIRARD illustrates a specimen inscribed "The
blood of Isis, the words of power of Isis, the might of Isis :
a talisman to protect the Great One and prevent any wrong
being done to him." The protective power of the buckle
is also shown in the *Book of the Dead*, where a buckle with

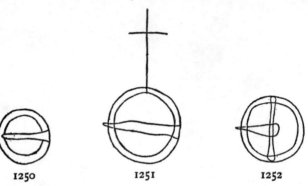

1250   1251   1252

human hands grasps the deceased by the left arm and
prevents him from going astray.[1] The emblems above are
evidently Buckles.

In fig. 1253 representing PARNASSUS, the centre tree is
guarded between two pyramidal rocks, and these Pillars of
HERCULES figure not infrequently on ancient coinage. King
ARTHUR is reported to have been buried between two
pyramidal stones. The goals of chariot- and other ancient
races were two great *stones*, and the word *goal* resolves, like
gaol, into the " Mighty or Ever-Existent God."

In GREECE the Dragon, a "crested serpent much resembling the Hindoo *cobra*," was sacred to MINERVA, and

---

[1] Cf. *Book of the Dead*, pp. 79, 80.

its image appears frequently upon her helmet. "The ancient Agathadæmon," says KING, "in the form of his congener, the Cobra, still haunts the precincts of the Hindoo temples as of old the shrines of Isis, and issues from his hole at the sound of fife to accept the oblation of milk from the attendant priest. As with the ancients so with the Hindoos, *he is the special keeper of concealed treasure;* and when a zemindar deposits his hoard in the prepared hiding-place, he, to make assurance doubly sure, builds up a serpent therewith to watch over the gold."[1]

1253

In PERSIA there prevailed a similar idea, and in PERU "we find the serpent, especially URCAGUAY, the keeper of subterranean gold, an object of great veneration."[2]

The figure of a Griffin with its paw placed guardingly upon a pearl, ball, or sphere, is a common subject of sculpture ; in fig. 668 (*ante*, vol. i., p. 276) Griffins were the supporters of the Water-Mother, and the Griffin seems everywhere to have been pre-eminently a symbol of Wardenship.

The belief in Griffins is considered to have come from the East, where they are mentioned as the fabulous animals that guarded the gold of INDIA. The Greeks believed that Griffins found gold in the mountains and built their nests

---

[1] *The Gnostics*, p. 218. (Italics mine.)
[2] Spence (L.), *Myths of Mexico and Peru*, p. 54.

of it, for which reason these nests were highly attractive to hunters, and the Griffins were forced to keep vigilant watch over them. The instinct of the Griffins led them to know where buried treasures lay, and they did their best to keep pilferers at a safe distance. According to BAR-THOLOMEW ANGLICUS, Griffins dwelt in "those hills that are called HYPERBOREAN," and they "keep the mountains in which be gems and precious stones, and suffer them not to be taken from thence." Other accounts state that the Griffins collected their gold from the sands of a river in SCYTHIA, and that the neighbouring ARIMASPIANS were constantly endeavouring to filch it from them. "These stories," says HERODOTUS, "are received by the Scythians from the ISSEDONIANS, and by them passed on to us Greeks ; whence it arises that we give the one-eyed race the Scythian name of ARIMASPI, *arima* being the Scythic word for ' one,' and ' spu ' for ' the eye.' "[1]

I have already suggested that the ISSEDONIANS or ISSEDONES, who, according to Herodotus, were the originators or fosterers of this fable, were the followers of ISIS—the enlightened ISSES', JESSEES', or ESSENES'—and that the ARIMAS-PIANS and other would-be thieves represent that semi-blind, one-eyed class that has no eye to recognise anything else than Matter. We may arrive at the more exact symbolism of the Griffin by a consideration of its composition, which was half-lion and half-eagle. The Lion born torpid but awakened by the roaring of its Sire was, I have suggested, a type of the regenerate man ; the eagle, according to DIONYSIUS, "denotes the kingly, and soaring, and swift in flight, and quickness in search of the nourishment which makes strong, and wariness, and agility, and cleverness, and the unimpeded, straight, and unflinching gaze towards the bounteous and brilliant splendour of the Divine

[1] Book iv. p. 27.

rays of the Sun, with the robust extension of the visual powers." [1]

The gold of which the Griffins built their nests and which was collected by them from the sands of a river, seems to have been the imperishable gold of Wisdom.

> "They wove bright fables in the days of old,
>   When Reason borrowed Fancy's painted wings,
>   When *Truth's clear river flowed o'er sands of gold.*" [2]

---

[1] *Heavenly Hierarchy*, section viii.

[2] T. K. Harvey.

A popular variant of this River of Golden Sands is found in the Slav Fairy-tale known as "The River of the Princess." The story runs that the land of Roumania was devastated by a disastrous drought, and men crept about like ghosts with their bones starting through the skin, their lips drawn back so that the teeth lay bare, and only a few rags upon their bodies. The beautiful Princess IRINA felt her heart breaking for pity, and wringing her hands, prayed thus :—

"'O good God! hast Thou, then, quite forsaken me? Wilt Thou bring our poor land to destruction? Have we sinned yet more that we must endure such searchings-out of Thy wrath?'

"Then a soft, cool breath stole in, bearing a perfume as from the most beautiful of gardens, and a silvery voice spoke :

"'Help shall arise for thee *out of a river*. Only seek.'

"Then, through the burning summer heat she began a weary pilgrimage toward the rivers. Sometimes she would still chance upon a poor, starved little horse, that would carry her a short distance, and then fall down dead, even beneath her light weight. She went up the *Olto* river, the *Gin*, the *Buzlu*, the *Sereth*, all the rivers, both great and small. They flowed but meagrely over their stony beds, and those once mighty waters scarcely whispered as they went, they that of old were wont to rush and roar.

"'Merciful God!' prayed the Princess, 'let but a little cloud appear when I have found the river that is to help us!' But there arose no cloud. She was wandering for a second time up the banks of the *Argesch*, and was just about to turn sadly back, when she caught sight of the mouth of *a little stream that she had not noticed before.*"

The Princess falls asleep, and upon awaking—"Behold! the river was no longer brown, but clear and blue as the air, and at the bottom of the water something shone and glittered like the sunbeams themselves. Irina again girt up her garments and waded in—she must see what it was that shone with so wondrous a gleam. And lo! it was pure gold. She fell on her knees, there in the stream, and gave God thanks, aloud and earnestly. Gold! gold! Now she could help! She went carefully on through the

The Hyperborean Mountains where the gems were found and where the Griffins had their nests, are manifestly the mountains of *hyper*[1] BOREAS, *i.e.* above the storms and blasts of BOREAS, the Northern Wind. The Hyperboreans, according to HERODOTUS, "extended to the Sea,"[2] and this sea, one may assume, was the same as that alluded to by Wordsworth—

> "Hence in a season of calm weather,
> Though inland far we be,
> Our Souls have sight of that immortal sea
> Which brought us hither."[3]

According to some accounts, the Griffin "layeth in his nest a stone that hight Smaragdus against venomous beasts of the mountain."[4] *Smaragdus* was a generic name applied to stones of a green colour, but more particularly to the Emerald, and the Emerald symbolised "hopes of immortality."[5] Precious stones were, as has been seen, considered to be symbols of Truths, and the stone Smaragdus[6] thus

water and gathered up the golden grains and little fragments, filling her mantle with them till the burden was almost too heavy for her. And now she hurried home with her treasure and poured it out before her husband. Her children were yet alive, though weak and sorely exhausted; and they scarcely knew her again, she was so emaciated and sunburnt. Yet now messengers went forth into distant lands and bought corn, maize and hay, seeds and cattle; and the river never grew weary of giving till the famine was at an end, and laughing green, and sleek cattle, covered the Roumanian meadows once more."—*Legends from River and Mountain*, Carmen Sylva, pp. 135-138.

[1] *Hyper*, meaning *over* or *above*, may be modernised into *High Power* or *Eye Père*. [2] iv. 13.

[3] *Intimations of Immortality*. [4] *Mediæval Lore*, R. Steele, p. 130.

[5] *Romance of Symbolism*, Heath, p. 217.

[6] The medical practitioners of the Middle Ages firmly believed that Emeralds gave relief in a great variety of ailments, but nothing appears to have possessed such admirable healing qualities as GOLD; and *Aurum Potabile* or Solar Oil, when mixed with Lunar Oil or Silver, was held to be "a Great Arcanum fit to be used in most diseases." Dissolved gold was considered to be an Elixir of Life and was idealised as a divine antidote to disease and death.

seems to mean that the Truth of Immortality is an efficacious balm against the ills and evils of Mortality.

The one-eyed ARIMASPIANS everlastingly on the prowl for the treasured gold of the Hyperborean Griffins *rode*, it is said, *on horses*, an implication that they were men of intellect. The Intellect *per se*, as symbolised by the horse, is a faculty neither moral nor immoral, except as it may be driven or applied to a good or a bad purpose. The two eyes, as has been exemplified, typified respectively Knowledge and Love, and one may reasonably infer from the very marked mention of horses, that the solitary eye possessed by the Arimaspians was the Eye of Intellect and the eye lacking was the Eye of Love. The never-ending tussle between the filching Arimaspians and the indomitable Griffins thus seems to allegorise the old-standing feud between those who heard the pipes of PAN and those who would deny them into ridicule and silence.[1]

In PERUGIA there is a well-known sculpture, representing a crowned Griffin clutching a writhing pig. Its meaning is probably expressed in the lines of TENNYSON :

> " Let me fly discaged to sweep
> In ever-highering eagle-circles up
> To the great Sun of Glory, and thence swoop

---

[1] Plutarch alludes to the Arimaspians of his own epoch as follows : " We shall also get our hands on the dull crowd, who take pleasure in associating the ideas about these gods either with changes of the atmosphere according to the seasons, or with the generation of corn and sowings and ploughings, and in saying that Osiris is buried when the sown corn is hidden by the earth, and comes to life and shows himself again when it begins to sprout. . . . They should take very good heed and be apprehensive lest unwittingly they write off the sacred mysteries and dissolve them into winds and streams and sowings and ploughings and passions of earth and changes of seasons. . . . There are consecrated symbols, some obscure ones and others more plain, guiding the intelligence toward the mysteries of the Gods. Not without risk, for some going entirely astray have stepped into superstition, while others, shunning superstition as a quagmire, have unwittingly fallen into atheism as down a precipice."

Down upon all things base, and dash them dead,
A knight of Arthur, working out his will,
To cleanse the world." [1]

It was said of the Almighty, "he rode upon a cherub, and did fly : and he was seen upon the wings of the wind." [2] In Fairy-tale the Cherub or Griffin figures very generally as a benign and powerful *transporter*. There is, for instance, a tale current in TIBET of a Griffin that rewarded the hero by taking him upon its back and flying "straight in through

1254

the Great Golden Gate," where it deposited the youth "in the centre of a vast courtyard round which were sitting numbers of Gods, fairies, and other denizens of the Sky. [3] In fig. 1254 the Griffin is supporting not only the oblong square that typified the Universe but also a *globus alatus* or winged circle, the ancient picture of the *anima mundi* or Divine Spirit. [4]

The Master-Griffin or CHRIST was illustrated *ante*, vol. i., p. 278, and the word *griffin* or *gryphon*, allied to *gryffe*, a *claw*, resolves into "the Mighty Fire, the Living One."

[1] *Gareth and Lynette.*   [2] 2 Samuel xxii. 2.
[3] W. F. O'Connor, *Folk-Tales from Tibet*, p. 100.
[4] Stukeley, *Avebury*, p. 76.

In Gnostic emblems the Gryphon is sometimes represented with its paw or claw upon a wheel; sometimes "the same gryphon's tail ends in a scorpion, whilst the wheel squeezes out of its chrysalis a tiny human soul that stretches forth its hands in jubilation."[1]

In the designs below, of which fig. 1255 is Egyptian and figs. 1256, 1257, and 1258 European, the little soul is emerging jubilantly from the mouth of a Dragon or Serpent, and these emblems evidently express the passage, "Osiris enters the tail of a great serpent, was drawn through its body and came out through its mouth, and was then born

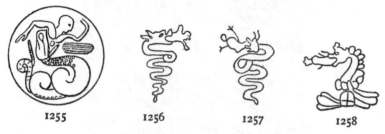

1255   1256   1257   1258

anew."[2] This progression of OSIRIS or Everyman through the body of the Agathadæmon or Good Genius, depicted as a huge serpent,[3] evidently typifies the purifying transit of the Soul through Wisdom. The story of Jonah is probably a garbled account of this ancient idea, and it is not unlikely that the sacred rites at Avebury and at other dracontian or snake-formed Temples included a perambulation by priests and people from the tail to the head, a ceremony typifying the healthful progress of the soul from the bondage of Ignorance into the Liberty of Light.

A belief in the efficacy of transit between sacred symbols was once widespread. Sometimes as a favourable omen

[1] King, *The Gnostics*, p. 129.
[2] Churchward, *Signs and Symbols of Primordial Man*, p. 275.
[3] *The Gnostics*, p. 217.

armies were purified by being led to pass between the split halves of a Dog,[1] and in Europe there are numerous round-holed stones by creeping through which it was believed that the old man was put off and the new man put on.[2] The passing through a split *Ash*-tree was regarded as equally efficacious, and sometimes a *Cherry* was considered the

1259

proper tree for the purpose.[3] The Stone or Rock hewn into the ring or circle of the Perfect One and the Ash-tree and the Cherry-tree all being alike symbols of the Great Spirit, may, it is obvious, be equated with the Dragon or Serpent.

In the printer's mark herewith the emerging Soul is

---

[1] Borlase, *Ant. of Cornwall*, p. 177.

[2] Baring-Gould, *Cliff Castles*, pp. 308, 309. Indra is said to have drawn a sick man thrice through a hole and thereby to have given him health and new birth.　　　　　　　　　[3] E. S. Hartland, *Folk-Lore*, p. 16.

rising above the tree-bending blasts of BOREAS to HYPER-
BOREAS or "Peacepool" in the form of a Dove. The Slavs
considered that the Soul after Death flew from the mouth
in the form of a *dove*, and they called the Milky Way "the
street of the birds," believing that the souls of the dead
fluttered along it in the shape of birds. The Latin for a
bird is *avis* or the "essence of Av," and the word *dove*
resolves into "resplendent Life." [1] The Hebrew and
Chaldaic for a *dove* is *juneh*, which is equal to the Latin

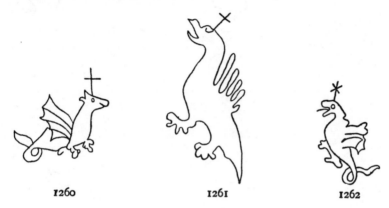

1260   1261   1262

JUNO, the Goddess of *Childbirth*, and to the Sanscrit *yoni*,
meaning *womb*.

It is believed by students of folk-lore that the legend of
St. George and the Dragon originated in that fabulously
remote period when mankind actually encountered "Dragons
of the Prime." [2] But the conception of the Dragon as a
beneficent monster must either have antedated this period
or the Dragon must, like the later Serpent, have served
simultaneously as the symbol of two direct opposites. We
shall probably be right in assuming that the giant saurian

[1] There are two rivers called DOVE in England, and the root enters
largely into place-names.
[2] See MacCulloch (J. A.), *Childhood of Fiction*.

was elevated into a symbol of the Infinite and the Omnipotent, because, like the elephant of later times, it was the vastest and the most powerful of all living things. Among the monsters here illustrated, which are doubtless emblems of that *agathadæmon* which the Albigeois were charged with heretically worshipping, two are marked with the cross

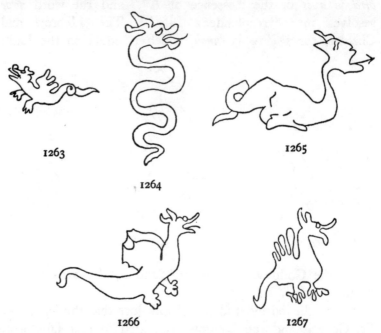

1263

1264

1265

1266

1267

and one with the star or *aster*. The word *monster* must indeed be the same as *minster* or *monastery*, and may be resolved into *mon as ter*, the "lone enduring light." The word *dragon* yields *dur ag on*, "enduring mighty one"; and the *Kraken* or great Sea Serpent, cognate with *kr*, the Sanscrit for *creator*, may be understood as *akeraken*, the "Great Fire, the Great One." According to Egyptian mythology, "*Aker keepeth ward*[1] over the wicked"; and the same root

[1] Budge, *Legends*, p. 13.

is perceptible in CERBERUS, the *three*-headed, serpent-tailed, monster-dog said to guard HADES.

According to Greek legend, the Dragon guardian of HESPERIA (or JASPERIA?) was named LADON, *i.e.* the "Everlasting Stronghold." In *Greece* there is a River LADON, and in LYCIA there is a volcano named CHIMÆRA. According to some versions, the guardian of the Hesperidian apples was GERYON, "the mighty fire, the ever-existent one," a *three*-headed Being possessing herds of the most splendid cattle.

The *three hearts* upon the back and the heart-like tongue of fig. 1268 stamp this emblem unmistakably as the *agathadæmon* or "good demon." But before the Greek word *agatha* came to mean *good* it must have meant *ag atha*, the Mighty A-Tau or the Ether. The father of King Arthur was UTHER PENDRAGON—emblemised *ante*, p. 10—and one of the Greek titles for ZEUS was ÆTHER. Thus EURIPIDES: "Seest thou the immense *æther* on high and the earth around held in its moist embrace? Revere Zeus and obey god."[1] And VIRGIL: "Thus the Omnipotent Father, great *Æther* with fecund showers, descends into the bosom of his rejoicing wife,[2] and, united in love with her great body, nourishes all her offspring."[3]

The word *agathadæmon* may thus be resolved into the fundamental "Mighty Ether or Author, the Resplendent Sole One."

In SOUTH AMERICA the alligator (*el agatha* ?) is known alternatively as the *cayman* or *ac ay mon*; and in *crocodile* the initial syllables are *kr*, the Creator or Great Fire.

In COREA the alligator is known as the *a-ke*; in CHINA the Dragon is termed *nake* or *naga*, and the word *leviathan* is no doubt cognate with the surnames LEVI and LEVEY, both of which may be compared with *lovey*. The Persian *mar*, which "may be supposed the same as that serpent which guards the golden fruit in the garden of the Hesperides,"[4] may be equated with the Egyptian *mer*, meaning *love*; and Love or *La Vie*, the "Everlasting Life,"

[1] *Heraclida.*   [2] JUNO or YONI.   [3] *Georgics*, ii. p. 324.
[4] Gould (C.), *Mystical Monsters*, p. 211.

may be identified with AMOR, the oldest and the first-born of the Gods.

In some localities CINDERELLA is known as AGATA,[1] and CINDERELLA—no larger than one's little finger—may, like the grain of mustard seed, be compared to that *agathadæmon* of which the Chinese mystics say: "The bright moon pearl is concealed in the oyster, the dragon is there."

It is believed in CHINA that "The dragon's skin has five colours, and he moves like a spirit; he wishes to be small and he becomes like a silkworm; great, and he fills all below heaven; he desires to rise, and he reaches the ether; he desires to sink, and he enters the deep fountains. The times of his changing are not fixed, his rising and descending are undetermined; he is called a god (or spirit)."[2]

It is further related of the Chinese dragon that when he opens his eyes it is day and when he shuts them it is night. He is said to have nine characteristics and eighty-one scales. The number eighty-one is nine times nine, and as the immutable nine was the symbol of immutable Truth, eighty-one may be obviously understood as a nine-fold nine or the fundamental Truth of Truths. KIAO, a Chinese name for the mystic Dragon, may be equated with *ak iao*, the great and ever-existent Beginning and the End. *Azhdaha*, the Persian name for *dragon*, resolves into the "blazing and resplendent A."

The Turks have a word *cove*, meaning the *sky*, and, according to STUKELEY, the old British term for the central stone of the sacred circles was *cove*. A cove is a shelter or haven, and the word is probably identical with *cave*. The Mithraic Mysteries were invariably practised within caves, and this curious custom may have survived from the time when caves were a refuge and a stronghold. The word *hole*,

---

[1] *Cinderella*, p. 315. [2] Gould (C.), *Mystical Monsters*, p. 400.

like *hill*, must once have meant *God*, and the French for hole is *trou*, which differs very little from our *true* and *tree*. Holes and Caves and Trees were Man's first home and refuge, and to the fugitive from some active ICHTHYOSAURUS or DINOSAUR Holes and Trees and Caverns must necessarily have implied a cogent symbol of the protective Spirit. In Cymric the word *tre*, as in COVENTRY and DAV- or DOVEN-TRY (?), means an abode, and the prefix *tre* still abounds in Cornwall. A *cove* is a *harbour*, and the Latin for *tree* is *arbor*. Among the Gypsies *hev*, the root of *cave*, means a hole and also a water-hole or *well*.

Once upon a time the words *ill*, *hell*, and *evil* must have meant *good*, just as DEVIL, LUCIFER, and DEMON once implied "Resplendent Living God," the "Lord of Light, the Living Fire," and "Resplendent Sole One." There is a tradition that SATAN was originally a Seraph, and the name SATAN allied to SET, the Lucifer of Egypt, may probably be Anglicised into the *Set* or immovable *One*. The antagonism between SET and HORUS was originally a poetic conception of the amicable and eternal rivalry between night and day, and in the AVEBURY Temple these twin circles lie tranquilly together within the greater circle of *Tem, the Lord of Life.*[1]

At that remote age when AVEBURY and the neighbouring DEVEREL were so named, *evil* and *devil* presumably had none other than a good significance. The Gypsy name for God is still *devel*; and the French for *hell* is *enfer*, the one Fire.

The writer of *The Hound of Heaven* has conceived that imperturbable "tremendous Lover" as unescapable; the poet of Psalm cxxxix. describes even the darkness of Hell as hiding not God; and the Egyptians entitled OSIRIS "Lord of the uttermost limit of everything."

The Dragon is known heraldically as a *wivern*; and there

[1] Budge, *Legends of the Gods*, p. 147.

is a minute kind of beetle termed a *weevil*. The name *weevil*, fundamentally the same as *devil* and *evil*, may be resolved into *wee evil*, and this tiny chafer had presumably the same symbolic significance as the *scarab* or *chepera*. About two hundred years ago part of the great circle at AVE-BURY was cut away by the then-there-resident Lord SCROPE —*is ak ur ope*, the " Essence of the great Fire Hoop "— and to this day there is living within its radius a family named KEM, " the Great Sun," one of the titles of the Land of Egypt.

According to an Egyptian account of Creation, Father NU, the celestial ocean, said : " Plants and creeping things (sprang up) from the God REM through the tears which I let fall. I cried out to my Eye and men and women came into existence."[1] The creative REM or *urem*, the " Fire of the Sun," does not differ from *kem*, the " Great Sun," nor from *ar*, the Egyptian for *Eye*.

The Egyptians conceived the sun-disc not only as the Eye of CHEPERA but also as a golden Boat that sailed daily across the azure ocean of the Sky. This so-called " Boat of Millions of years," or " Boat of RA," was named sometimes UR, sometimes URU, and sometimes MAKAA, the last meaning in Egyptian " great Protector," but resolvable fundamentally into *om ak aa*, the Sun, the great AA.

In fig. 1277 the " Boat of RA " is associated with the letters I O, and in fig. 1278 this moon-shaped boat is rigged with the P of the protective Parent.

The Egyptian believed that eventually his soul would be allowed to enter the Boat of the Sun, and that in the company of the Gods he would then sail into the source of immortal Light. Hence he placed model Boats in the tombs and prayed, " Come to the earth, draw nigh, O boat of RA, make the boat to travel, O mariners of Heaven."[2] The

---

[1] Budge, *Legends of the Gods*, p. 11. [2] *Ibid.*, p. 193.

Gnostic Manichees of the Dark Ages supposed that souls passed upwards primarily to the Moon, which they conceived to be a celestial Ship, whose brightness waxed or waned as it filled with souls or rendered them back to the Sun.[1] These Manicheans termed the Mother of Life or Living Spirit, Omoforos, a title resolving into "the Sun, the Living Fire Light."

It is obvious that such a maritime, seaborn notion as that of the Sun and Moon being *ships* could not have originated in the centre of Asia nor anywhere except among some nautical seafaring people. It must also have been

1277

1278

among *islanders* who were able to track the coming and the going of the sun-disc to the Sea, that there first originated the idea that *mare*, the ocean, was the Mother of RA. The word *home* means *sun*, and the terms *come* and *go* represent the daily movements of *ac ome* and *ago*, the "Mighty O." The Sanscrit for *go* is *gam*, and a symonym for *come* is *approach*, i.e. *ap er oche*, the "Eye of Fire, the O ever-existent."

Similarly the words *vanish* and *evanescent* allied to *vannus*,[2] a *fan*, express the fading and disappearance of the great Fan or EVAN. *Evening* is the evanescent time, and

---

[1] Conybeare, "The Religion of the Mani," *The Quest*, iii. 1, p. 7.

[2] *Vannus* = VENUS, who was often represented as seated in a *shell*-like car drawn by *doves*. AMPHITRITE = *am fi tur yte*, "the Sun Fire, the Enduring Heat."

even,[1] meaning *level*, may be equated with *elevel* or el Evil, "Lord Living Lord."

In BABYLONIA several of the Gods were assigned ships, and that of SIN, the God of Wisdom, was called "the ship of Light." JASTROW says "that it resembled a moon's crescent not differing much therefore from the ordinary flat-bottomed Babylonian boat with upturned edges."[2]

The word *ship* does not differ from *sheep* or *cheop*. The Latin for *sheep* is *ovis*, and for *ship*, *navis*, *i.e.* the one *avis* or *ophis*. The chief star in the constellation of "the Ship" is

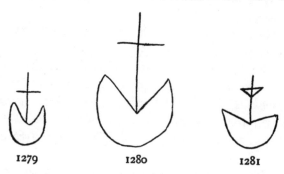

1279   1280   1281

named CANOPUS, which may be Anglicised into the "great one, the snake, sheep, ship, or hoop-light." *Hippos*, the Greek word for *horse*, was used also to mean *ship*: in Chaldee *ship* was *hipha*.

The main part of a Christian church is termed its *nave*; CHRIST, the Sheep or "Lamb of God," uttered some of his parables from a ship, and the likening of Christ's church to an ark or barque of safety is a frequent similitude.

The skin-covered canoes of the ancient Britons were known as *coracles*, and to this day the *ak* or *ak el* is in use in WALES. The little ships in which COLUMBUS sailed to the "New World" were termed *carvels*, and a synonym for *carvel* was *chaloupe*. The root *oop*, meaning *hoop*, eye, or

[1] *Haven=Heaven.*   [2] *Religions of Babylonia and Assyria*, p. 654.

disc, is preserved not only in the word *ship* but likewise in *shallop* or *chaloupe*, and in *sloop*. In North European languages *ship* becomes *skip*, *skib*, and *skepp*, whence our English *skipper* or *captain*. *Cap* is the "Great Eye" and *skipper* is the "Great Eye Father," and to the same root are resolvable the terms *schooner* and *skiff*.

A Persian and Arabian term for a boat is *sumbuk*, which is allied to the Spanish and Turkish *xebec* or *xabeque*. *Ek se bek*, the "Great Fire Buck" or the Roebuck, must be allied to the Serpentine "SABAK, Lord of the Bat in the East" (*ante*, p. 208).

The word *bateau* or *boat* is fundamentally akin to the Latin *beatus* which means *happy*; the term *pinnace* is allied to *benison*, and *punt* to the Blessed and Exquisite Land of PUNT or *op un te*, the "Eye of Unique Splendour." The word *sumbuk* is initially the same as *smack* or *sumak*; the Anglo-Saxon for a *smack* was *snace*—otherwise *snake*; the Icelandic for a swift vessel is *snekkja*, and the Swedish is *snacka*.

There is a kind of *sloop* known as a *hoy*—which is the way some people pronounce *Eye*. The Dutch term for a *hoy* is *heu* or *heudie*; *hodie* is Latin for *daily*; and by reversing the order of the two syllables *heu die* or *ho die*, the result is *dhow*—the African name for a sailing boat. In CEYLON the native name for a canoe is *dhoney*, which may be resolved into "resplendent one Eye" or "On High." *Galley* yields the "Mighty God Eye"; and *dao*, an alternative form of *dhow*,[1] may be understood as "resplendent O, HU, or *Ewe*."

The word *canoe* is a native term reaching us via SPAIN from HAYTI, the Island of the "Splendid AY." The Greek for ship is *naos* or *naus*, and there is still preserved the notion of the one Lord AY or Aw in our English *yawl*.

---

[1] Compare also aujourd'hui.

In *barge, brig,* and *barque,* there is fundamentally the notion of Everlasting, Mighty, and Great Bear or *Père.* The arms of BERKSHIRE are the Dragon, and the Northmen built their Dragon-headed barges, barques, or brigs in Dragon form. To this day there is held in CHINA an annual festival of the Dragon Boat. A Dragon was the standard of the Phœnicians, and at the prow of the Phœnician galleys stood a figurehead of the goddess ASTARTE, holding a cross in one hand and pointing the way with the other.[1]

In fig. 1282 the Bow *sprit, sprout, sprite,* or *spirit* is a cross, and the word *prow* (French *proue*) presumably origi-

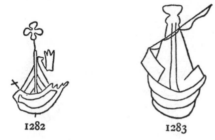

1282   1283

nated from the custom of the forefront of the ship, once consisting of an image, figurehead, or mascot of "*père* HU." The Gypsy word for ship is *berro.*

The name ASTARTE, "the resplendent Tower of Light" or the "splended lasting Light," is an amplified form of AST, the Egyptian name for the Goddess whom the Greeks entitled ISIS. Within historic times, a symbolic but very material "Ship of ISIS" used to be carried through European towns and villages,[2] and the ceremony was only suppressed when it degenerated into too scandalous license. *Eiss* was the Celtic for *ship.* The Spiritual Ship of ISIS or, as PLUTARCH explains it, *knowledge,* may be equated with the magic ship of the fairy Princess SUDOLISU. This Slav

[1] Donnelly, *Atlantis,* p. 441.
[2] Cf. *Curious Myths of the Middle Ages,* S. Baring-Gould, p. 334.

story runs, that Sudolisu, "the sustainer, the resplendent Lizu," dwelt beyond the nine kingdoms, far beyond the ocean, within a silver vessel with golden masts. The magic steed of her lover Niezguinek, says to its master : "Do you see that silver ship with golden masts that rides on the waves yonder? The first thing to be done is to get the diamond key that opens the ship. In order to procure this you must kill me and then throw into the water one end of my entrails, by which bait you will trap the King of the Lobsters. Do not set him free till he has promised to get you the key, for it is this key that draws the vessel to you

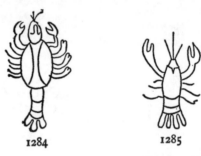

1284   1285

of its own accord." Niezguinek, Cinderella-like, demurs against slaughtering his trusty friend, but the horse exclaims : "Do as I tell you ; you can bring me to life again as you did before." Niezguinek then carries out his injunctions, whereupon, runs the tale, "there came a crowd of crawfish, and amongst them a gigantic lobster as large as a year-old calf."

This key-guarding, calf-like lobster illustrated in the emblems herewith is evidently a variant of the Sunguarding *calf, acalif,* or "Great Lord of Life"-like *Scorpion,* and it was presumably the similarity in form between scorpion and crayfish, and the likeness between these creatures' extended claws and the protecting form of a pair of horns that led to the crayfish being held sacred. Plutarch wrote : "I hear that the inhabitants of SERIPHOS bury dead crawfish. If a living one falls into their nets, they do not keep it, but throw it into the water again. They mourn over the dead ones and say they are the delight of PERSEUS, Son of ZEUS."[1] The French for *crayfish* is *écrevisse* or *écrefish*, and the root of both these words is "Great Fire A." The term *lobster* (Anglo-Saxon *loppestre*) resolves into "Lord Eye of Light Enduring."

" 'Give me,' says NIEZGUINEK to the calf—*ac Aleph* or Great-A-like lobster—'the diamond key which belongs to the silver ship with the golden masts, for in that vessel dwells Princess SUDOLISU.' The King of the Crawfish whistled, whereupon myriads of his subjects appeared. He spoke to them in their own language and dismissed one who soon returned with the magic diamond key in his claws. While speaking he saw the marvellous ship sparkling white in the sun. She was made entirely of pure silver, with golden masts. The rigging was of silk, the sails of velvet, and the whole was enclosed in a casing of impenetrable steel network. NIEZGUINEK sprang down to the water's edge armed with his club, and rubbing his forehead with the diamond key, said :

" ' Riding on the ocean waves a magic ship I see ;
Stop and change thy course, O ship, here I hold the key,
Obey the signal known to thee,
And come at once direct to me.'

" The vessel turned right round and came at full speed towards land, and right on to the bank, where it remained motionless. NIEZGUINEK smashed in the steel network with his club ; and opening the doors with the diamond key, there found Princess SUDOLISU."[2]

[1] *De sera Num. Vindic.*, 17.
[2] *Fairy-Tales of the Slav Peasants and Herdsmen*, pp. 257, 261.

The Greek for a ship is *naus*, which may be equated with *nous*, meaning the *Mind, Intellect*, or *Reason*. Silver was the symbol of Knowledge, gold of Wisdom, and the gold-rigged, silver ship of SUDOLISU cannot but be an emblem of the *Gnosis* or *agonisis*, the " Mighty One ISIS." Several of our London publishers still use this well-recognised sign of the Ship of Knowledge, and one of them combines with it the castle of KRONUS and the Tree of Life.

Fig. 1287 is the sign of Messrs CHATTO & WINDUS, copied by them from an Egyptian papyrus, and it will be noticed how curiously this ship is rigged. The rig of fig. 1288 forms a simple cross, and it was presum-

| 1286 | 1287 |

ably this sign that caused the earliest mariners to employ the word *rig*. The Gypsy term for *mast* or *tree* is *rook* or *rukh*.

The stays of figs. 1289 and 1290 form a firm *set A, stay*, cone, or pyramid, and the triangular *lug*sail [1] of fig. 1291 identifies this emblem as a mystic *lugger*. At the masthead of fig. 1282 (*ante*) is a fourfold Rose of Fire, the oriflamme of the Master of Life. The sail or lantern of this same small *Rose*-tipped ship of EROS—the little *chap* [2]—is

---

[1] The sail as an emblem was illustrated (*ante*, p. 38, vol. i.).
[2] *Lad*=LADON ? *Knave*=KNEPH ?

seemingly an *iris*. *Chap* is a variant of the word *ship*; and *chiel*, the Scotch for *child*, is a variant of *ceol*, the Anglo-Saxon for a *keel* or *ship*.[1] The sail of fig. 1278 is P, and of fig. 1290 a fiery, fluttering flag. An *iris* is alternatively called a *flag*, and the word *flag*,[2] meaning the "living Almighty," is also used to mean a stone. *Stone* reappears in *standard*, and *étendard*, the French for *standard*, points to the probability that the earliest standards were signs or models of *aten dar de*, the "enduring, brilliant sun-disc." At the battle of NORTHALLERTON in 1138, the English standard con-

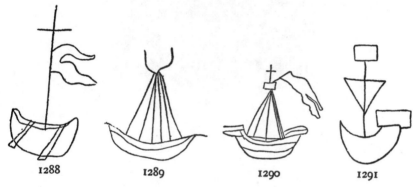

sisted of the mast of a ship fitted into a high four-wheeled carriage, and on the top of this mast was a silver pix with a consecrated host.[3] One sees frequently to-day a golden ball at the summit of a flagstaff, and this golden ball or Pearl of Price is portrayed in fig. 1277. The French for *flag* is *drapeau*, the *dur ap o*, the "one sign" or *ensign*. A *pennon* is the "universal one"; a *banner* or "good fire" is the same as *bonheur*, which means *happiness*, i.e. "*hoopyness*."

---

[1] The *chil* of *child* occurs in CHILTERN, etc., and, meaning *keel*, in place-names such as CHELSEA or *chel's ea*, the "port of the ships." The French for *child* is *enfant*, and *infant* may be resolved into *in fan te*.

[2] To *flag* is to *wane*, otherwise to *go*. To *wax* is to *grow*.

[3] *Chambers's Encyclopædia*, iv. p. 663.

In the emblem herewith a Ship is buffeting towards the rising Hoop or "Hope," to the motto *Espérance me Guide*. HESPERUS was known to the Latins under the name VESPER, the "Father of Living Light." *Vesper* is the Latin for *even*ing, and to the same root—*vis* (strong), *ovis* (sheep), or *ophis* (serpent)—may be referred the word *vessel*, *i.e.* the Living Light, Power, or God.

1292

CHAPTER XXI

VIA DOLOROSA

"Of all who have sailed the seas of life, no men have experienced a range of vicissitude more wide than has fallen to the lot of some among the mystics. Theirs have been the dazzling heights; the lowest depths also have been theirs. Their solitary vessels have been swept into the frozen North, where the ice of a great despair has closed about them like the ribs of death, and through a long soul's winter they have lain hidden in cold and darkness, as some belated swallow in the cleft of a rock."—VAUGHAN.

"We are scattered like sheep. We have been compelled to forsake house and home. We are as night ravens, which abide in the rocks. Our chambers are in holes and crags. They watch for us as fowls that fly in the air. We wander in the woods; they hunt us with dogs. They lead us away seized and bound, as lambs that open not their mouths. They cry out against us as seditious persons and heretics. We are brought like sheep to the slaughter. Many sit oppressed, and in bonds which even decay on their bodies. Some have sunk under their sufferings, and died without fault. Here is the patience of the saints in the earth. We must be tried by suffering here. The faithful have they hanged on trees, strangled, hewn in pieces, secretly and openly drowned. Not only men, but likewise women and maidens, have borne witness to the truth, that Jesus Christ is the truth, the only way to eternal life. The world still rages, and rests not: it raves as if mad. They invent lies against us. They cease not their fires and murders. They make the world too narrow for us. O Lord, how long wilt thou be silent?"

LEONARD SCHOENER, 1528.

THE road of mysticism has materially been a *via dolorosa*, and its track is thickly strewn with the bones of unremembered martyrs. Speaking of what he calls the "True Christians," or the "Invisible Church," KOMENSKY says: "Human fury attacked some of them shamefully. Bands of tyrants and hangmen, with countless followers, surrounded them. Sometimes powerful kings and whole kingdoms strove unto exhaustion to destroy them. Yet . . . they stood together, or went their way merrily, pursuing their callings."[1]

"Nothing unexpected," continues KOMENSKY, "can, indeed, befall such men ; for they count wounds, prison, torture, and death among God's gifts. To live joyfully or dolefully is indifferent to them, except that they consider the former more dangerous, the latter safer. Therefore they delight in their troubles, wounds, and stripes, and are proud of them. In all things they are so hardy in God's

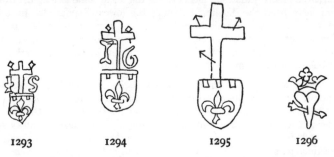

| 1293 | 1294 | 1295 | 1296 |

faith, that if they suffer not somewhat, they imagine that they are idling and losing time. . . . Some who fared not thus envied the others with holy envy, fearing God's wrath if they received no correction, and separation from Christ if they had no cross. Therefore they kissed the rod and stick of God whenever they touched them, and gratefully took His cross upon them."

In the emblems herewith, representing the three bent spikes or nails of the Passion, the designers adopted the Cross of Christ as their sign or trade-mark. The crowned and transfixed heart was, it may be assumed, a symbol of the grief-acquainted Man of Sorrows.

Continuing to describe the "True Christians," KOMENSKY

[1] *The Labyrinth of the World.*

says : " Now it is true that the evil world granted them but little rest, and, indeed, did everything it could to spite and mock them ; it grinned at them, bit its thumb at them, pelted them, spat at them, tripped them up, and whatever worse things can be imagined. Of this I saw many examples, and I understood that it befell, according to the orders of God the Highest, that those who wish to be good here must wear cap and bells ; for the ways of the world bring it with them that what is wisdom before God is to the world sheer folly. I saw, therefore, that many to whom God had granted His noblest gifts had to endure the contempt and derision of the others, often even of those who were nearest to them. Thus, I say, did it befall ; but I saw also that the godly heeded this not, that they, indeed, gloried therein, that the worldly stopped up their noses before them as before a stench, averted their eyes from them as from something loathsome, scorned them as fools, put them to death as malefactors. For they said that their watchword, by which it was known that they belonged to Christ, was " not to please the world." They said also that he who knows not how to suffer wrongs gaily hath not yet fully the spirit of Christ ; thus spake they of these things, and fortified each other."

The device of the Foolscap or the Cap and Bells—a paper-mark so widely customary that it has originated the term " Foolscap "—was seemingly a symbol of the determination to suffer wrongs gaily. It reflects the words of Paul : " For I think that God hath set forth us the apostles last, as it were appointed to death : for we are made a spectacle unto the world, and to angels, and to men. *We are fools for Christ's sake* . . . we are weak . . . we are despised. Even unto this present hour we both hunger, and thirst, and are naked, and are buffeted, and have no certain dwelling-place ; And labour, working with our own hands : being reviled, we bless ; being persecuted, we suffer it : Being defamed, we entreat : we are made as the filth of the world, and are the offscouring of all things unto this day." [1]

The notion that one must be considered a fool for the

1297   1298

1299   1300   1301

sake of Christ is common in the writings of A KEMPIS, BEHMEN, and other mystics, and it is akin to the declaration of Francis of Assisi, " We be the Troubadours of God." The rôle played in the past by the Troubadours and their intimate connection with the Vaudois or Albigeois has been

[1] I Corinthians iv. 9–13.

considered elsewhere.[1] Aroux, a devout Catholic, maintained that it was under the disguise of Jesters or Troubadours that the Albigeois disseminated their insidious doctrines,
and he further maintained that the Horn of Roland was a
symbol of this sectarian preaching.[2] It is common knowledge that the Troubadours[3] were fanners of the fire against
Rome; in the emblems herewith they are depicted with
open lips, and figs. 1302 and 1304 are associated with the
Horn of the Holy Spirit, *i.e.* the theme of their persistent
preaching. In one of the Cornish churches there is a piece
of carving representing a cock-hooded Jester, and this the
Rev. R. S. Hawker explains by the statement, "The Jester

1302   1303   1304

or Fool in a church is symbolic of the sectarian heretic or
scoffer at the mysteries, doctrines, or ritual of the Sanctuary."[4]
The traditional costume of a mediæval fool—the cockscomb of the dawn guarded between two horns—seemingly

[1] Bayley (H.), *A New Light on the Renaissance.*
[2] E. Aroux, *Dante: Hérétique, Révolutionnaire, et Socialiste*, p. 463.
[3] The geometrical design at the base of figs. 1299 to 1301 may, as I
first supposed, represent the various grades of the Troubadour's Organisation;
but I now think it more probably depicts the words of St Augustine, where,
after referring to the passage in St Paul, "What, know ye not that the saints
shall judge the world?' and explaining that the twelve thrones represent
the twelve apostles, he goes on to say: "The parts of the world are four:
the east, the west, the north, and the south. From these four, saith the
Lord in the Gospel, shall the elect be gathered together. Called, and how?
By the Trinity. Not called except by baptism in the name of the Father,
and of the Son, and of the Holy Ghost; so four parts each called by the
Three make twelve."
[4] J. T. Blight, *A Week at Land's End*, p. 135.

originated from the symbolism of their at-one-time high calling as preachers of the living Spirit in preference to formality and mere literalism.

The conception of a long-suffering but eventually victorious Fool is common to Fairy-tale and must be infinitely older than Christianity. "Who can understand the ways of God?" asks the Slav story-teller, and he answers : "It sometimes happens that the wisest men are not happy, while the foolish, when harmless and gentle, lead contented lives." The legend from which this passage is taken tells of a Fool who wound a waistband [the girdle of righteousness?] round his loins, put a helmet [of salvation?] on his head, secreted a tablecloth in his breast, took a magic wand [the *caduceus*?] in his hand and started off for the Royal Court. "Tell me, fool," says the king, "what price you want for these goods." "Not money, sire, a fool of my sort cares very little about money. Has not the king promised my mother that he will give me in exchange the half of his kingdom and the hand of his daughter in marriage. These are the gifts I claim."[1]

There is a Gaelic *Lay of the Great Fool* relating a

> "Tale of wonder that was heard without lie,
> Of the idiot to whom hosts yield ;
> A haughty son who yields not to arms,
> Whose name was the Mighty Fool."

CONALL, the hero of this legend — which may be regarded as embodying a whole cycle of mystical tradition —is first despised for his homely appearance and seeming weakness, but in the end he triumphs over all obstacles and wins the hand of the king's daughter who, like BRYNHILD and "Briar Rose," is imprisoned in a fastness. The name of this maiden is "Breast of Light," and the

[1] *Slav Tales*, p. 350.

tale relates that CONALL stood a little while gazing at her. At last, putting his palm on the point of his spear, he gave a springing bound, and "was in at the window beside the Breast of Light." In the sequel this tale repeats itself: the King of the Green Isle has a daughter who, like DANAË, is imprisoned within a tower, and various warriors try vainly to set her free, till CONALL "struck a kick on one of the posts that was keeping the turret aloft and the post broke and the turret fell, but Conall caught it between his hands before it reached the ground. A door opened and Sunbeam, the daughter of the King of the Green Isle, came out, and she clasped her two arms about the neck of Conall, and Conall put his two arms about Sunbeam and he bore her into the great house, and he said to the King of the Green Isle, 'Thy daughter is won.'"[1]

This Gaelic maid named "Breast of Light" is evidently the same as that forlorn but glorious "Daughter of Zion," of whom ISAIAH wrote: "Rejoice for joy with her, all ye that mourn for her; That ye may suck, and be satisfied with the breasts of her consolations; that ye may milk out, and be delighted with the abundance of her glory."[2]

It was one of the dicts of ST PAUL that, "If any man among you seemeth to be wise in this world, let him become a fool that he may be wise, for the wisdom of this world is foolishness with God," and from the device blazoned on the Bird of Fire herewith, it is evident that the Wisdom which the Holy Ghost teacheth, but which to the world is folly, was symbolised as The Great "Fool." "But the natural man receiveth not the things of the Spirit of God: for they are foolishness unto him."[3]

It is well known that the word *silly* meant originally *simple*, *innocent*, and *blessed*. *Silly*, like *zeal*, is allied to the

---

[1] Cox, *Mythology of Aryan Nations*, pp. 81, 392.
[2] lxvi. 10, 11.   [3] 1 Corinthians ii. 14.

German *seelig*,[1] which resolves into *se el ig*, the "fire of God Almighty." *Fou*, the French for *fool*,[2] is fundamentally the same as *feu*, the French for *fire*, and *fey*, the Scotch for *inspired*. *Oaf*, the English for *simpleton*, *booby*,[3] or *baby*, is the same as *ouphe*, the Scandinavian for *elf* or *fairy*, and *crazy* may be understood as smitten with a *craze*, or the "fire of the Great Fire A." The Old British name for the

1305

sacred *frenzy*, a familiar feature of all ancient divination and inspiration, was *awen*. The Old Irish term for a *simpleton* was *omadhawn*, of which the first two syllables may be equated with *mad*, or "hot sun" struck. The *hawn* of *omadhawn* is the British *awen*, *i.e.* the same "one A," as is the root of *crazy* or *ac* ERA *zy*, the "fire of the great ERA." Mythology relates that the Goddess HERA (=ERA[4]) struck DIONYSOS "crazy," and that in this state he wandered

---

[1] Compare German surnames SELIG and SELIGMANN.
[2] Compare Scotch surname FOULIS, also FULLJAMES and FOLJAMBE.
[3] Spanish *bobo*.   [4] *Era* now means a period of TIME.

throughout the world teaching its inhabitants the elements of civilisation and the arts of cultivation. JESUS CHRIST was charged by His contemporaries with being "crazy," "and many of them said, He hath a devil and is mad ; why hear ye him ? "[1]

The Latin for *mad* is *amens*, which may be resolved into *a men se*, the "fire of the sole A," and it must be assumed that this word has, like *silly*, changed almost completely in its meaning, owing partly to the inanities by which fanatics brought and still bring Spirituality and Religion into contempt.

In fig. 1306 the G of GESU is identified with the emblems of the Cap-and-Bells, and in the designs herewith this letter G or *jee*, the Ever-Existent, is treated as a separate symbol. In figs. 1307 and 1308 it is associated with a star or *aster*, to which must be allied *hysteria*. The hysterics of the Pythonesses or priestesses at the oracles of Apollo were, as we know, regarded as the utterances of *as tur*, the Enduring Light. The word has now, like Bedlam,[2] fallen entirely into disrepute.

In fig. 1318 a Fool is posed upon the Lodge or House of Wisdom. Among the Mexicans the *calli* or house was regarded as a symbol of fire, supposedly because a house or hut was warm.[3] In the most ancient Greek mythology the idea of VESTA, "the living light resplendent," stood for the *house* and the *hearth* and the domestic *fire*.[4] Prehistoric and native dwellings are nearly always circular or in Sun form, and were apparently named after the warm sun. Thus the English *hut* (Old English *hotte*) may be equated with *hot* and *heat*. *Cot* or *cote*, the Great Heat, must be cognate with *kotla*, the Zulu term for a gorsedd or parliament *circle*.[5] One of the Old British terms for

---

[1] John x. 20.
[2] Bedlam = Bethlehem.
[3] *Ruins of Sacred and His. Lands*, p. 290.
[4] *Ibid.*, p. 291.
[5] Bent, p. 25.

cottage was *cab*, the Great Orb ; another was *hove*,[1] the root of *cave* and *hovel* and cognate with *hof*, the Russian for a house. *Crella*, the Cornish for a round hut, is evidently the Zulu *kraal*; *calli*, the Mexican for *house*, is *ac al li*,

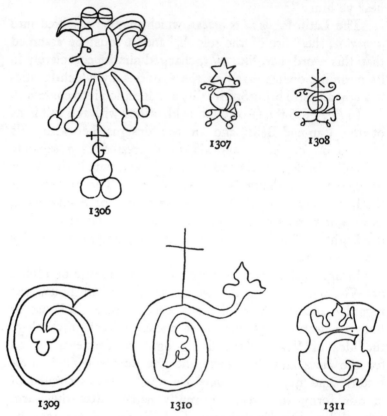

1306

1307

1308

1309

1310

1311

"Great God Everlasting," and *home*, the radical of *hamlet*, is *hom*, or *aum*, the *sun*. The Zulus term a coterie of kraals *umzi*, to which is in all probability cognate the French *maison* or *um zone*, the "Sun zone." Our *house*[2]

[1] HOVE, near Brighton, was once the Hovel Town.
[2] The word *housel* means the Eucharist, originally sacrifice.

(Anglo-Saxon *hus*) is the "immutable Light," and *castle* or
CASTILE is the "Great Light, the resplendent God."
The Gaelic for *house* is *aros*, the "Fire light," which

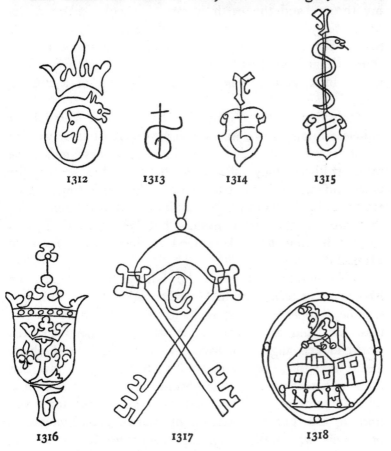

1312 1313 1314 1315

1316 1317 1318

may be equated with EROS or Love, and in Scandinavian
an abode was known as *bo* or *by*.[1] *Heresy* is derived by
the dictionaries from Greek *airetikos*, "able to choose." But
more truly *heresy* was EROSY, and most *heretics* were heroic
erotics.

[1] Whence DERBY, APPLEBY, etc.

The personal application of the Simpleton's house within a hoop, eye, or circle, illustrated in fig. 1318, is perhaps to be found in the passage : " The heaven is my throne, and the earth *is* my footstool : *where is the house that ye build unto me?* and where *is* the place of my rest ? For all those *things* hath mine hand made, and all those *things* have been, saith the Lord : but to this *man* will I look, *even* to *him that is* poor, and of a contrite spirit." [1]

Referring to the " True Christians," those Parsifals or guileless Fools, grown wise through pity, KOMENSKY writes : " But let all hold their hands aloof from these men ; the more willingly they offer their back to the stripes, the more difficult it is to strike them ; the more similar they are to fools, the more dangerous it is to mock them. For they are not their own masters, but belong to God ; and all that is done unto them God considers as done unto Himself."

This invulnerability of the faithful is explained by KOMENSKY as being due to Guardian Angels. " Nothing," says he, " appeared so exposed and subject to divers dangers than the band of the godly, at which the devil and the world looked angrily, menacing to strike and smite them. Yet I saw that they were well sheltered : for I saw that their whole community was encompassed by a wall of fire. When I came nearer I saw that this wall moved, for it was nothing else but a procession of thousands and thousands of angels who walked around them ; no foe, therefore, could approach them. Each one of them also had an angel who had been given to him by God and ordained to be his guardian, that he might guard him and preserve him, and protect him against all dangers and snares, pits, ambushes, traps, and temptations. They are, no doubt

[1] Isaiah lxvi. 1, 2.

(I understood and saw this), the friends of the men who are their fellow-servants, and watch them that they may uphold the duties for which they were created by God;

1319   1320   1321   1322

thus they serve men readily, guard them against the devil, evil folk, and unhappy accidents; and carrying them, if necessary, on their own hands, they shield them from injury. Here, too, I understood how great is the import

1323   1324   1325   1326

of godliness; for these beautiful and pure spirits remained only where they smelt the perfume of virtue, while they were driven away by the stink of sin and uncleanliness."

The Angelic trade-marks here reproduced served without doubt as an incentive, a strengthening, and a consolation to their designers.

It will be remembered that one of the faculties of the Holy Spectacles was to reveal to the Pilgrim his invisible fellow-pilgrims, dwelling unknown in this world, and dispersed here and there "among the others." "It is worthy of wonder," says KOMENSKY, "that (as I here saw with pleasure) men who had never seen each other, heard each other, and who were separated by the whole world, were quite similar the one to the other; for, as if one had been in the body of the other, they spoke alike, saw alike, felt alike."

Symbolism has been described as "the language of the angels," and in the Middle Ages it was eloquent and cosmopolitan. To the scattered, persecuted, and labour-loving mystics it was the silent speech of the "Invisible Church," and the method whereby its members fortified themselves and were able to commune one with another. "There was," says KOMENSKY, "great intimacy among them, openness, and holy companionship; therefore all, however different their gifts and their callings may be, consider and hold themselves as brethren." As the mystics were scattered throughout EUROPE, from the RHINE to SPAIN, and from ITALY to GREAT BRITAIN, so do we find traces of their tenets in their hitherto mysterious trade-marks. The tenacity with which from century to century the sectarians clung to their cherished traditions and maintained their persecuted doctrines was expressed by an extended hand, the symbol of Fidelity and Faith maintained. The motto *Foy* on fig. 1327 is the Old French form of *foi* (Spanish *fe*), *Faith*—to the World *fou*—and these numerous and almost innumerable Hand-watermarks, embroidered with supplementary symbols of the secret faith of Mysticism, may be regarded as silent vouchers to the resolution, "I WILL MAINTAIN."

It was at one time a custom in the West of England for village Friendly Societies to assemble at certain festivals and march in procession carrying symbols fixed to the point of rods. One of these old Friendly Society's badges, a brass hand pierced in the palm with the form of a heart, and obviously denoting Fidelity to Charity, is in my possession, and a variety of similar processional emblems were illustrated in *Country Life* of 1st January 1910. In their representative processions the Chinese still carry at the end of long silver rods figures in silver of strange animals, hands, scales, fishes, and other mysterious things.

When clasped in friendship, as in fig. 1330, the Hand was obviously an expression of concord and brotherly love ;

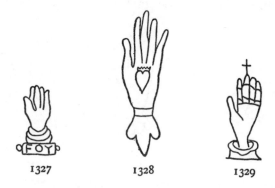

| 1327 | 1328 | 1329 |

when the third and fourth fingers were bent downwards, it formed the well-recognised symbol of benediction. Very rarely (only one instance is on record) the deviser came boldly into the open and proclaimed the sentiment, *Valete* = "health be with you !" "may you fare well !" In fig. 1332 this valediction has been amplified by the Fleur-de-lys of Light and the heart of Charity.

BEHMEN, the enlightened cobbler, has something to say about the wireless telegraphy or telepathy that existed among his fellow-workmen. "When," he writes, "the soul is *winged up*, and above that which is temporal, he hath all the angels for his friends, and he gets the hearts of all good men into his possession." "But," objects his disciple, "how is it that he can get his good friends into his possession?" BEHMEN replies: "He gets the very hearts and souls of all those that belong to our Lord Jesus to be his brethren, and the members of his own very life. For all the children of God are but One in Christ, which is Christ in All. And therefore he gets them all to be his fellow-members in the Body of Christ, whence they have all the same heavenly goods in common, and all live in one and the same love of God, as the branches of a tree in one and the same root, and spring all from one and the same source of life in them. So that he can have no want of

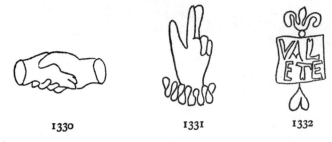

1330   1331   1332

spiritual friends and relations, who are all rooted with him together in the Love which is from above, who are all of the same blood and kindred in Christ Jesus; and who are cherished all by the same quickening sap and spirit diffusing itself through them universally from the one true Vine, which is the tree of life and love. These are friends worth having; and though here they may be unknown to him, will abide his friends beyond doubt to all eternity. But neither can he want even outward natural friends, as our Lord Jesus Christ, when on earth, did not want such also. For though, indeed, the High Priests and Potentates of the World could not have a love to Him, because they belonged not to Him, neither stood in any kind of relation to Him, as being not of this world, yet those loved Him who were capable of His love and receptive of His words. So, in like manner, those who love truth and righteousness will love that man, and will associate themselves unto him, yea, though they may perhaps be outwardly at some distance or seeming disagreement, from the situation of their worldly affairs, or from other reasons, yet in their hearts they cannot but cleave to him. For though they be not actually incorporated into one body with him, yet they cannot resist being of one mind with him, and being united in affliction, for the great regard they bear to the truth, which shines forth in his words and in his life. By this they are made either his declared or his secret friends : and *he doth so get their hearts* that they will be delighted above all things in his company, for the sake thereof, and will court his friendship and will come unto him by stealth, if openly they dare not, for the benefit of his conversation and advice ; even as Nicodemus did to Christ, who came to Him by night, and in his heart loved Jesus for the truth's sake, though outwardly he feared the World. And thus thou shalt have many friends that are not known to thee ; and some known to thee, who may not appear so before the World."[1]

The hands here reproduced depict the winning of unseen friends and the acquisition of their hearts. The base of fig. 1333 consists of hearts, and in fig. 1334 these emblems of Love centre in the clover leaf of the Great Lover. Komensky likens the unseen servants of Christ to the iron needles of a compass which once having been touched by the magnet, point one and all into the same quarter, " so," says he, " the souls of these men touched by the spirit of love, all turn to one and the same direction."

In INDIA a golden hand is the symbol of labour and of the productive power of the Sun. In EUROPE during the first eight centuries of Christianity, and even until the

---

[1] *Dialogues on the Supersensual Life.*

twelfth, God the Father was invariably represented by a Hand, the origin of which symbol, says Mr Heath, "is lost in pagan obscurity."[1]

Among the Indians of NORTH AMERICA the figure of a human hand is used to denote supplication to the Master of Life or Great Spirit, and it stands in their system of picture-writing as the symbol of strength, power, and mastery, thence derived. "In the great number of instances which I have met with of its being employed," says an American traveller, "both in the ceremonial observances of their

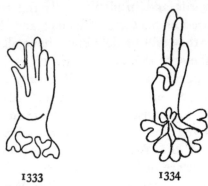

1333   1334

dances and in their pictorial records, I do not recollect a single one in which this sacred character is not assigned to it. Their priests are usually drawn with outstretched and uplifted hands."[2]

In the Latin Church, as among the Indians, the Hand plays an important rôle and is regarded as minutely symbolic. "The thumb, stout and strong, denotes the Chief Person of the Godhead ; the third finger, taller than the others, denotes Christ, the most important Person in man's salvation ; and the second finger, as between the others, denotes the Holy Ghost proceeding from the Father and the Son. The two

[1] *Romance of Symbolism*, p. 117.
[2] Quoted in *Ruins of Sacred and Historical Lands*, p. 293.

digits upon the palm denote respectively the Divine and the human nature of Jesus." [1]

From the supplementary emblems upon the Hands here illustrated it is evident that they symbolised the "Unique and Incomparable Heart Enslaver" of Sufi [2] poetry.

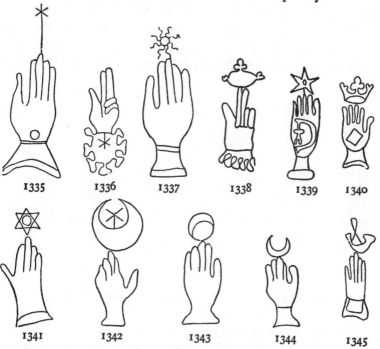

"Thou art Absolute Being : all else is naught but a phantasm,
For in Thy universe . . . all things are one.
Thy world captivating beauty, to display its perfections,
Appears in thousands of mirrors, but it is one.
Although thy beauty accompanies all the beautiful,
In truth the Unique and Incomparable Heart-Enslaver is one." [3]

---

[1] See Heath (S.), *Romance of Symbolism*, p. 118.

[2] The Sufis themselves connect this word with the Arabic root *safi—saf*, which signifies what is *pure*. It is equally related to our *safe* and *Saviour*, and to the Greek *sophos*, meaning *wisdom*.

[3] Quoted from *Sufiism* in *Religious Systems of the World*, p. 327.

On the palm of fig. 1335 is the Union or Pearl of Price, and from the middle finger rises the cross of Lux, the Light. Over figs. 1337 and 1338 are representations of the Solar Fire ; on the palm of fig. 1339 is the D of Dionysos or the Dayspring from on high ; and on fig. 1340 there appears the Diamond of unconquerable Light.

In fig. 1342 the cross is sheltered within the crescent horns of the virgin moon, LUNA or *lune*, the One ; and over fig. 1345 is the mystic horn whose notes rally the Hosts of Heaven.

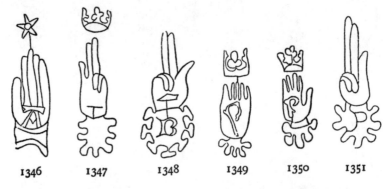

| 1346 | 1347 | 1348 | 1349 | 1350 | 1351 |

On fig. 1346 is the A-TAU of the First and Last, the Author of the Universe ; on fig. 1347 the T of THOR ; and on fig. 1348 the hammer of the creative Word. On fig. 1349 is the pastoral Crook of the Good Shepherd of All Souls, and on fig. 1351 is the P of PAN. The term Pantheism has been applied in two different senses which should be heedfully distinguished. There is a materialistic Pantheism that equates God with the physical world or Nature, and there is also a spiritualistic Pantheism that sees in the universe unending reflections and manifestations of one Invisible, Omnipotent, and Omnipresent Spirit.

It was one of the schemes of KOMENSKY, who was an ardent educationalist, to organise what he termed a "Pansophic " academy, and for this purpose he came to ENGLAND in 1641, visiting among others John Evelyn and Lord Herbert of Cherbury. The Moslem SUFIS, like the Christian

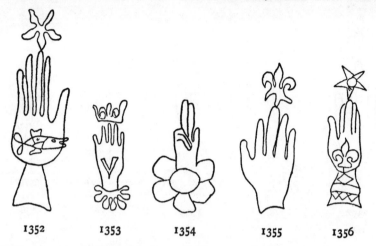

1352   1353   1354   1355   1356

Pan*sophists*, were adherents of the idealistic pantheism expressed by Elizabeth Barrett Browning :

> " If a man could feel
> The spiritual significance burn through
> The hieroglyphic of material shows,
> Henceforward he would paint the globe with wings,
> And reverence fish and fowl, the bull, the tree,
> And even his very body as a man. " [1]

On fig. 1352 is the mystic Fish or *vish* surmounted by a Flower of Flame, and on fig. 1353 the V of *La Vie* and VISHNU. Fig. 1354 is partly a five-petalled Marigold, and on fig. 1356 is the Flower of Light surmounted by a five-rayed Star.

---

[1] *Aurora Leigh* ; cf. also

> " Earth's crammed with heaven,
> And every common bush afire with God,
> But only he who sees takes off his shoes."

On fig. 1357 the twin pearls of Love and Knowledge appear unaccompanied, but in fig. 1358 they support the Holy One or MONAD of the Great Unity. On figs. 1360

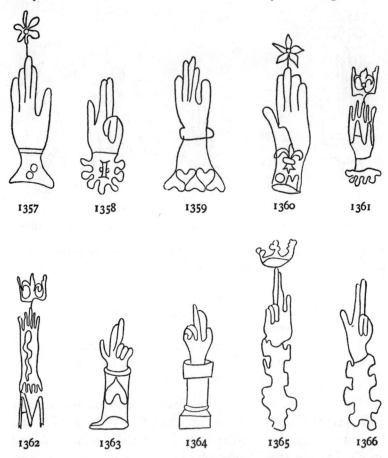

1357   1358   1359   1360   1361

1362   1363   1364   1365   1366

to 1362 is the sacrosanct OM or AUM, and in fig. 1359 the Hand of I O is thrust, Maypole-like, through the ring or bracelet of O. On the palm of fig. 1385 is a representation of the Tree of Life, and fig. 1362 has very much the appearance of a Tree Trunk or Holy Rod. Figs. 1363 and 1364 are unquestionably Columns or Pillars, and figs. 1365 and 1366 represent the Rugged Staff, the Root of all Existence, and the *tat* or backbone of OSIRIS.

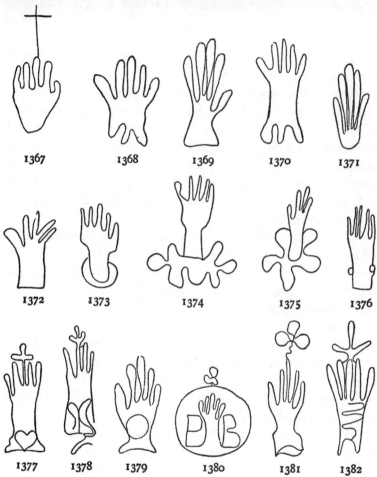

Toot, the Egyptian word for *hand*, may be equated with *tat* or *dad*, the parent Pillar of the Universe.

In the group of designs herewith—all of which are classified by Mons. BRIQUET as "Hands"—the designers seem to have aimed at combining the idea of hands, tree trunks, and palm leaves. The words *palm*, meaning a tree, and *palm*, the inner part of the hand, are identical, and may have originated from the same root because of the similitude between a palm leaf and the outspread fingers of the human hand.

In describing some of the most remarkable features of the ruins at UXMAL in MEXICO, Stephens remarks : " Over a cavity in the mortar were two conspicuous marks, which afterwards stared us in the face in all the ruined buildings of the country. They were the prints of a red hand with the thumb and fingers extended, not drawn or painted, but *stamped by the living hand, the pressure of the palm upon the stone.* He who made it had stood before it alive as we did, and pressed his hand, moistened with red paint, hard against the stone." [1]

It is highly probable that these *red* hand-marked seals, which were common all over AMERICA, were intended like the modern horseshoe to ward off evils, and that originally they symbolised the Flaming Sun. This seeming sign of the Sun was presumably the earliest form of a seal. The word *seal* is " fire-god," and legal sealing is still accomplished by applying a ceremonial *finger* to a *round, red* seal.

The word *hand* (Anglo-Saxon *hond*) resolves ultimately into "immutable, resplendent one," and may be equated etymologically and symbolically with the *Hound* of Heaven and the *Hind* of the Dawn.

The French word *main*, a hand, is the same as our *main*, meaning *chief* or *principal*. The Latin *manus* is "sole light," [2] and the Greek *chier* is the "Great Fire."

Fig. 1383 herewith is identified with the Four or Fire of the Divine Equity or Level, and figs. 1384 and 1385 with

---

[1] See *Ruins of Sacred and Historic Lands*, p. 292.

[2] *Om an us*, "the sun, the one light."

the *Three* and the *Tree* of the *True*. On fig. 1386 is the Dove or Pigeon of the Holy Ghost.

The S S or *Sanctus Spiritus* on fig. 1387 is exactly like the sound holes of viols, violas, violins, and other stringed

instruments, whence it may perhaps be inferred that by the early artists Music was regarded as the voice of the Holy Spirit.

The G and I C herewith stand for GESU or JESOUS CHRISTOS, and the L in all probability for LOGOS or the Word made Flesh.

Vast numbers of symbolic hands have been discovered

among the ruins of POMPEII and elsewhere in EUROPE, and many of these elaborate *ex votos* are illustrated in *Horns of Honour*.[1]

As a paper-mark the Hand was so common that among paper-makers it has become a generic term. Similarly frequent was the device of a Crown, and this also has become a technical term, appearing in publishers' advertisements of to-day as *crown 8vo* or *crown 4to*.

The Crown of Life was the symbol of Paul's charge : " Endure afflictions, do the work of an evangelist, make full proof of thy ministry." [2] To quote an Anabaptist under sentence of death : " With Paul we may say, *We have fought a good fight, we have finished our course, we have kept the faith ; henceforth there is laid up for us a crown of righteousness which the Lord Christ shall give unto us.* And may God the Father of mercies, the God of all comfort (on the behalf of whom it is given us, not only to believe in His name, but to suffer for His sake), who must strengthen us with His Holy Spirit, confirm and establish us that we faint not under our sufferings for the truth, but that we continue steadfast to the end."

Some of the Crowns here illustrated are simply coronals of olive leaves, or, as in fig. 1394, of Hearts ; others are associated with the Circle of Perfection or the Pearl of Price, and figs. 1402 and 1403 have the appearance of wings or horns guarding Good Thought, Good Deed, and Good Word. But the majority of Crown emblems evidently express the words of ISAIAH : " In that day shall the Lord of hosts be for a crown of glory, and for a diadem of beauty, unto the residue of his people, And for a spirit of judgment to him that sitteth in judgment, and for strength to them that turn the battle to the gate." [3] One of the titles of MERODACH—" the Creator," " the Merciful One,"

---

[1] Elworthy (T.). [2] 2 Timothy iv. 5. [3] xxviii. 5, 6.

" He with whom is Salvation "—was " the Glorious Crown."
MITHRA was " the Crown," and one of the appellations of

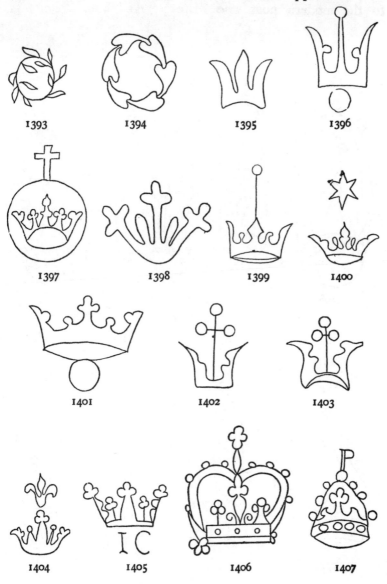

Osiris was "Lord of the lofty white Crown." The identification of the Deity with a crown has persisted even to the modern poet who writes: "Ah! but I rejoice in

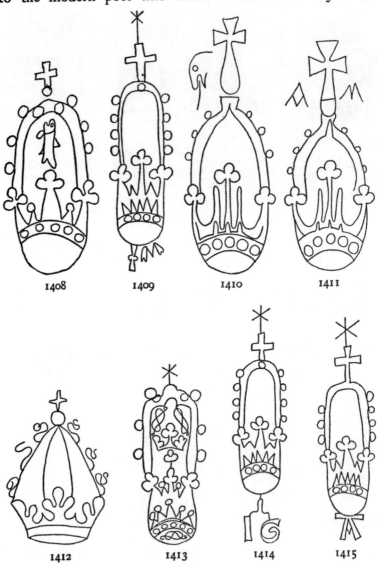

1408   1409   1410   1411

1412   1413   1414   1415

Thee, O Thou my God, Thou Crown of unutterable loveliness, Thou feather of . . . hyalescent flame ; I rejoice, yea,
I shout with gladness till I mount as a white beam unto the
Crown, and as a breath of night melt into the golden lips
of Thy dawn in the Glory and Splendour of Thy Name." [1]

The lofty white *crowns* or *couronnes* here illustrated are
elaborately symbolic, and some of them are representative
of the " Great Fire One," or all the powers and principalities of Heaven.   From the summit of fig. 1410 the

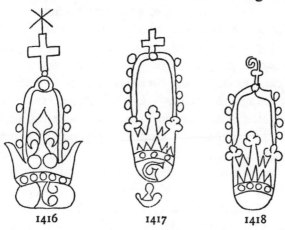

1416   1417   1418

head of *eeg* EL, the Mighty Power or *Père*, the Bird of
Fire, or the Good and Perfect Serpent, is looking down ;
and associated with fig. 1411 is the sacrosanct Name AUM.
The flaming twists on fig. 1412 form twice three *esses* of
Sanctus ! Sanctus ! Sanctus ! and into fig. 1413 are introduced
three Solomon's or S S knots.   A more or less general
feature is the fivefold zigzag of effulgence, and the majority
of examples are surmounted with the Cross of Lux.

The Gnostics deemed the Crown to be a symbol of the
Supreme, and refer to it, according to King, under " the
synonym of *Or*, ' Light ' (possibly the same as *Our*, the

[1] A. Crowley.

name of a Sabean genius)."[1] This syllable is obviously the
root both of *crown* and *couronne*, "the Great One Fire."
PARMENIDES terms the Godhead *Stephanos*,[2] which is the
Greek for *crown*. The cognate STEPHEN may be Anglicised
into the firm *set heaven*, and to the designers of the emblems
here illustrated the Crown served manifestly as a sign of
that expected time when everything irregular, disjointed, and
awry, would be *set even*.

It is proverbial that WISDOM is a Crown of Beauty.
"Her roots are eternal life, and her branches length of
days. Blessed is the man who meditates upon her, for she
is better for him than all treasures. Blessed is the man
who approaches her, and makes use of her commandments.
She will place upon him an eternal crown, and victory for all
eternities among the saints. He will rejoice over her, and
she will rejoice over him, and she will not reject him in all
eternity. The angels of God will rejoice over him, and
will recount all the glories of the Lord. Behold! scripture
is altogether full of life. Blessed is the man who hears and
acts. Listen to me, ye who fear God; observe and give
heed to my words, whoever will inherit life, eternal gain,
and great joy. Hear and obey all my words, and thou
shalt be written in the books of life. Love the fruit of the
Lord, and make thy heart firm in it, and fear not. Approach
and delay not, and thou shalt find life for thy spirit, even
when thou approachest like a hero and a mighty one."[3]

[1] *The Gnostics*, p. 35.
[2] *Ibid.*
[3] Ecclesiasticus i.

CHAPTER XXII

CONCLUSION

"Facts are only stopping-places on the way to new ideas."

DION CLAYTON CALTHROP.

"Perhaps in spite of every disillusionment, when we contemplate the seemingly endless vistas of knowledge which have been opened up even within our own generation, many of us may cherish in our heart of hearts a fancy, if not a hope, that some loophole of escape may after all be discovered from the iron walls of the prison-house which threaten to close on and crush us; that, groping about in the darkness, mankind may yet chance to lay hands on 'that golden key that opes the palace of eternity,' and so to pass from this world of shadows and sorrow to a world of untroubled light and joy."

J. G. FRAZER.

"The one Spirit's plastic stress
Sweeps through the dull, dense world, compelling there
All new successions to the forms they wear;
Torturing the unwilling dross that checks its flight
To its own likeness, as each mass they bear;
And bursting in its beauty and its might
From trees and beasts and men into the Heaven's light."

SHELLEY.

KOMENSKY attributes the recondite and supernormal knowledge possessed by his "True Christians" to Intuition or Inspiration. Following his description of ministering angels, he says: "I saw also (and it is not beseeming to conceal this) another advantage of this holy, invisible companionship—to wit, that the angels were not only as guards, but also as teachers to the chosen. They often give them secret knowledge of divers things, and teach them the deep secret mysteries of God. For as they ever behold the

347

countenance of the omniscient God, nothing that a godly
man can wish to know can be secret to them, and with
God's permission they reveal that which they know, and
which it is necessary that the chosen should know. Therefore the heart of the godly often feels that which has
befallen elsewhere, mourns with the mournful, and rejoices
with the joyful. Therefore, also, can they, by means of
dreams and other visions, or of secret inspirations, imagine
in their minds that which has befallen, or befalls, or will
befall. Thence comes also other increase of the gifts of
God within us, deep, valuable meditations, divers wondrous
discoveries, by means of which man often surpasses himself,
though he knows not how he has that power. Oh, blessed
school of the sons of God ! It is this which often causes
the astonishment of all worldly-wise men, when they see
how some plain little fellow speaks wondrous mysteries ;
prophesies the future changes in the world and in the
Church as if he saw them before his eyes ; mentions the
names of yet unborn kings and heads of states ; proclaims
and announces other things that could not be conceived
either by any study of the stars or by any endeavour of
human wit."

The history of Heresy is conspicuous for these claims
to supernatural guidance. It was a main tenet of the
Montanists, and the Albigeois similarly claimed that they
received daily visitations from their Invisible Chief, the
Holy Spirit. In his account of the Huguenots SMILES
relates that after the revocation of the Edict of Nantes,
"The rapidity with which the contagion of convulsive
prophesying spread was extraordinary. The adherents
were all of the poorer classes, who read nothing but the
Bible, and had it nearly by heart. It spread from Dauphiney
to Viverais, and from thence into the Cevennes. 'I have
seen,' said Marshal Villars, 'things that I could never

have believed if they had not passed under my own eyes
—an entire city, in which all the women and girls, without
exception, appeared possessed by the devil ; they quaked
and prophesied publicly in the streets.' "

To account at all rationally for the facts accumulated
in the preceding chapters one must necessarily accept either
some theory of inspiration or the only alternative theory of a
mystic tradition transmitted secretly by word of mouth from
a vast period anterior to Christianity. There is plentiful
testimony to the existence of some such esoteric knowledge,
and in many Literatures are to be found references to certain
" hidden wisdom," and claims to the stewardship of a Secret
Doctrine. We meet them among the priesthoods of EGYPT
and AMERICA, and in the Mysteries of GREECE and ROME.
To the Jews the writer of Esdras stated it as a command
from the Highest that " Some things shalt thou publish
and some things shalt thou show secretly to the wise." [1]
In the *Advancement of Learning* BACON refers to the dis-
cretion anciently observed of publishing part and reserving
part to a private succession. Of this *Traditionem Lampadis*,
the handing on of the traditive lamp or the Method be-
queathed to the Sons of Sapience, he observes : " The
pretence thereof seemeth to be this : that by the intricate
envelopings of delivery the profane vulgar may be removed
from the secrets of Sciences, and they only admitted which
had either acquired the interpretation of parables by
Tradition from their teachers or by the sharpness and
subtlety of their own wit could pierce the veil." [2]

The writer of the Epistles of St Paul — which are
admittedly tinged strongly with Gnosticism — claims to
speak the wisdom of God in a mystery, *even the hidden
wisdom, which God ordained before the world.* [3]

It is now very generally recognised that Christianity

[1] 2 Esdras xv. 26.   [2] Bk. vi. cap. ii.   [3] I Corinthians ii. 7.

did not originate in JERUSALEM or in PALESTINE or indeed from any unique focus, but that it arose simultaneously from many geographically independent *foci*. The current diction of the primitive Christians, as exemplified in the Gospels, was more or less symbolic, and it was, thinks Professor W. B. SMITH, "a misconstruction of this symbolism (by second-century Ecclesiasticism) that has for 1800 years concealed the true nature of Proto-Christianity, which was an organised crusade of Greek-Jewish monotheism against the prevalent polytheism." [1]

When CORTEZ landed in MEXICO he reported that "the Devil had positively taught to the Mexicans the same things which God had taught to Christendom," and TERTULLIAN complained with characteristic bitterness that in the mysteries of MITHRA the Evil One had "emulously mimicked" even the precise particulars of the Divine sacraments. We have it on the notable authority of ST AUGUSTINE that "That very thing which is now designated the Christian Religion was in existence among the ancients, nor was it absent even from the commencement of the human race up to the time when Christ entered into the flesh, after which true religion, which already existed, began to be called Christian."

Mysticism was the core and kernel of Primitive Christianity, and Symbolism was the language of Christian and every other form of Mysticism. "The earliest Christian Symbolism," says Mrs JENNER, "was for the most part constructed so that it should be understood fully by the initiated only. At the time at which Christianity was revealed to the world esoteric religions were common; and though Christianity differed from Mithraism and various Gnostic sects in that it had received and obeyed a command to go into all the world and preach the Gospel

[1] *Ecce Deus.*

to every creature, nevertheless there were many details which were only explained to those who had accepted the preliminary teaching. These, as in other religions, were often represented by signs to which the uninitiated would attach either some other, or perhaps no meaning at all, but which would remind the initiated of what they had learnt. As there has been an unbroken tradition of Christianity, from those troublous times of its beginning, through the days when it no longer needed to hide itself in caves and catacombs, until now, we know fairly well what these symbols meant. But had Christianity died out before the cessation of persecution, many of them would be as great puzzles to antiquaries as some of the Mithraic devices still remain. Even after the Peace of the Church the tradition of esoterism lingered on, as St John Chrysostom's not infrequent phrase, "The initiated will understand," shows us ; and the same symbols and types continued to be used, even after their meanings had become common property. It is not at all certain that what is known as the *disciplina arcani* had any real existence, and certainly if it had, some of the Apologists, such as St Justin, did not make much account of it. But a natural instinct of self-preservation, coupled with an objection to casting the pearls of the new religion before the Pagan swine, would lead to a considerable amount of unsystematic concealment, which would result in signs and emblems analogous to those of modern Freemasons."[1]

The Founders of Christianity were uneducated, hardworking men, and the workers of the Middle Ages persistently claimed that they and not the luxurious clergy were the real possessors of the truths of Christianity.

There is on record the unwilling testimony of Roman Catholic inquisitors that the Vaudois "heresy" had

[1] *Christian Symbolism*, xv.

"existed in these valleys from all antiquity." The Vaudois themselves maintained that the religion they followed had been preserved from father to son "from all time, and from time immemorial," and most of their historians support this same opinion.

It was said by Julian that "There is no wild beast like an angry theologian," and the "schismatics" of the Middle Ages have been assailed with such sulphurous rhetoric by their antagonists, that it is now almost impossible to disentangle the truth from fiction. But it is sufficiently evident that during the darkest periods of ecclesiastical corruption the Mysticism of the common man was in the main a shrine preserving the living kernel of Christianity, and that most of the so-called New Thought, New Theology, Christian Science, and Higher Criticism of to-day is merely recrudescence under new *formulæ* of very ancient and well-nigh universal ideas.

The Troubadours, like the Templars and the later Freemasons, claimed to be the depositaries of a *Noble Savoir* or "Noble Knowledge," and their rôle in connection with a Mystic Tradition has been lucidly presented by Mrs I. Cooper-Oakley in *Mystical Traditions and Traces of a Hidden Tradition in Masonry and Mediæval Mysticism*.

One of the most potent influences on the Thought of Europe was the *Romance of the Rose*, and this encyclopædic poem of 23,000 lines—about twice the length of *Paradise Lost*—was evidently committed to memory, the poet exhorting his readers

"To learn the whole by heart,
In view that whereso ye depart,
In city, castle, thorp, or town,
Ye may right widely make it known."

From time immemorial the most illustrious Bards and Poets have claimed to be vehicles of a supremely ancient

Wisdom. It is related, for instance, of VAINOMOINEN in the *Kalevala* that

> "Day by day he sang unwearied,
> Night by night discoursed unceasing,
> Sang the Songs of bygone ages,
> Hidden words of ancient wisdom :
> Songs which all the children sing not,
> All beyond men's comprehension ;
> In these ages of misfortune,
> When the race is near its ending." [1]

Among the three Orders of the Druids were the so-called Bards or Masters of Wisdom, and a corresponding class flourished among all primitive and ancient races. The Druidic precepts which it was unlawful to set down in writing, were expressed in rhymed triplets amounting, it is said, to 20,000 in number. The whole of these were committed to memory and handed on from mouth to mouth. The memories of the American natives were, and still are, a matter of amazement. The entire *Popul Vuh* was memorised, and the Spaniards were struck with astonishment at the ease with which the Mexicans recited poems of stupendous length.

Tradition is not infrequently more truthful and more trustworthy [2] than script, and the tendency of modern research is to reinstate the accuracy and reputation of Tradition. The two most current traditions are the lapse of mankind from a Golden Age, and the destruction of the world by water, and I venture to think that both these beliefs are based upon actual fact.

Scattered over the world is material evidence in the

---

[1] Runo, iii. 7, 14.

[2] Tradition always maintained the existence of buried cities at HERCULANEUM and POMPEII, but the idea was long ridiculed by scientists as a vulgar superstition.

form of ruins, majestic in conception and colossal in execution, proving beyond controversy the past existence of a civilisation in comparison with which much so-called "progress" is a fall rather than an advance. To some unknown prehistoric people the world is indebted for the development of wheat, of maize, and of the many fruits and edible grains which millions of years ago must have been scientifically evolved from wild plants.

The original unity of the human race is admittedly proved by the universal similarity of folk-lore customs, fairy-tales, and superstitions, but more especially by *language*. Philology has already established such affinities as can only be accounted for by the supposition that mankind had a common cradle, the relation between all languages being that of sisters—daughters of one mother who perished, as it were, in giving them birth. It is believed that no monuments of this Mother Tongue have been preserved, and that we have no history or even tradition of the nation that spoke it.[1]

The mysterious ancestors from whom many modern races have supposedly sprung, have been termed *Aryans*, a Sanscrit word meaning "excellent" or "honourable," and the beneficent character of the Aryans has been deduced

[1] "That such a people existed and spoke such a tongue is an inference of comparative philology, the process of reasoning being analogous to that followed in the kindred science of geology. The geologist, interpreting the inscriptions written by the finger of Nature herself upon the rock-tablets of the earth's strata, carries us back myriads of ages before man appeared on the scene at all, and enables us to be present, as it were, at creation itself, and see one formation laid above another, and one plant or animal succeed another. Now languages are to the ethnologist what strata are in geology ; dead languages have been well called his fossils and petrifactions. By skilful interpretation of their indications, aided by the light of all other available monuments, he is able to spell out, with more or less probability, the ethnical records of the past, and thus obtain a glimpse here and there into the grey cloud that rests over the dawn of ages."—Article "Aryans," *Chambers's Encyclopædia.*

from the fact that the most ancient words all relate to peaceful occupations. "It should be observed," says MAX MÜLLER, " that most of the terms connected with chase and warfare differ in each of the Aryan dialects, while words connected with more peaceful occupations belong generally to the common heirloom of the Aryan language. The proper appreciation of this fact in its general bearing will show how a similar remark made by Niebuhr, with regard to Greek and Latin, requires a very different explanation from that which that great scholar, from his more restricted point of view, was able to give it. *It will show that all the Aryan nations had led a long life of peace before they separated,*[1] and that their language acquired individuality and nationality as each colony started in search of new homes—new generations forming new terms connected with the warlike and adventurous life of their onward migrations. Hence it is that not only Greek and Latin, but all Aryan languages, have their peaceful words in common ; and hence it is that they all differ so strangely in their warlike expressions."

There is thus already—apart from any etymological evidence that I may have accumulated—good ground for the tradition of a Golden Age when, as the Indians say, "all men were well happified." I think that there is equally good ground for supposing that the world-wide legend of a Deluge was based upon some physical disaster, and that in all probability this tradition preserves the memory of the destruction of Atlantis, *circa* 10,000 years ago. SOLON, who knew nothing of the findings of modern Philology, described the Atlanteans in very much the same terms as the scientist now applies to the hypothetical Aryans. According to SOLON, "For many generations, as long as the divine nature lasted in them, they were obedient to the laws, and well-affectioned toward the gods, who were

[1] Italics mine.

their kinsmen ; for they possessed true and in every way great spirits, practising gentleness and wisdom in the various chances of life, and in their intercourse with one another. They despised everything but virtue, not caring for their present state of life, and thinking lightly on the possession of gold and other property, which seemed only a burden to them ; neither were they intoxicated by luxury ; nor did wealth deprive them of their self-control ; but they were sober, and saw clearly that all these goods are increased by virtuous friendship with one another, and that, by excessive zeal for them, the honour of them, the good of them is lost, and friendship perishes with them. By such reflections, and by the continuance in them of a divine nature, all that which we have described waxed and increased in them ; but when this divine portion began to fade away in them, and became diluted too often, and with too much of the mortal admixture, and the human nature got the upper hand, then, they being unable to bear their fortune, became unseemly."

It is stated that in ancient EGYPT even the very games and dances had a religious significance, and that the sublimer portions of Egyptian religion are those which are *the most ancient*.[1] The inference is that the remoter the time the purer and simpler was Humanity. There can be no older human monument than Language, and it is already an axiom among Philologists that " Language is fossil poetry ; in other words, we are not to look for the poetry which a people may possess only in its poems, or its poetical customs, traditions, and beliefs. Many a single word also is itself a concentrated poem, having stores of poetical thought and imagery laid up in it."[2]

By the unveiling of an unsuspected beauty underlying many commonplace and supposedly unpoetic words, I am

[1] Renouf, *Hibbert Lectures*, pp. 91, 132.   [2] Trench.

simply extending an already accepted principle. To what extent this New Philology may be sound, and to what extent fantastic, must be gauged by Criticism, but the inherent probabilities are *prima facie* in favour of my having let loose an imprisoned Poetry rather than imposed something supposititous, self-made, and non-existent. I did not cunningly invent or contrive some half-a-dozen roots to fit a preconceived idea ; most of those used are already familiar and well-recognised, and to those few which are novel I was surprisedly led by the lamp of the Comparative Method.

Hitherto, this modern tool has been used almost solely as a weapon of destruction, and at present it is the vogue either to resolve the material of Mythology and Romance into the soulless unity of physical phenomena or to regard it as " lewd, foul, revolting, and unnatural, as the gross growth of disgusting savagery." [1]   On the contrary, I believe it to be like many of the seemingly senseless and insane tribal customs of " savages," the survival of some infinitely ancient simple civilisation.   The mere fact that certain savage tribes who are now unable to count beyond five, possess the mysterious and marvellous art of Language—an art they certainly have not now the wit to invent—is presumptive evidence of decadence.

The age of this Earth, estimated from Radium deposits, is now calculated by some scientists as upwards of 750 million years, and there are said to be proofs of Man having existed in the MISSISSIPPI Valley 50,000 years ago.   There is thus abundant time for the Human race to have evolved from a supposed bestiality, and risen to a culminating point of morality, whence they have since declined.   Whether the ancient culture-centre of this Earth was some island in the ATLANTIC or a vague site in ASIA is a problem that has no

[1] Dr Andrew Lang, M.A.

necessary relevance to Symbolism, but the Atlantean theory seems to me to offer the line of least difficulty. Primitive sounds and forms are, it is now generally believed, preserved more faithfully in EUROPE than in INDIA, and Sanscrit has already been dethroned from the high place it occupied a few years ago.[1]

It is not impossible that our profusely numerous monosyllabic words and place-names are due to " phonetic decay," but it is far more probable that elementary words of one syllable are more primitive and more ancient than well-developed and complicated terms of two, three, four, or six syllables. It is more difficult to suppose that there was once intimate intercommunication between BRITAIN and MEXICO than it is to believe that both lands derived their customs and ideas from some common intermediate source— a parent-people who, like the British of to-day, circum-navigated and colonised the world.

Dr FRAZER observes that :—" The comparative study of the beliefs and institutions of mankind is fitted to be much more than a means of satisfying an enlightened curiosity, and of furnishing materials for the researches of the learned. Well handled, it may become a powerful instrument to expedite progress, if it lays bare certain weak spots in the foundations on which modern society is built— if it shows that much which we are wont to regard as solid rests on the sands of superstition rather than on the rocks of nature. It is indeed a melancholy and in some respects thankless task to strike at the foundations of beliefs in which, as in a strong tower, the hopes and aspirations of humanity through long ages have sought a refuge from the storm and stress of life. Yet sooner or later it is inevitable that the battery of the comparative method should breach these venerable walls, mantled over with the ivy and

---

[1] Sayce, *Principles of Comparative Philology*, Preface.

mosses and wild flowers of a thousand tender and sacred associations. At present we are only dragging the guns into position ; they have hardly yet begun to speak. The task of building up into fairer and more enduring forms the old structures so rudely shattered is reserved for other hands, perhaps for other and happier ages. We cannot foresee, we can hardly even guess, the new forms into which thought and society will run in the future. Yet this uncertainty ought not to induce us, from any consideration of expediency or regard for antiquity, to spare the ancient moulds, however beautiful, when these are proved to be outworn."

Dr FRAZER is our leading exemplar of the Comparative Method, and it is evident—*vide* the extract with which I have headed this chapter—that he is writhing uneasily at the pessimism of his own conclusions. It is true that Christianity—its symbols having grown too stark and solid —has been cast into the melting-pot, whence it will never emerge except in a more rational, more widely sympathetic, less parochial, less petty, and less literalistic form. But the ancient moulds—to the degree that they are beautiful— will never prove outworn, and it would be a curious revenge if the irresistible guns of the Comparative Method instead of wreaking fresh and ever greater destruction, recoiled from the present dismal mud-and-dust Materialism, and became an instrument of the armies above, a trumpet-call of the Eternal Reason, and a weapon of the poetic dictum : " Beauty is truth, truth beauty."

Poets have from all time claimed to be the Tongues of an Unseen World, the custodians of an interior certainty, of a Knowledge standing behind and apart from evidence, and of an Understanding that makes darkness light. "Poets," to quote SHELLEY, "are the hierophants of an unapprehended inspiration ; the mirrors of the gigantic shadows which futurity casts upon the present; the words which express what they understand not; the trumpets which sing to battle, and feel not what they inspire; the influence which is moved not but moves." And he adds: "The persons in whom this power resides, may often, as far as regards many portions of their nature, have little apparent correspondence with that spirit of good of which they are the ministers. But even whilst they deny and abjure, they are yet compelled to serve the power which is seated on the throne of their own soul."[1]

Although every scruple of due weight may be given to the force of Memory, to the possible existence of a Secret Tradition, and to the world-wide influence of Freemasonry; yet these causes are alone not adequate to account for the phenomena of Symbolism.

There are manifold problems in Literature that are insoluble except by the supposition that the mind is at times an instrument played upon by the fingers of an Unseen Force. "When I sit down to write my book," said CHARLES DICKENS, "some beneficent power shows it all to me and tempts me to be interested, and I don't invent —really do not—but see it and write it down." Dickens, like most other imaginative artists, is said to have declared that every word uttered by his characters was distinctly heard by him before it was written down. Yet, on the other hand, he averred: "I work slowly and with great care, and never give way to my invention recklessly, but constantly restrain it." We have it on the authority of MILTON that the Muse "dictated" to him his "unpremeditated song." WAGNER was astonished at the gulf existing between his intuition and his reason, *i.e.* between his inspiration as an artist and his intellectual ideas as a philosopher. "Seldom perhaps," he writes in this con-

[1] *A Prelude to Poetry.*

nection, "have a man's ideas and intuitions been at such marvellous variance as mine."[1] In his essay on The Oversoul, EMERSON says, "I am a pensioner ; not a cause, but a surprised spectator of this ethereal water ; I desire and look up, and put myself in the attitude of reception, but from some alien energy the visions come."

It is curious that Etymology, unable to account for the curiously fluctuating and seemingly whimsical variations of speech, is now perplexedly falling back upon old and discarded ideas. The author of *The English Language*,[2] published only just recently, writes : "When the early physicists became aware of forces they could not understand, they tried to escape their difficulty by personifying the laws of nature and inventing 'spirits' that controlled material phenomena. The student of language, in the presence of the mysterious power which creates and changes language, has been compelled to adopt this mediæval procedure, and has vaguely defined, by the name of 'the Genius of the Language,' the power that guides and controls its progress. If we ask ourselves who are the ministers of this power, and whence its decrees derive their binding force, we cannot find any definite answer to our question. It is not the grammarians or philologists who form or carry out its decisions ; for the philologists disclaim all responsibility, and the schoolmasters and grammarians generally oppose, and fight bitterly, but in vain, against the new developments. We can, perhaps, find its nearest analogy in what, among social insects, we call, for lack of a more scientific name, 'the Spirit of the Hive.' This 'spirit,' in societies of bees, is supposed to direct their labours on a fixed plan, with intelligent consideration of needs and opportunities ; and although proceeding from no fixed

[1] Cleather and Crump, *Ring of the Nibelung*, pp. 127, 153.
[2] Logan Pearsall Smith, M.A.

authority, it is yet operative in each member of the community. And so in each one of us the Genius of the Language finds an instrument for the carrying out of its decrees."

The Brahmins in the Hymns of the Veda raised Language to a Divine rank, as they did all things that they were unable to explain. They addressed hymns to Her in which she is said to have been with the Gods from the beginning, achieving the most wonderful things, and never revealed to man except in part. It is impossible to fix the exact number of known languages, but they number, it is supposed, not less than nine hundred. When we consider that the myriads and myriads of human aspirations and ideas are all microscopically expressed by the mere permutations of some two dozen elementary sounds, the results without question are not far distant from the miraculous.

The present is a period when the walls of matter are crumbling momentarily down and the Fairy-land of Electricity, Radium, Röntgen Rays, Wireless Telegraphy, Gramophones, Cinematographs, and other scientific wonders, is becoming a reality. I believe with MILTON in the Fairies and that—

"Millions of spiritual beings walk this earth,
Unseen, both when we wake and when we sleep."

I believe with Sir THOMAS BROWNE that "We do surely owe the discovery of many secrets to the discovery of good and bad angels, and I do think that many mysteries ascribed to our own inventions have been the courteous revelations of spirits ; for these noble essences in Heaven bear a friendly regard unto their fellow natures on earth."[1]

I am in sympathy with the poet who wrote :

[1] *Religio Medici.*

"Verily I was wrong,
And verily many thinkers of this age ;
Ay, many Christian teachers, half in heaven,
Are wrong in just my sense who understood
Our natural world too insularly, as if
No spiritual counterpart completed it,
Consummating its meaning, rounding all,
To justice and perfection, line by line,
Form by form, nothing single nor alone ;
The great below clenched by the great above,
Shade here, authenticating substance there,
The body proving spirit, as the effect,
The cause : we meantime being too grossly apt
To hold the natural as dogs a bone,
(Though Reason and Nature beat us in the face)
So obstinately that we'll break our teeth
Or ever we let go.   For everywhere
We're too materialistic . . . ay, materialist
The age's name is.   God himself with some
Is apprehended as the bare result
Of what his hand materially has made."[1]

[1] E. B. Browning, *Aurora Leigh.*

APPENDIX

THE LETTERS OF THE LATIN ALPHABET AS SEEMINGLY UNDERSTOOD BY THE MYSTICS

A = A cone, mountain, or pyramid, the Primal Cause.

B = The Feeder (?).

C = The crescent moon, the Great Mother, the Sea.

D = The Brilliant.

E = The letter of Apollo or the Sun, as at DELPHI.

F = The Fire or Life.

G = The Self-Existent.

H = Twin pillars, the Aged and Immutable Gateway or Door.

I = The " Holy One," the Pole or Axis of the Universe.

L = God or Power.

M = When angular, twin mountain-peaks ; when cursive, the waves of the sea or the undulations of a serpent.

O = The Sun disc, the perfect One, the Pearl of Price.

P = A Shepherd's crook.

R = A Shepherd's crook.

S = A twisted serpent.

T = A hammer, or twin axes.

U = JUPITER's Chain.

V = Twin rays.

W = Gemini, The Twins.

X = The Cross of LUX.

Y = The Three in One, the Great Unit.

Z = The zigzags of the Lightning Flash.

A SUMMARY OF THE PRIMITIVE ROOTS
USED IN THE FOREGOING PAGES

P or B

OP = *hoop* or *eye*, as in *hoop, optics*.

PA = *Father*, as in *pa, pater, parent*.

T or D

OT = *hot*, as in *hot*.

DI = *brilliant*, as in DIANA, *diamond*, etc., and Sanscrit *dyu*, DYAUS.

CH or J

AJ = *aged*, as in *age*.

JA, IA, or YA = *ever-existent*, as in JAH, JEHOVAH, JAHWE.

K or G

AK = *great* or *mighty*, as in KARNAK, CARNAC, *Zodiac*.

L

EL = *God* or *Power*, as Semitic EL.

LA = " *That which has existed for ever.*"

M

OM = *Sun*, as in Hindoo OM or AUM.

MA = *Mother*, as in *ma, mama, mater*.

N

ON = *one*, as in *one*.

NE = *born of*, as in French *né* (I have not made any use of this root, which is seemingly apparent in *né*, *natal*, *navel*, *naître*, *natus*, *naissance*, *nascence*, *nucleus*, *new* (or just born), and *Noël*, the Birth of God).

R

UR = *Fire* and *Light*, as in Semitic *ur*.

RA = *The Sun-God Ra* or *Re*—fundamentally *ur A*, the *Fiery A*.

S or Z and SH or ZH

ES = *essence* or *light*, as in *esse, to be.*
ZE = *Fire* and *Life*, as in ZEUS, *Zoology*, Zodiac.

F or V

EF = *Life*, as in EVE, *alive*, and *ivy.*
FI = *Life* and *Fire*, as in *feu* and *vie.*

INDEX

Note.—The entries in *italics* relate to the etymologies of those words.

367

VOL. II.

24